Library of
Davidson College

THE CHANGING ROLE OF
THE INDIVIDUAL INVESTOR

THE TWENTIETH CENTURY FUND

The Twentieth Century Fund is an independent research foundation that undertakes policy studies of economic, political, and social institutions and issues. The Fund was founded in 1919 and endowed by Edward A. Filene.

Board of Trustees of the Twentieth Century Fund

Morris B. Abram
Peter A. A. Berle
Jonathan B. Bingham
Arthur F. Burns (on leave)
Erwin D. Canham (on leave)
Hodding Carter III
Benjamin V. Cohen
Brewster C. Denny
Charles V. Hamilton
Patricia Roberts Harris
August Heckscher
Matina S. Horner

David E. Lilienthal
Georges-Henri Martin
Lawrence K. Miller
Don K. Price, *Chairman*
James Rowe
William D. Ruckelshaus
Arthur M. Schlesinger, Jr.
Harvey I. Sloane, M.D.
Charles P. Taft
David B. Truman
Shirley Williams, M.P.
Jerry Wurf

M. J. Rossant, *Director*

MARSHALL E. BLUME • IRWIN FRIEND

THE CHANGING ROLE OF THE INDIVIDUAL INVESTOR

A Twentieth Century Fund Report

A WILEY-INTERSCIENCE PUBLICATION
JOHN WILEY & SONS
New York • Chichester • Brisbane • Toronto

332.6
B658c

Copyright © 1978 by John Wiley & Sons, Inc.

All rights reserved. Published simultaneously in Canada.

Reproduction or translation of any part of this work beyond that permitted by Sections 107 and 108 of the 1976 United States Copyright Act without the permission of the copyright owner is unlawful. Requests for permission or further information should be addressed to the Permissions Department, John Wiley & Sons, Inc.

Library of Congress Cataloging in Publication Data
Blume, Marshall.
 The changing role of the individual investor.

 "A Twentieth Century Fund report."
 "A Wiley-Interscience publication."
 1. Stockholders—United States. 2. Investments —United States. I. Friend, Irwin, joint author. II. Title.
HG4910.B594   332.6'42   78-18303
ISBN 0-471-04547-0

Printed in the United States of America

10 9 8 7 6 5 4 3 2 1

To our wives

Foreword

Of all the dramatic changes that have taken place in the securities markets since World War II, perhaps the most significant is the increasing participation of institutional investors and the diminishing role of individual investors. Transactions by individuals have always been regarded as essential to both the liquidity and the efficiency of the market. In recent years, individual investors have been not only selling their direct holdings of common stock but also redeeming more shares of mutual funds than they have purchased. Many observers believe that these developments have helped bring about the decline in securities prices and the dwindling in the number of firms in the securities industry.

The Twentieth Century Fund has a venerable tradition of research on the securities markets. In 1974, the Trustees of the Fund decided that the changing role of the individual investor and the consequences of those changes for the markets merited a thorough study. They chose for this assignment Marshall E. Blume and Irwin Friend of the University of Pennsylvania's Wharton School.

Blume and Friend, along with Jean Crockett, also of the Wharton School, had earlier examined the influence and significance of institutional investors in *Mutual Funds and Other Institutional Investors: A New Perspective,* published for the Fund by McGraw-Hill in 1970. In their new study, they have sought to determine why individual investors left the market in such large numbers and what their exodus portended for the efficiency of the market and its ability to meet the needs of American enterprise for new capital, and have reviewed various proposals for attracting back individual investors and have presented their own policy recommendations.

In *The Changing Role of the Individual Investor,* based on a wealth of data, including the results of a special survey, are offered fresh insights into the past, present, and future participation of individual investors in the securities markets. It refutes much conventional wisdom about individual investors and presents a great deal of fascinating material on the expectations of investors and their attitudes toward risks and rewards. This material should be invaluable to practitioners in the marketplace and to policy-makers in Washington.

The Fund is grateful to the authors for a report that is a worthy addition to the body of Fund-sponsored literature on the securities market, dating back to the great crash and including Blume and Friend's own earlier work on institutional investors. As always, the Fund has made no attempt to interfere or influence the findings of the authors. Their interpretations and conclusions are their own. But by offering a much fuller understanding of individual investors than we have had until now, these interpretations and conclusions should stimulate debate and the formulation of wiser public policy.

M. J. ROSSANT, DIRECTOR
The Twentieth Century Fund
May 1978

Preface

Observers of the stock market have watched, sometimes with much apprehension, the declining relative importance of the individual investor and the increasing relative importance of the institutional investor. The purpose of this study is to document the current role of the individual investor in the stock market and to assess what he is likely to do in the future. In formulating effective public policy, it is of utmost importance to know who the individual investor is, why he invests in stocks, and finally how his actions impact upon the efficiency of the stock market and ultimately the economy as a whole. It is hoped that the analyses presented in this study will not only be of interest in themselves but will also serve to stimulate a more effective dialogue among the makers of public policy.

Of the five chapters making up the study itself, Chapter 1 summarizes the major findings; and Chapter 5 examines the implications of these findings for the formation of public policy and discusses the desirability of various measures currently under discussion to encourage greater relative participation of the individual investor or to restrict the actions of institutional investors. Of perhaps the greatest interest, we find no persuasive reason at present to restrict the amount of stock that any single institutional investor can own—a restriction that has often received serious consideration in Washington.

The three central chapters contain the detailed analyses undertaken as part of the study. Chapter 2 examines the historical trends in the asset holdings and sociodemographic characteristics of the individual investor in order to place in perspective his current role in the stock market. Chapter 3 reports on a survey of individual stockholders designed to assess what the individual is likely to do in the future and how he might react to various changes in the tax law and in the economic environment. Chapter 4 analyses the effect of the decreasing relative role of the individual investor upon the economic efficiency of the stock market. Much of the data in these three chapters were collected from sources unavailable before the undertaking of the study.

x Preface

Many individuals and organizations contributed in one way or another. Of particular help were the Department of Commerce, the Internal Revenue Service, the Federal Reserve Board, and the New York Stock Exchange. A number of people in these organizations, particularly George Jaszi, Vito Natrella, and Helen Tice, were very generous in providing special tabulations and in answering questions about the definitions of existing data series. We were fortunate to have the benefit of unusually competent statistical and programming assistance from Kun Yuan Chen, Robert Goodrich, Michael Granito, Bulent Gultekin, Eleanor Noreika, Jay Rechter, Kathy Tama, James Tandy, Bruce Terker, and Elliot Weiss. Phyllis Hess, Virginia A. Mace, Evelyn Mayo, and Janet Parsons did a superb job in preparing various drafts and the manuscript. Jean Steinberg edited the entire manuscript and thereby greatly improved its readability. Finally, we are, of course, greatly indebted to the Twentieth Century Fund, whose support made this study possible, and to the Director, Murray Rossant, who provided many valuable suggestions.

MARSHALL E. BLUME
IRWIN FRIEND
Philadelphia, Pa.
August 1978

Contents

Chapter 1:   Introduction, 1

    Individuals and Institutions, 4
    Individual Balance Sheets, 7
    The Balance Sheets of the Rich, 9
    The Retired and Other Investors, 10
    Realized and Expected Returns, 11
    Risk-taking Behavior, 13
    The Use of Speculative Mechanisms, 15
    Market Efficiency, 16

Chapter 2:   Characteristics and Overall Trends in the Assets Held by Individuals, 23

    The Assets Owned by Individuals, 23
    Sociodemographic Characteristics of Individual Investors, 30
    The Extent of Diversification, 46

Chapter 3:   The Individual Investor: Recent and Prospective Behavior, 62

    Characteristics of Stock Trading in 1975, 66
    Sources and Uses of Funds for Stock Purchases and Sales in 1975, 78
    Comparison of 1975 Trading with Earlier Years, 80

xii   Contents

    Reasons for Recent Trading Activity, 82
    Current and Prospective Importance of Stock in Balance Sheet, 86
    Impact of Institutional and Tax Changes on Market Behavior, 94
    Stockholders' Reactions to Risk, 113
    Required and Expected Rates of Return on Stock, 129
    Characteristics of Stockholding Families, 133

Chapter 4:   Market Efficiency and the Individual Investor, 143

    The Meaning of Market Efficiency, 143
    The Role of the Individual, 147
    Operational Efficiency, 150
    Informational Efficiency, 168
    The Two-Tier Market, 172
    Allocational Efficiency, 178

Chapter 5:   Implications and Recommendations, 186

    Limitations on Institutional Stockownership and Trading, 186
    Stimulation of Individual Investment in Stock, 195
    Disclosure: Basic Mechanism for Efficient and Equitable Markets, 202
    Restrictions on Speculative Activity, 208
    Movement Toward a Central Market System, 214
    Other Changes in Market Arrangements, 216
    Concluding Comments, 221

Appendix: Estate Tax Data, 230

Index, 235

CHAPTER 1

Introduction

The last twenty-five years have brought about dramatic changes in every aspect of American life. Among the enormous changes that have taken place in the economy of the United States since World War II is the sharp increase in the proportion of stock owned by institutional investors and the corresponding decrease in ownership by individual investors.

Little is known about either the relative contributions of institutions and individuals to market efficiency or the effect of the shift to increased institutional ownership on the functioning of the market. Some observers believe that this shift has interfered with market efficiency and have suggested a variety of solutions for this problem. In the Ford administration, Secretary of the Treasury Simon proposed various tax incentives to entice the individual investor back to the stock market. Spokesmen for the New York Stock Exchange have made similar proposals. But the statistical analyses carried out for this book do not support the belief that institutions have significantly altered the efficiency of the market for common stocks.

Although there are large gaps in our knowledge of the individual investor, the decline in the *proportion* of stock owned by individuals is a well-established fact. Nevertheless, surveys conducted by the New York Stock Exchange (NYSE) show that the *number* of individual stockholders increased steadily from 1952 through 1970 and then declined somewhat through 1975. The number of stockholders in 1975 was estimated to be 25.2 million, down 18.1 percent from its peak in 1970, but still much greater than the 6.5 million owning stock in 1952 or the 20.1 million in 1965. The actual decrease in the number of stockholders after 1970 was probably somewhat smaller than the NYSE figures indicate, but it was a decrease nonetheless. Moreover, virtually all of the decrease was accounted for by investors whose holdings did not include NYSE stock.

This book is intended to fill in some of the gaps in our knowledge of

2 The Changing Role of the Individual Investor

the individual investor—what he has been doing, what he plans to do, and how changes in governmental policy or the economic environment would affect his actions. The two main sources of new information for this book are a survey of dividends reported on 17,056 federal income tax forms for 1971 and the responses of 1041 stockowning families to a mail and telephone survey conducted in the latter part of 1975. In the analyses of the federal income-tax forms, the principle of confidentiality was rigidly observed; no one outside the Internal Revenue Service had access to the original forms or any clue to the identity of the individual taxpayer. The mail and telephone survey of stockholders, conducted by the NYSE under the auspices of the Wharton School and financed by the Twentieth Century Fund, is referred to here as the Wharton Survey. In addition, the authors made use of numerous existing sources of data, often with substantial adjustments to obtain comparability.

This book also attempts to determine whether the shift of stockownership from individuals to institutions has adversely affected the efficiency of American equity markets. Both market aggregates and the price behavior of individual issues were examined to help in the evaluation. Two of these analyses went back as far as 1928, after which time there have been some obvious changes in the characteristics of the market that might be related to market efficiency. Yet these changes do not appear to be linked to the growth of institutions; often they preceded the growth of institutions or occurred after their growth had leveled off. These analyses thus do not support the proposition that the growth of institutions has harmed the market for common stocks in any significant way. This conclusion, however, does not mean to imply that the overall level of investment by both individuals and institutions has or has not been optimal; this study has collected no new evidence on the question of absolute levels, only relative levels.

Although this book found no strong economic reasons for encouraging greater *relative* participation of the individual investor, it did survey individuals for reactions to potential tax and other governmental policy changes and to improvements in the economic environment. The replies to the stockholder survey indicate that by 1980 families owning stock would increase the proportion of their financial assets held in stock by 5.5 percentage points if capital gains taxes were reduced by 50 percent. Applied to the amount of stock currently held by individuals, this increase would almost equal the net total of new stock issued by corporations in any three-year period in the past. Although it is unlikely that families would exactly raise their holdings by 5.5 percentage points by 1980 as a result of such a change in taxes, it is highly probable that there would be a significant increase.

Introduction 3

Another frequently recommended method for encouraging individual stockownership is to reduce taxes on dividends. Of the three approaches examined in the Wharton Survey of 1041 stockholders, the one held to be most effective was the abolition of personal taxes on dividends received by individuals, and the next most effective was the elimination of corporate taxes on dividends paid out. It might be noted that the latter would involve a potentially greater tax reduction than the former because the average corporation pays a higher percentage of its income in taxes than does the average individual stockholder and because not all dividends are paid out to individuals. The least effective would be doubling the existing dividend exclusion in the calculation of the individual income tax. The respondents also indicated that an overall reduction in personal income-tax rates of 10 percent would on balance increase their desired holdings of stocks, but the magnitude of the increase was generally considerably less than that from tax reductions specifically targeted toward common stocks.

Any increased demand for common stocks by individuals would probably stem more from a shift from existing assets to stocks than an increase in overall savings. Thus the effect of these tax changes on aggregate investment would be considerably less than the effect on stock alone. Instituting any of these tax reductions while maintaining the same level of government revenue would involve shifting the tax burden from stockholders to those not owning stock, a shift that would raise obvious questions of equity.

If, for some reason, it should be thought desirable to increase the absolute participation of the individual investor in the stock market without major shifts in the tax burden, the responses from the Wharton Survey pointed to a scheme that might work. When asked about their reactions to a substantial increase in the proportion of corporate earnings paid out as dividends, and a corresponding reduction in retained earnings, 41.8 percent of the respondents indicated that they would want to increase their stockholdings, whereas only 10.5 percent indicated that they might reduce them. The rest stated that such a change would have no effect on their investments or that they had no opinion. In view of the lower tax rates on capital gains in 1975 and the expectation then that any tax-reform bill in the immediate future would not totally eliminate this advantage, the opposite response might have been anticipated. Perhaps the respondents were not fully aware of the impact of reduced retained earnings on subsequent capital gains; however, those with stock portfolios valued at more than $100,000, who would presumably be the more knowledgeable investors, indicated the greatest readiness to increase their stock investment.

Since the early 1970s was generally an unfavorable period for common stocks, it is possible that, given a prolonged buoyancy in the market, stockholders might moderate their indicated preference for higher payout in the future. This moderation would become an even likelier possibility if capital gains continue to receive more favorable tax treatment than ordinary income. If this indicated desire for increased dividends turns out to be a cyclical rather than a permanent phenomenon, the encouragement of changes in dividend payout over the cycle could be regarded as an anticyclical policy measure with no significant efficiency cost.

If investors indeed prefer dividends to retained earnings, it should be possible to stimulate greater individual stock investment by inducing corporations, through tax incentives, to raise their dividends. By balancing the tax reductions to corporations against the additional taxes paid by individuals on their increased dividends, the government may be able to induce greater participation of the individual investor with no loss of tax revenue. The survey results suggest that such a change in tax policy may work. Even if, contrary to the responses, an increase in dividends failed to increase demand for stock, the costs of such a tax scheme would be minimal.

Sizable reductions in either interest rates or inflation would substantially stimulate stock investment by individuals. Wage and price controls would moderately dampen the desire of individuals to hold stock. The establishment of an Investor Protection Office by the Securities and Exchange Commission (SEC) to process investor complaints on trade executions and related problems would moderately stimulate the desire of individuals to hold stock, particularly individuals with stockholdings of less than $10,000. If properly set up, such an agency might be able not only to encourage individual investment but also to reduce or discourage the growing number of suits—many of them of dubious validity—being brought against brokers, corporations, their officers, and directors.

Individuals and Institutions

Perhaps the most publicized development in the stock market over the last twenty-five years has been the rapid growth of institutional volume. Figures compiled by the NYSE indicate that in 1961 institutions accounted for only 38.7 percent of the value of its public volume but that by 1974 this share had increased to 69 percent,[1] and by 1977 to 70 percent. Because of this increase and the decrease in the number of individual stockholders from 1970 to 1975, much of the public apparently has the impression that institutions are now the dominant force in the stock market.

However, these figures are somewhat misleading, in part because individuals are much more important in stockownership than in trading. Even though the share of stock owned by individuals has been decreasing at a steady pace over the last twenty-five years, individuals in 1975 still owned more stock than did institutions. Depending on the treatment of shares issued by mutual funds and the classfication of personal trusts, individuals in 1975 owned somewhere between 53.4 percent and 66.9 percent of all stock. In 1950 individuals owned roughly 85 percent of all stock. There has thus been a substantial reduction in the relative importance of individuals, but not nearly as great as the volume figures would suggest.[2]

Virtually all of this decrease in the proportion of individual holdings occurred in direct holdings. This means that even though investors may, on balance, have channeled no new funds into personal trusts and investment companies, or perhaps may even have redeemed some mutual fund shares, these beneficial holdings have nonetheless taken on relatively greater importance in individual stockholdings.

Over the last twenty-five years, 85.4 percent of the total growth of institutional stockownership was due to three types of institutions: private noninsured pension plans, life-insurance companies, and state and local retirement funds. In the last decade these three types of institutions have accounted for an even greater percentage of the increase in institutional ownership. Since 1965 the ownership share of investment companies, which grew quite rapidly in the 1950s and early 1960s, has remained roughly constant, with a slight decrease in the most recent years.

These overall ownership figures obscure the fact that institutions and individuals tend to concentrate their holdings in different types of stocks. Institutions invest the bulk of their assets in the 500 largest NYSE stocks.[3] They put very little of their money into over-the-counter (OTC) stocks. Almost as a mirror image, individuals are the principal investors in OTC and the smaller listed stocks. And since individuals still own more than half of all stock, they are also important investors in the largest NYSE stocks. The tendency for institutions to invest heavily in the largest NYSE stocks has given rise to the notion of a two-tier market, in which the buying power of institutions is presumed to push the prices of stocks in the upper tier to unreasonably high levels. (Adherents of this view have presumably forgotten the market of 1967 and 1968, when the price performance of the stocks of smaller companies, particularly those on the AMEX, far exceeded

6 The Changing Role of the Individual Investor

that of the larger companies. Even in those two years, despite the publicity given to the so-called go-go funds, the bulk of institutional purchases was still in the larger NYSE issues.) We have found no statistical evidence that the tendency of institutions and individuals to invest more heavily in different segments of the market has produced any differences among these segments in expected rates of return adjusted for risk.

Apart from the potential impact of the Employee Retirement and Income Security Act of 1974 (ERISA), it would not be surprising to see a continued decline in the importance of the individual investor over the next four or five years, but at a slower rate than in the past. Individuals under forty-five years of age will make up an increasing proportion of the work force over the next several years, and they tend to save less in the form of stock than do older workers. Moreover, after adjusting for market movements, the portfolios of those who will be retiring in the course of several years will tend to be relatively smaller than those of their counterparts in the early 1960s, suggesting that the average size of the portfolios of the retired may decrease over the next several years.

If the capital required to support a worker and the proportion of new capital financed by equity do not decrease over the next several years, the increasing proportion of individuals under forty-five years of age in the work force and the decreasing relative size of the portfolios of the retired would suggest that the share of stock owned by institutions may continue to increase. As the average age of the work force increases, this tendency for increased institutional ownership would be expected to moderate.

According to the Wharton Survey, pension plans have had little impact on the propensity of employees to invest directly in stocks. It seems unlikely that this situation will continue when employees start to understand the insurance provisions of ERISA, which would be expected to decrease direct savings, while encouraging individuals to place a greater proportion of their direct holdings in stock. In addition, the funding requirements under ERISA, which will undoubtedly be in excess of current funding levels, should create additional institutional demand for many types of financial assets, including common stock. The proportion of funds actually invested in stock will hinge ultimately on the risks which trustees are willing to bear. One initial effect of ERISA was to make trustees more aware of their financial responsibilities. This awareness might lead initially to some reduction in the proportion of institutional funds invested in common stock, but its ultimate effect is uncertain.

Individual Balance Sheets

In mid-1962 the assets owned by individuals, including personal residences, consumer durables, and land, were valued at $1.9 trillion. By mid-1969 that value had risen to $3.1 trillion—an annual compound rate of 7.2 percent. By the end of 1972 these assets had grown to $4.1 trillion—an annual compound rate of 7.6 percent from mid-1969.

A breakdown of this aggregate wealth by type of asset reveals that common stock represented 23.3 percent of all individually held assets in mid-1962, 24.8 percent in mid-1969, and 22.5 percent at the end of 1972. This drop in the proportion of assets invested in stock from mid-1969 through 1972 is consistent with the relatively poor performance of common stocks during this period and the reported decrease in the number of individual stockholders from 1970 through 1975.

According to the Wharton Survey, present stockholders, on the average, plan by 1980 to reduce the proportion of their assets in common stock by about 2.2 percentage points. With the expected growth in total assets and the entry of new stockholders, individuals, even if they were to realize this planned reduction by 1980, would still hold roughly the same dollar value of stock as they do today, assuming no substantial changes in stock prices. Thus stockholders are not likely over the next few years to liquidate their stockholdings at the substantial rates of recent years, although a number may. In 1975 a greater proportion of stockholders registered net purchases than net sales. Since individuals in 1975 had net sales of $1 billion, what apparently happened is that a large number of stockholders were accumulating small amounts of stocks and relatively few were selling large portions of their stockholdings, let alone liquidating their entire holdings. The same phenomenon appears to have occurred in the two-year period 1973–1974. Although individual stockholders, on the average, plan slight reductions in the proportion of their assets invested in common stock through 1980, there is wide disparity among individuals as to their exact plans. As might be expected, the largest percentage decreases are anticipated by stockholders with the greatest proportion of their assets currently invested in common stocks.

The sources used by investors to finance stock purchases were as disparate as their investment plans for the ensuing years. Of those who were net purchasers of common stock in 1975, 44 percent financed their acquisitions out of current income. Next in importance were withdrawals from savings accounts (17 percent), profits from earlier stock transactions (11 percent), withdrawals from checking accounts (7 percent), borrowing from either bankers or brokers (6 percent), and

8 The Changing Role of the Individual Investor

sales of other assets (5 percent). More than one source may have been used by a single investor. The most frequently cited reasons for buying stock on balance in 1975 were the availability of surplus funds from profits or cash resources (18 percent), the expectation of higher return (including price appreciation) on stock than on other investments over the next two to five years (14 percent), the expectation of improvement in the general economy or investment climate (13 percent), the participation in employee stock purchase or monthly investment plans (13 percent), the expectation of higher return over the next year (8 percent), a hedge against inflation (8 percent), and technical market conditions (7 percent). The relatively large number of families that acquired stock through stock-purchase plans or monthly investment plans is of particular interest. This sizable group accords with the evidence that more stockholders were accumulating than liquidating stock, although individuals in total were net sellers of common stock in 1975.

Among net sellers of common stock in 1975, the most common utilization of these funds was for increases in bank deposits; 25 percent used their proceeds in this way. Presumably, many of these deposits were subsequently used for some other purpose. Next in importance was diversification of previous holdings (15 percent), repayment of debt (10 percent), education, illness, and emergency expenses (over 8 percent), and the purchase of tax-exempt bonds (8 percent). It is interesting that tax-exempt bonds were more frequently purchased from the proceeds of stock sales than the reverse. The most frequently cited reasons for selling stock were poor investment performance (17 percent), realization of capital gains on earlier stock purchases (12 percent), a need for funds for a specific purpose or emergency (10 percent), concern about technical conditions in the stock market (10 percent), concern about adverse effects on the investor's portfolio stock (10 percent), and establishment of a tax loss (10 percent). Various other reasons were given, but none by as many as 10 percent of the respondents.

The Wharton Survey also disclosed that approximately 75 percent of all families owning stock maintained an account with one or more brokerage firms. Families with annual incomes below $10,000 typically had no regular brokerage account, whereas those of incomes of $100,000 or more generally had accounts with two or three firms. Somewhere between 11 percent and 16 percent of all stockholding families changed brokerage houses or ceased to do business with a particular firm in 1975. The major reasons given were: better services elsewhere (41 percent), poor advice (27 percent), and departure of the investor's regular representative (26 percent). Only 2 percent switched to take advantage of lower commissions. The wealthier investors, particularly those with large stock portfolios, were less likely to switch brokerage houses, which would suggest that small investors were more apt to be displeased with the brokerage services they received.

Balance Sheets of the Rich

Investment practices vary with income and other determinants of wealth. The rich tend to invest much more heavily in what might be termed "long-term financial assets" than does the average individual. In mid-1962 the wealthiest 1 percent of all households held 57 to 61 percent of their assets in corporate stock, as compared with 23 percent for the population as a whole. The rich are much more heavily invested in bonds and mortgages, and relative to the population as a whole, they tend to hold less cash, short-term assets, and life-insurance policies. In 1962 residences made up over 50 percent of the assets of families with net worths between $10,000 and $100,000, but less than 5 percent of the assets of families with net worths of over $1 million.

Unlike the population as a whole, the rich reduced the importance of corporate stock in their balance sheets from mid-1962 through mid-1969, with the very rich showing the greatest reductions. This means that the rich were reducing their investments in common stock as a proportion of their assets during the long bull market of the 1960s.

The rich continued to reduce the importance of stock in their balance sheets through 1972, a three-year period when all individuals were reducing the importance of stock in their balance sheets; the rich, however, were doing it at a faster rate. The Wharton Survey indicates that this trend may have reversed in 1973 and 1974, when the wealthier families were more likely to show net purchases than the population as whole. In 1975 no relationship of net purchases or sales to wealth could be established. Measured by their anticipated holdings of common stock in 1980, those households with the highest incomes appear somewhat more likely than others to increase their holdings, although the relationship is not strong.

Ownership of common stock is much more concentrated than total wealth. On the basis of the lower bound estimates, the wealthiest 0.5 percent of all families held 40.4 percent of all individually held corporate stock in mid-1962, 32.6 percent in mid-1969, and 33.4 percent at the end of 1972. These changes in concentration suggest that more of the recent shift of stockownership from individuals to institutions in the 1960s is due to the actions of the rich than to the actions of others. The trends from mid-1969 through 1972, as well as the responses to the Wharton Survey, suggest that this decline in concentration of stockownership may have been arrested.

These concentration ratios are based on the wealthiest families rather than on those households owning the most stock. A household may be quite wealthy and yet own little stock, as, for example, a farmer with extensive land holdings. In 1971, those families with stock portfolios valued above $1 million owned fully 40 percent of all individually held stock. These families represented at most 1.1 percent of all families owning stock but, of course, a very much smaller percentage of the population as a whole. Those families with stock portfolios valued at more than $100,000 owned roughly 80 percent of all individually held stock and represented at most 14.2 percent of all households owning stock. In contrast, over half of those families owning stock had portfolios of less than $10,000, but they held only 2.4 percent of the market value of all individually held stock. These figures would suggest that the benefits of many types of tax reductions targeted toward common stocks would, at least initially, flow primarily to a limited number of families.

The Retired and Other Investors

Despite the drop in the proportion of stock owned by individuals over the past twenty-five years, the proportion owned by retired persons actually increased from 11.2 percent of all stock outstanding in 1960 to 14.5 percent in 1971—the only two dates for which these figures are available. Measured against stock held solely by individuals, the growth in stock owned by the retired would appear even more pronounced. Thus the retired increased their share of individually held stock from 13.6 percent in 1960 to 19.3 percent in 1971—a 41.9 percent increase.

The age profile of the population might provide part of the explanation for the growing importance of the retired, but certainly not all of it. Apparently, the size of the portfolios of the employed compared to those of the retired was greater in 1960 than in 1971. Over the next several years the stock portfolios of the newly retired are likely to be smaller in comparison to those currently retired than to those of their 1960 counterparts, suggesting a further decrease in the importance of individual stockholdings. Of course, new savings in the form of stock or a difference in the rates of return between the retired and other individuals as well as other factors could offset this tendency.

Another important difference between the retired and other individuals lies in the degree of risk these groups were and are willing to assume. The retired tend to be more risk averse than others. This conclusion is based on both the survey of federal income tax forms and the Wharton Survey. On the basis of the federal income-tax survey, it was possible to construct quantitative and objective measures of the risk inherent in the stock portfolios of individuals. These quantitative measures indicate that the retired held the least risky portfolios of common stocks, and managers the most risky. The Wharton Survey asked stockholders to describe the amount of risk they were willing to incur. These responses also indicated that the retired had a greater aversion to risk than other individual stockholders.

Realized and Expected Returns

Numerous previous studies have found no long-range differences in the investment performance between individuals and institutions. Since individuals tend to invest more heavily than institutions in the smaller listed companies and much more heavily in OTC issues, they may occasionally do better than institutions when these types of issues perform comparatively well. Likewise, individuals do worse when these issues perform comparatively poorly. Since most individuals and institutions do not appear to shift their portfolios in anticipation of these differential movements, any observed differences in realized returns are probably due simply to chance. The only groups that appear to perform consistently better than the market are specialists and insiders, who have access to inside market or company information.

In 1970 the survey of federal income-tax forms showed that individuals realized about the same returns on their dividend-paying NYSE issues as they would have obtained had they invested in the market basket of all dividend-paying NYSE issues. Individuals realized 1 percent on these types of stocks, including both capital gains and dividends, whereas the market basket of these issues returned 0.7 percent.

From July 1971 through December 1972, individuals, on average, realized 5 percent on their dividend-paying NYSE issues, but their overall return on all their dividend-paying issues was 11 percent. The substantially larger overall return in this period was due to the better performance of OTC issues, which were held predominantly by individuals. Since the market basket of all dividend-paying NYSE stocks returned 8.8 percent, individuals realized lower returns than the market on these types of stocks. On balance, these results and many other forms of evidence over longer periods of time suggest that there has been virtually no consistent differences in the investment performance of individual and institutional investors.

To obtain more up-to-date data, the Wharton Survey asked investors how they would rate their investment performance from May 1974 through the fall of 1975 compared with the performance of the Dow Jones Industrial Average. The tabulations showed that 40 percent thought they did worse, 34 percent about the same, and 26 percent better. On the face of it, these responses suggest that on balance individuals did slightly worse than the market over this period, but this conclusion may be unwarranted for several reasons. First, the Dow Jones Industrial Averages over this period experienced a slightly greater rate of return than did most other market indexes. Second, individuals bear some transaction costs, and if the returns on the Dow Jones were adjusted for such costs, the responses might have been different. Third, it is not unusual for more than 50 percent of the stocks to realize rates of return less than the average. This can occur when a limited number of stocks with relatively large returns pull up the average. The pattern of responses as well as the diversification structure inherent in many individual portfolios are consistent with this type of skewness. Finally, the psychological aftermath of several years of weak markets may have affected the responses.

Investors' perceptions of their rates of return were not strongly related to any socioeconomic–demographic characteristics, except for age and income. Younger stockholders tended to evaluate their performance less favorably than did older ones. Upper-income stockholders on balance believed their performance to be above average, whereas low-income stockholders believed theirs to be below average.

The mean expected rate of return over the next five-year period that would induce investors to buy stock was 12.9 percent, a figure cited by investors in the fall of 1975. To provide some perspective, the market yield on three-month Treasury bills was 6.42 percent in September 1975, and it fell rapidly to 5.48 percent by November 1975. The yield on three- to five-year government issues was 8.22 percent in September, and again fell rapidly to 7.51 percent by November. Triple A corporates yielded 8.95 percent in September, 8.86 percent in October, and 8.78 percent in November. The rate of return required to induce investors to buy stock was positively correlated with the rate required to induce them to buy government bonds, but surprisingly there was only a modest positive relationship with the rate of inflation anticipated by them.

The mean required rate of return of 12.9 percent in the fall of 1975 is roughly consistent with the past relationship between the average realized returns on bonds and stocks. For example, the risk differential implied by the difference between 12.9 percent and the yield on a new long-term U.S. government bond would be somewhat below 5 percent. This differential is somewhat less than the average difference between the realized rate of return on NYSE and high-grade bonds since the latter part of the nineteenth century.

Required rates of return tended to decrease with age but to increase with income. Stockholders under thirty four indicated a median required return of 14.2 percent, and those over sixty five, 12.4 percent. Stockholders in families with incomes of less than $10,000 required 12.1 percent, whereas those with incomes of $50,000 or more required 13.6 percent. The differences in rates of return required by different groups of stockholders reflect not only variations in their willingness to assume risk, but also variations in the riskiness of the stock they would consider purchasing. Therefore, whereas the older and lower-income stockholders are more risk-averse than others, the rates of return that they claim to require on their stock investment are generally lower than those of other stockholders, perhaps because they buy less risky stock.

Risk-taking Behavior

According to the Wharton Survey, individuals generally do not like to take on substantial risks in the hopes of realizing substantial gains; less than 3 percent of families owning stock indicated willingness to assume such risks. The remaining 97 percent varied in their willingness to take risk from a minimal to a small to a moderate amount. Based on the responses of the 97 percent unwilling to assume substantial risks, it can be concluded that risk-taking behavior is postively related to income and negatively to age. Moreover, male stockholders are much less risk-averse than are females, and the level of education is positively correlated with risk-taking behavior.

When purchasing stock, 82 percent of all stockholders "customarily evaluate the degree of risk involved as well as the amount or percent of profit" they expect. The three most commonly used measures of risk are: earnings volatility (42.2 percent), price volatility (30.3 percent), and published beta coefficients (17.3 percent). The last is a relatively new and sophisticated measure that is now readily available through standard advisory services and indicates how a security tends to respond to general market movements, both upward and downward.

14   The Changing Role of the Individual Investor

In spite of this obvious concern about risk, many individuals apparently do not understand the fundamental principles underlying the concept of risk. To begin with, the portfolios of an inordinate number of stockholders are so poorly diversified as to be effectively undiversified; also, when asked hypothetical questions about diversification and risk management, the answers of many of the respondents to the Wharton Survey were inconsistent with the mechanics of minimizing risk.

The survey of federal income-tax forms revealed that at least 34 percent of all families receiving dividend income held only one dividend-paying equity issue in 1971 and another 16 percent held only two. Such portfolios represent, by value, slightly less than 20 percent of all individually held stock—a not inconsequential amount. Roughly 38 percent of all stockholding families owned between three and nine dividend-paying issues and, coincidentally, also 38 percent of the value of all individually held stock. Many of these portfolios did not even show the potential diversification possible with holdings of three to nine securities because the portfolios were concentrated in only one or two issues.

Not only does the Wharton Survey confirm that many individuals hold poorly diversified portfolios, but it also gives additional insight into the relationship between socioeconomic–demographic characteristics and the level of diversification. Not surprisingly, the larger the portfolio, the more diversified it tends to be. For portfolios of stocks valued under $10,000, the median percentage invested in the largest holding other than mutual funds and trusts was 75.9 in 1975. For portfolios valued in excess of $100,000 the corresponding figure was 24.8 percent—a figure still much too large for effective diversification. Families with incomes in excess of $50,000 tended to hold more diversified portfolios than did those with lower incomes. The amount of diversification was positively related to education levels and to age, even after holding income constant. Age was a lesser factor than education.

The less diversified a portfolio, the greater the risk of loss or of less than average performance. The objective measures of return derived from both sample of federal income-tax forms and the investors' perceived returns as reported in the Wharton Survey bear this out. From mid-1971 through mid-1972, at least 66 percent of all families with the least diversified portfolios realized a loss, as compared with only 30.8 percent of those with the most diversified portfolios. The returns realized in 1970 tell a similar story. Moreover, from May 1974 through the fall of 1975, a greater proportion of investors with poorly diversified portfolios rated their investment returns below average than those with more diversified portfolios. The same was found to be true when other family characteristics, such as income, are held constant.

The responses to the Wharton Survey clearly indicate that, although investors wish to minimize the risk for a given level of expected return, many do not know how to do it. The Wharton Survey elicited knowledge of risk management by asking respondents how they would act in specific situations. For instance, one question asked:

> Suppose the expected rates of return of two stocks, A and B, are about the same, and . . .
>> Stock A had a much wider price variation both upward and downward;
>> Stock B had a narrower price variation both upward and downward.

Would you prefer to invest in Stock A or Stock B?

Modern portfolio theory would clearly opt for Stock B. And although many gave this answer, roughly 36 percent picked Stock A.

A large number of investors thus unknowingly expose themselves to unnecessary risks. Many of them are of limited means and cannot afford the losses their ill-conceived investment strategies might incur. These people are unwittingly engaged in gambles of great risk. It is thus not surprising that when the market falls, as it did in the early 1970s, many investors with poorly diversified portfolios suffer catastrophic losses, become disillusioned, and ultimately get out of the market. Undoubtedly, this in part explains the drop in the number of stockholders from 1970 through 1975.

The investment community could well serve the small investor by educating him as to the principles of risk management and by providing products that permit him to obtain effective diversification at minimal costs. Index funds, whose sole purpose is to match the return of a particular index like the Standard & Poor's 500, are one such product. A limited number of the more sophisticated corporations are utilizing index funds in the management of their pension plans; properly constructed mutual funds could offer the same benefits to a broad segment of the population.

Use of Speculative Mechanisms

Despite the publicity given to the option market, only a relatively few individual investors have participated in it. From the beginning of 1975 through the fall of the same year, only 5.7 percent of all families owning stock wrote an option, whereas 8.1 percent bought an option. The story for other speculative mechanisms is similar; 6.3 percent used a margin account, and 3.7 percent sold a stock short.

It has been asserted that options can be used advantageously by all types of investors. The argument is that options provide a way to both increase and decrease the risk of a specific portfolio. The responses to the Wharton Survey, however, show that those who wish to minimize risk tend to avoid the option market. Indeed, there is a positive relationship between the propensity to take risks and participation in the option market. The use of the two other speculative mechanisms, buying stock on margin and selling short, is likewise positively related to the propensity to take risks.

No single sociodemographic–economic group accounted for a major share in the use of these speculative mechanisms; yet there were some interesting differences among groups. The utilization of margin accounts and the writing and buying of options were positively correlated with income and the value of the stock portfolio, but there was no apparent relationship of these two variables to selling short. The older the head of the family, the less likely the use of margin accounts or the purchase of stock options. The thirty-five to forty age group was the most likely to write options and, together with the under-thirty-four age group, to buy stock options.

With income and other family characteristics held constant, education significantly reduced a family's tendency to buy stock options. However, if these other characteristics are disregarded, the level of education was positively correlated to the use of all three types of speculative mechanisms examined. Those families that sold stock short or used margin accounts were on the average willing to assume more risk than were those participating in the option market. Finally, women were less likely to make use of these speculative mechanisms than were men.

Market Efficiency

As already mentioned, there was no evidence that the shift to stockownership from individuals to institutions over the past twenty-five years has harmed the efficiency of the common stock market. There thus appears to be no economic reason for encouraging greater relative participation of the individual investor in the stock market. This finding does not necessarily mean that the level of total investment has been optimal, which constitutes a subject outside the scope of this study. Moreover, all tests of market efficiency, both in this book and in other sources, are subject to considerable margins of error and often to ambiguity in interpretation. Thus the finding that institutions have had no *substantial* effect on market efficiency does not mean that they have had *no* effect whatsoever.

The actual analyses covered only NYSE stocks in which institutions invest the bulk of their equity assets and examined three aspects of market efficiency: operational, informational, and allocational efficiency. Although other definitions are possible, a market was termed *operationally efficient* if the purchase and sale of securities involved no explicit or implicit costs. A market was termed *informationally efficient* if stockholders and other participants in the market correctly perceived the risks and expected cash flows of assets available to them and priced them accordingly. Finally, a market was termed *allocationally efficient* if managers used the information available to them to operate their firms in the best interest of their stockholders. It should be noted that informational and allocational efficiency are not equivalent concepts. It is quite possible for stockholders to price a mismanaged firm correctly or a well-managed firm incorrectly.

These three characteristics of an efficient market are, of course, ideal traits and do not describe any real market. Nonetheless, they do set standards to which a specific market can be compared. Specifically, the question addressed in this book was whether markets dominated by individuals were closer to these ideals than were markets dominated by institutions. The answer is "no."

The costs of trading are both explicit and implicit. Explicit costs would include commissions, for instance. The recent abolition of fixed commissions on listed issues has probably made the market relatively more efficient in an operational sense. Commission rates have generally dropped. Institutions enjoyed the greatest reductions, but even the majority of individual investors can transact at lower rates if they wish. The growth of institutional ownership and the ability of institutions to utilize the third market were undoubtedly important factors in the elimination of fixed commission rates. In this respect, the growth of institutional ownership has probably enhanced the operational efficiency of the market.

Perhaps the most important implicit cost in trading securities is the so-called bid–ask spread or some portion of it. The bid–ask spread is the difference between the asking price (the price at which an investor can buy a security) and the bid price (the price at which an investor can sell a security). To examine the impact of institutional growth on bid–ask spreads, two principal analyses were undertaken. The first, covering the 1928–1974 period, sought to determine whether there have been any major changes in the pattern of bid–ask spreads that could be explained by institutional growth. The second examined the bid–ask spread of two days in greater detail, one in 1968 and the other in 1971, to see whether the magnitudes of the bid–ask spreads for individual stocks varied according to the amount of stock owned by institutions. In view of the concentration of institutional assets in the larger NYSE issues, the analysis was confined to this stock exchange. The occasionally cited instances of institutional participation in the OTC make interesting headlines but so far have probably had little overall economic impact.

The bid–ask spread for the average stock on the NYSE in 1928 was estimated to be 2.7 percent. To remove obvious scale effects, the bid–ask spreads used in this study were always expressed as a percentage of the price of the stock. The bid–ask spread for the average stock increased dramatically to 11.1 percent in 1932 and 12.2 percent in 1941. The average spread then decreased to 1.7 percent in 1955, 1.6 percent in 1959, 1.2 percent in 1968, and 1.6 percent in 1974. These percentages have been estimated from a random sample of stocks for a specific day within each year. The day itself was selected at random. For the purposes of this book, the most pertinent conclusion to be drawn from these averages is that their values have shown little change during the period of rapid institutional growth in the 1950s and 1960s.

While some of the movement in these averages may have been due to technological changes, the low levels of volume in 1932 and 1941 undoubtedly were the primary reasons for the increase from 1928 through 1941 and the subsequent decrease. In all these years, the bid–ask spreads for individual stocks were negatively related to volume. Moreover, the bid–ask spreads in 1932 and 1941 for actively traded stocks, such as Standard Oil of New Jersey, were of the same magnitude as those in the post-World War II period. The differences observed between 1928 and the post-World War II period may be explained in several ways: (1) the 1928 data were based on a different source than that used in subsequent years and therefore may not be exactly comparable; (2) technological changes over this almost fifty-year period may have led to reduced costs; (3) changes in the volume distribution of stocks could, as a statistical matter, explain these differences even in the absence of technological changes; and (4) there may have been nontechnological changes, such as increased competition and more effective disclosure.

The bid–ask spreads in 1968 and 1971 were examined in greater detail. It was found that spreads on individual stocks were negatively correlated with the proportion of the stock outstanding owned by institutions. Holding constant such variables as dollar volume and the number of exchanges on which the stock was listed, the relationship between the bid–ask spreads and this measure of institutional ownership was statistically insignificant in both years, although still negative.

In both years the bid–ask spread expressed as a percentage of the price of the issue was negatively related to volume. Since institutions tend to trade more actively than individuals, it is probable that, because of this volume effect, the bid–ask spreads of stocks in which institutions are the dominant traders are smaller than they would ordinarily have been. These smaller spreads and lower commission costs would be expected to lead to a slight increase in the operational efficiency of the market. It is difficult to know whether the total resources devoted to trading by the public have increased or decreased with the growth of institutional trading. Whereas the reduction in commission rates paid by institutions has undoubtedly resulted in an absolute decrease in the resources devoted to trading from this source, the empirical results of this study show that, as volume increases, bid–ask spreads fall but at a slower pace, implying an increase in resources devoted to trading from this source. Whether the total resources devoted to trading have increased or decreased thus depends on the magnitude of these two offsetting effects.

It has been alleged that institutional trading has increased the variability of short-run price movements and thereby harmed the operational efficiency of the market. Actually, it is not clear whether increased variability is a sign of decreased market efficiency. In a truly efficient market, one would expect prices to adjust quickly and accurately to the new equilibrium on the receipt of new information. In this case, increased volatility would be associated with increased efficiency. Because of the importance occasionally placed on volatility as a measure of efficiency, several analyses of price volatility were performed. The first examined changes in the day-to-day volatility of the market from 1928 through 1976. Not surprisingly, the market was found to have its greatest post-1928 volatility roughly from October 1929 through October 1933. The period of next greatest volatility began in September 1937 and lasted through mid-1939. From mid-1939 through the mid-1970s market volatility remained fairly constant and relatively low by the standards of the 1930s. Thus the rapid growth of institutions during the 1950s and 1960s appears to have had little effect on overall market volatility.

Another analysis examined the daily price changes of all common stocks listed on the NYSE in each of three six-month periods: one from 1962, another from 1969, and the last from 1976. There appears to have been little change in the volatility of daily returns of individual stocks from the last half of 1962 to the second and third quarters of 1969. During the last half of 1962 the average of the maximum daily rates of return realized by each individual stock within this period was 7.1 percent, and the average of the minimum daily rates was −5.8 percent. The corresponding figures for the two quarters of 1969 were 7.0 percent and −6.3 percent, roughly the same as that of 1962. In contrast, the average of the maximum daily returns during the first two quarters of 1976 was 8.9 percent, and the average of the minimums was −6.6 percent—a slightly greater range than in 1962 and 1969.

These analyses indicate a reasonably constant level of price volatility in the 1960s, which is low by historical standards. There is some evidence that the volatility of the market as well as of the prices of individual stocks were slightly greater in the mid-1970s than in the 1960s. Thus no great change in volatility was detected over the 1960s, which was a period of rapid growth of institutional investment. The reason for the increased volatility in the mid-1970s is not clear. Some might attribute it to institutions and others, to real changes in uncertainty. This last view has much to recommend it in view of the major worldwide economic and political changes during the past several years.

Covering the two months August 1972 and March 1975, a more detailed analysis of within-day fluctuations in prices for individual NYSE stocks found no meaningful relationships between these fluctuations and two measures of institutional holdings. Thus the argument that institutions tend to make price volatility more severe in the stocks they hold finds no support from this analysis. One can always cite specific cases linking institutional activity to large price changes. What this analysis suggests is that one can probably also find isolated cases in which individual activity was associated with large price changes.

As discussed later in the book, there are various ways of measuring the effect of individuals and institutions on the informational efficiency of the market, but perhaps the most telling evidence about their relative contributions is indirect. If institutions were more (or less) able to discover mispriced securities, their investment performance would theoretically be consistently better (or worse) than that of individuals. In fact, this book and numerous other previous studies have found no consistent differences in the respective investment performance of these two groups. This absence of significant differences in investment performance suggests that a market dominated by institutions would be neither more nor less informationally efficient than one dominated by individuals.

The final aspect of market efficiency is allocational efficiency. Do managers always act in the best interest of their stockholders? The distribution of stockownership between individuals and institutions may affect the propensity of management to optimize the welfare of the stockholders. It might be hypothesized that when ownership is widely dispersed, management is more likely to optimize its own interests at the expense of the stockholder than if ownership is more concentrated. It is undoubtedly true that institutions, particularly the larger banks, possess much greater potential to influence management than do individuals.

The evidence cited in this book indicates, however, that institutions are generally loath to exercise this potential power. Concerned about conflicts of interest, they generally register their displeasure with management by selling out. Such selling would ultimately lead to a decline in the price of the stock, making the company a more likely candidate for a takeover bid, but this would be a slow process. Hence it could be argued that allocational efficiency would be enhanced if institutions were to take a more active role, but other considerations, particularly those of conflict of interest and concentration of power, would argue against such a position.

This book has found no evidence that the growth of institutional investors has significantly harmed the efficiency of the market for common stocks. This does not mean that a specific institution has never harmed the efficiency of the market through its trading activities and in other ways. It means only that the incidence of such harmful behavior has been so small that the various statistical analyses conducted as part of this study could not detect any significant relationship between market efficiency and institutional ownership. Until explicit (as distinct from imagined) abuses of institutional ownership are documented, there is no apparent reason at the current time to restrict institutional ownership of common stocks or to encourage greater relative participation of the individual investor.

NOTES

1. If many so-called institutional trades such as those of investment clubs or nonbank trusts and estates were reclassified as individual trades, institutions would have ac-

counted for only 54 percent of nonbroker to broker trades in 1974 (*New York Times*, September 18, 1975).

2. These percentages are based on figures contained in the SEC Statistical Bulletin, various issues; SEC Worksheets; and *Mutual Fund Fact Book*, 1974. The smaller figure excludes stock issued by investment companies and treats personal trusts as institutional holdings. The larger figure treats stock issued by investment companies and personal trusts as individual holdings.

3. Marshall E. Blume, "Changes in the Structure of Share-Holders and Their Impact on Decision Making within the Firm," *Gesellschaft für Wirtschafts und Sozialwissenschaften—Verein für Socialpolitik* (Aachen, Germany: September 9, 1975).

CHAPTER 2

Characteristics and Overall Trends in Assets Held by Individuals

This chapter begins with an analysis of trends in the type and value of assets held by individuals as a whole and by the rich separately. A comparison of these trends in turn reveals the trend in the concentration of wealth. The chapter then analyzes the stockholdings of individuals in terms of both the economy as a whole and sociodemographic categories.

According to the new data, the stock portfolios of a large proportion of individuals are poorly diversified. By value, close to 20 percent of all individually held stock is in portfolios that contain only one or two issues. Empirical evidence indicates that, although some undiversified portfolios perform much better than the market, a majority perform poorly and a few sustain heavy losses in any type of market.

Assets Owned by Individuals

In mid-1962 the assets—including personal residences, consumer durable goods, and land—owned by individuals were valued at $1.9 trillion. The value of these assets increased at an annual compound rate of 7 percent through mid-1969, at which time it amounted to $3.1 trillion. By the end of 1972, it had increased to $4.1 trillion—a 7.6 percent annual compound rate from mid-1969.[1]

A breakdown of these aggregate wealth levels by type of asset reveals that common stocks represented 23.3 percent of all individually held assets in mid-1962, 24.8 percent in mid-1969, and 22.5 percent in 1972

Table 2-1. Percentage Distributions of Assets and Liabilities of Households for Three Dates

Type of Asset	Mid-1962	Mid-1969	Mid-1972
Cash and short-term assets	14.0	15.8	17.8
Corporate stock	23.3	24.8	22.5
Bonds and mortgages	7.2	6.4	5.2
Life insurance[a]	4.7	3.9	3.5
Remaining assets	50.8	49.1	51.1
Total assets	100.0	100.0	100.0
Liabilities	12.4	13.4	13.8

[a]Life insurance measured by cash value.
SOURCE: Work sheets provided by Helen Tice and various Federal Reserve Board flow-of-funds statements.

(see Table 2-1). In contrast to the absence of any trend in the holdings of common stock, the percentage held in cash, demand deposits, and time and saving accounts increased steadily, from 14 percent in mid-1962 to 17.8 percent by the end of 1972. The percentage holdings of both bonds and the cash value of life-insurance policies decreased steadily over these years. The remaining assets, including for the most part nonfinancial assets like real estate, decreased modestly in importance from mid-1962 through mid-1969 and then increased slightly through 1972. Finally, the amount of debt used in financing these assets has increased modestly, although steadily, from 12.4 percent in mid-1962 to 13.8 percent in 1972.

These changes in relative holdings of different types of assets could stem from either or both of the following: (1) differences in the relative performance of the assets themselves and/or (2) purchases of assets financed by new savings or by sales of existing assets. In this regard, it is interesting to note that, according to the flow-of-funds accounts, households and nonprofit institutions annually sold, on balance, an average of $3.9 billion of corporate equities over the four-year period 1969–1972. They then stepped up their net sales activity to $8.2 billion in 1973, but decreased their sales substantially to $1 billion in both 1974 and 1975. Thus the amount of stock liquidated by individuals and nonprofit institutions on an average annual basis between 1973 and 1975 did not differ much from that in the preceding four years. Yet not since the late 1950s or early 1960s have their net sales been as low as they were in 1974 and 1975.

To examine the rich separately, one must turn to data other than the flow-of-funds accounts. No totally satisfactory data are available for this purpose, but perhaps federal estate-tax filings constitute the best source for estimating overall levels of wealth and the value of many of its components over a period of years. Such filings are supposed to include a listing of all a decedent's assets and liabilities at fair market value, which is usually the quoted price where a market exists. Viewing each filing as a random drawing, occasioned by death, from a sample stratified according to age, sex, and other variables, one can use the actual mortality rate for each stratum as a measure of the sampling probability. For example, if the probability of a woman dying at the age of 50 were one in a hundred, any woman of this age in the estate-tax sample would be assumed to be representative of 100 women in that age group.

As might be expected, the rich tend to invest their assets differently from the average household (see Tables 2-2 and 2-3).[2] Although the exact numbers differ according to the data and the method of estimation, it is clear that the rich tend to invest more heavily in what might be termed "long-term financial assets" than does the average household. In mid-1962 the richest 1 percent of all households held somewhat between 57 percent and 61 percent of their assets in corporate stock, as compared to 23 percent for the population as a whole. The 57-percent figure assumes that the richest spouse was married to a

Table 2-2. Percentage Distribution of Assets and Liabilities of Richest Households for Three Dates (Lower-bound Estimates)

Type of Asset	Mid-1962	Mid-1969	1972
A. The richest 0.5 percent			
Cash	5.4	5.3	5.3
Corporate stock	64.5	59.2	54.8
Bonds and mortgages	12.6	12.6	15.3
Life insurance	0.8	0.5	0.5
Remaining assets	16.8	22.3	24.2
Total assets	100.0	100.0	100.0
Liabilities	7.0	8.0	6.7
B. The richest 1 percent			
Cash	6.3	6.5	6.6
Corporate stock	60.9	56.2	52.3
Bonds and mortgages	12.2	12.4	14.7
Life insurance	0.9	0.7	0.6
Remaining assets	19.6	24.3	25.8
Total assets	100.0	100.0	100.0
Liabilities	7.0	8.2	7.0

Table 2–3. Percentage Distribution of Assets and Liabilities of Richest Households for Three Dates (Upper-bound Estimates)

Type of Asset	Mid-1962	Mid-1969	1972
A. The richest 0.5 percent			
Cash	5.8	5.8	5.8
Corporate stock	62.3	56.7	52.9
Bonds and mortgages	12.3	12.3	14.4
Life insurance	0.8	0.6	0.6
Remaining assets	18.9	24.7	26.4
Total assets	100.0	100.0	100.0
Liabilities	6.6	8.8	7.5
B. The richest 1 percent			
Cash	6.5	7.1	7.0
Corporate stock	56.9	54.4	49.2
Bonds and mortgages	11.8	12.0	13.7
Life insurance	1.0	0.7	0.8
Remaining assets	23.7	25.8	28.5
Total assets	100.0	100.0	100.0
Liabilities	7.7	8.4	8.3

relatively poor spouse; the 61 percent figure assumes that the richest man was married to the richest woman. The rich are also much more heavily invested in bonds and mortgages. Compared with the population as a whole, the rich tend to hold less cash and fewer short-term assets as well as less life insurance.

In view of this heavy concentration in long-term financial assets, it is not surprising that the rich hold a much smaller percentage of their portfolios in a variety of assets, primarily real estate and equity in unincorporated businesses. Some insight into the composition of these remaining assets can be gained from a 1962 special survey of the Federal Reserve Board, which collected financial information for a large stratified sample of households. According to that study, households of smaller means invest more heavily in homes than the rich. Homes represented over 50 percent of the assets of households with net worth of between $10,000 and $100,000, whereas they represented less than 5 percent of the assets of households with net worth of more than $1 million.[3]

Although the estate tax data are certainly adequate for making these gross comparisons between the rich and the population as a whole, they are much less adequate for determining trends over time. With this proviso in mind, it is nonetheless interesting to examine the trends they reveal, of which the most striking is the waning importance of corporate stock in the balance sheets of the rich from mid-1962 through mid-1969. The richest 0.5 percent showed a much greater decrease than did the richest 1 percent, whereas over this same period, the flow-of-funds data (Table 2-1) show a slight increase for the population as a whole. If these figures are correct, it means that the rich were reducing their stock investments as a proportion of their assets over the long bull market of the 1960s—in retrospect, at the right time. There appears to have been a further reduction in the share of the assets the rich invested in common stocks from mid-1969 through 1972.

However, virtually no change seems to have occurred in the proportion of the assets of the rich invested in bonds and mortgages from mid-1962 through mid-1969, but thereafter a sizable increase through 1972. Again, the richest 0.5 percent showed a slightly greater increase than did the richest 1 percent, a group that of course includes the richest 0.5 percent as well.

Having examined the composition of the balance sheets of both the rich and all households, let us now look at the concentration of wealth in the hands of the rich. Overall, there appears to have been a modest decline in the proportion of individually held assets owned by the rich

Table 2-4. Percentage Distribution of Individually Held Assets in Hands of the Rich (Lower-bound Estimates)

Type of Asset	Mid-1962	Mid-1969	1972
A. The richest 0.5 percent			
Cash	5.6	4.6	4.1
Corporate stock	40.4	32.6	33.4
Bonds and mortgages	25.5	26.8	40.9
Life insurance	2.4	1.9	1.8
Remaining assets	4.8	6.2	6.5
Total assets	14.6	13.6	13.7
Net worth	15.5	14.5	14.9
B. The richest 1 percent			
Cash	8.8	7.9	6.6
Corporate stock	51.3	43.8	41.5
Bonds and mortgages	33.4	37.3	50.9
Life insurance	3.9	3.3	3.0
Remaining assets	7.6	9.5	9.0
Total assets	19.6	19.3	17.8
Net worth	20.8	20.5	19.2

from mid-1962 through 1972. On the basis of the lower bound estimates (Table 2–4), the proportion of individuals' asssets held by the richest 0.5 percent of all households decreased from 14.6 percent in mid-1962 to 13.7 percent in 1972. The proportion of the richest 1 percent decreased similarly, from 19.6 percent in mid-1962 to 17.8 percent in 1972. If valid, this decrease would continue the trend begun in the 1930s toward a more egalitarian distribution of wealth.[4] Because these estimates may be subject to error, the only safe conclusion is that a decrease, rather than increase, in concentration is more likely to have occurred, although whatever changes did occur have not been great. Even if there was a further decrease, the rate of change in concentration has probably moderated in recent years.

In terms of the components of the balance sheets, the estate-tax data suggest that the rich decreased their share of individually held stock from mid-1962 through mid-1969 and thereafter maintained it (see Tables 2–4 and 2–5). These figures suggest that the shift to stockownership from individuals to institutions starting in the 1960s was the result primarily of the actions of the rich.

The share of bonds and mortgages held by the rich increased gradually from mid-1962 through mid-1969 and then very rapidly through 1972. The increase through 1972 is quite large—so large as to suggest that at least in part it may be due to a statistical error in either the

Table 2–5. Percentage Distribution of Individually Held Assets in Hands of the Rich (Upper-bound Estimates)

Type of Asset	Mid-1962	Mid-1969	1972
A. The richest 0.5 percent			
Cash	7.5	7.0	5.5
Corporate stock	48.1	43.5	40.2
Bonds and mortgages	30.7	36.3	47.9
Life insurance	3.1	3.0	2.7
Remaining assets	6.7	9.6	8.9
Total assets	18.0	19.0	17.1
Net worth	19.2	20.0	18.4
B. The richest 1 percent			
Cash	11.6	10.3	9.0
Corporate stocks	60.7	50.5	50.0
Bonds and mortgages	40.9	43.0	60.9
Life insurance	5.5	4.2	4.9
Remaining assets	11.6	12.1	13.1
Total assets	24.9	23.0	22.9
Net worth	26.2	24.4	24.4

estate-tax data or the flow-of-funds data; although there may have been some increase in the concentration of bonds and mortgages, the increase indicated by the estate-tax data may be too large.

In apparent contradiction to the decrease in the concentration of stockownership shown by the estate-tax data during 1962–1969, an analysis of the distribution of stockownership by income, prepared from income-tax samples, found little change in the concentration of stockownership of the 1 percent of the families with the highest income.[5] This analysis, based on income-tax forms, however, does find some decrease in the concentration of stockownership among the 5 percent of the families with the largest incomes—71.3 percent of all individually held stock in 1960, 66.6 percent in 1969, and finally 67.1 percent in 1971. Figures on the market value of stock held by individuals derived from income-tax forms would be expected to be reasonably accurate, considerably more accurate than those from the estate-tax data.

Whereas the data derived from income-tax returns should be more reliable than those from estate-tax data, there is a conceptual difference between these two sets of concentration ratios. The estate-tax data ratios are based on the wealthiest households, whereas those from the income-tax forms are based on the households with the highest incomes. The relationship between these two groups is subject to change from year to year. For instance, in 1960 salaries and wages made up 28 percent of the income received by those with incomes in excess of $50,000.[6] On the assumption that in the distribution of income a $100,000 income in 1969 is roughly equivalent to $50,000 in 1960,[7] the comparable figure for 1969 is 21 percent. The corresponding percentages for the sum of capital gains and dividends were 45 percent in 1960 and 56 percent in 1969. Thus in 1969 it is likely that more stockholders were included among those with the largest incomes. The differences in the sources of income could potentially explain the differences between the trends in the two series on the concentration of common stock.

The greater the income range, the more likely it is that the group will contain the large stockholders. For this reason, the percentage of stock owned by the 5 percent of the families with the largest income might be judged more likely to parallel the trend in concentration of stockholdings by the richest families. As already noted, this series does decline through 1969 and then levels off. In sum, it thus appears safe to conclude that the concentration of stockholdings declined throughout the 1960s and began to stabilize sometime in the early 1970s.

Sociodemographic Characteristics of Individual Investors

Our knowledge of the sociodemographic characteristics of individual investors is not nearly as great as that of the characteristics of institutional investors. Institutional investors are required to submit substantial information about themselves to government bureaus. Individuals are subject to no such requirements. What do we know of the individual investor?

On the Design of Stockholder Studies

Perhaps the most publicized studies of individual investors are those undertaken by the NYSE, which has produced the often-quoted estimates of the number of individual stockholders. The most recent study, in 1975, concluded that there were 25.2 million stockholders, a decrease of 18.1 percent from the earlier study in 1970, with virtually all of the decline attributable to holders of non-NYSE stock. This decrease may be slightly overstated because the NYSE did not adjust its figures for individuals whose only stock was held in trust in employee stock option plans. Based on unpublished data from the 1970 and 1975 studies, it appears that such plans were more prevalent in 1975 than in 1970.

Although the NYSE studies are adequate for estimating the number of stockholders and certain other information, for two reasons they are less than ideal for estimating the financial characteristics of stockholders. First, they have relied on telephone interviews to obtain financial information, and as is well known, financial information obtained by interviews may be subject to substantial error.[8] Second, and perhaps more important, the NYSE has selected its sample completely at random, with no stratification as to wealth or any variable correlated with wealth. Since a small percentage of shareholders account for the bulk of holdings, a fixed sample size must oversample the wealthy to minimize the sampling error in estimates of the market value of stock held.

One source of financial information on individuals not subject to substantial reporting errors and biases is the Federal Income Tax Form 1040. Moreover, the income reported on the tax form itself provides a basis for selecting a sample of stockholders that oversamples the wealthy. To utilize these data, the Internal Revenue Service drew a special sample, according to our specifications, of 17,056 returns for the fiscal year 1971.[9] The sample was highly stratified according to the geo-

Characteristics and Overall Trends in Assets 31

graphical location of, and the sources and amounts of various income items reported by, the filer.[10] In 1971 filers were required to list all dividends received and the names of the respective payers, provided the total dividends received were in excess of $100.

The dividends and the names of the associated payers on each of the sampled forms offered sufficient information to estimate the total value as well as the characteristics of a household's stock portfolio. From the total dividends received from a specific company, one can calculate the average number of shares owned of that company in the year. Using the average number of shares of each issue, one can value the dividend-paying portion of a portfolio at any point in time. With an adjustment for issues not paying dividends, the total value of the portfolio can ultimately be estimated with reasonable accuracy.

To preserve the complete confidentiality of the individual income tax forms sampled, all processing of the data was performed by government agencies to our specifications. Only employees of the Internal Revenue Service had access to the basic data.

The following sections present detailed results of these analyses for the year 1971. Where possible, these results are placed in a historical perspective, especially with respect to a similar study of 1960 income-tax forms.[11]

The Employed, Unemployed, and Retired

In 1971 households headed by employed or self-employed persons owned 36.8 percent of all stock held by American institutions and individuals and by foreigners; in 1960 this group held 45.3 percent (see Chart 2-1). The percentage of stock which this group owned thus declined 18.8 percent over these eleven years—a compounded rate of 1.9 percent per year.

At the same time that the share owned by this category was declining, the retired heads of households increased their share of all stock outstanding from 11.2 percent in 1960 to 14.5 percent in 1971. A large amount of stock was held by households whose heads were not gainfully employed or who failed to indicate their occupations on their tax forms. Many of them undoubtedly failed to do so because they were retired and thus technically not employed. Any adjustment for these persons would increase the estimated share of stock owned by the retired in both 1960 and 1971.

Relative to stock held only by individuals, the retired show an even more pronounced growth in their share ownership. Thus they increased their share of individually held stock from 13.6 percent in 1960

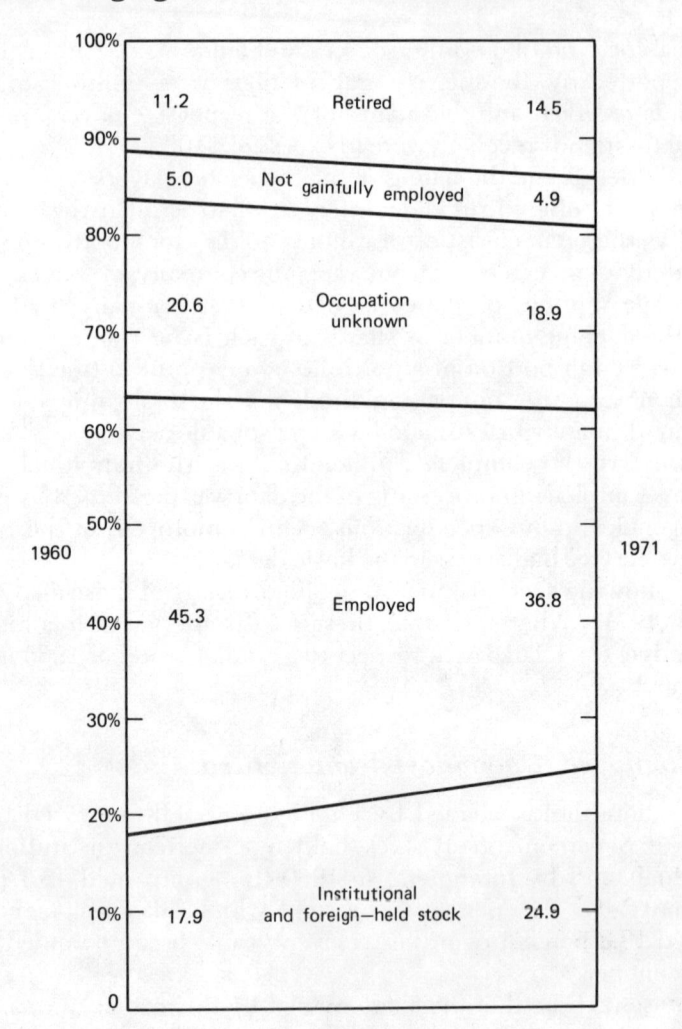

32 The Changing Role of the Individual Investor

	1960	1971
Retired	11.2	14.5
Not gainfully employed	5.0	4.9
Occupation unknown	20.6	18.9
Employed	45.3	36.8
Institutional and foreign-held stock	17.9	24.9

Chart 2–1. Changes in share of stock owned by major investment groups.

to 19.3 percent in 1971—a 41.9-percent increase. Over the same period, the employed reduced their share of individually held stock from 55.2 percent to 49 percent—an 11.2-percent decrease.

One reason for the increase in the stockholdings of the retired may be the relative increase in their number. For instance, persons sixty-five and over represented 9.2 percent of the population in 1960 and 9.9 percent in 1971. Perhaps a more meaningful base for measuring the relative number of the retired is the number of persons forty-five and over since most stock appears to be accumulated and held by individuals in their later years.[12] Relative to this base, the percentage of persons sixty-five and over increased from 31.5 percent in 1960 to 32.6 percent in 1971. If, on the other hand, one examines the trend for males, there is virtually no change from 1960 through 1971 in the position of males sixty-five and over, whether measured relative to all males of all ages or those only forty-five and over.[13] If one were to adjust for any trend toward early retirements, the relative numbers of retired males may have shown some increase.

Although population trends might explain some of the shifts in share ownership as between the retired and the employed, they certainly cannot explain all of the shifts. Apparently, the difference in size between the portfolios of the employed and those of the retired was greater in 1960 than in 1971. Over the next several years, the newly retired are likely to hold smaller portfolios of stocks relative to those currently retired than their counterparts in 1960. Of course, new savings in the form of stock, or differential returns as between the retired and the employed, might alter this tendency.

On the assumption that the assets of the typical employed stockholder compared with the typical retired stockholder have remained unchanged, this change in the relative sizes of stock portfolios of the employed and the retired would suggest that from 1971 to the present there may have been some decline in the proportion of stockholders' assets invested in common stocks. Even if employed stockholders were to increase the proportion of their assets in stocks in the future, it would take some time before such an increase would overcome the inertia from the existing differences in the relative sizes of the stockholdings of the retired and the employed.

Whether the proportion of assets invested in stock by those owning stock declines or perhaps even increases in the future, it is likely that the ratio of individually owned stock to the assets held by all individuals will continue to decline over the next several years, but at a decreasing rate, because of changes in the age composition of the population. Through 1980 the eighteen through forty-four age group is expected to become relatively more numerous than the forty-five and over group (see Table 2-6). Through 1985, the twenty-two through forty-four age group is projected to become relatively more numerous than the forty-five and over group. Since the bulk of stock is accumulated and held by those over forty-five, these shifts in the age composition of the population would expectedly result in some further reduction in the proportion of individual assets invested in stock. Given the changes in the age distribution of the over-eighteen population between 1980

Table 2-6. Historical and Estimated Distribution of the Population over Eighteen by Age

Percentage

| | Male and Female ||| | Males ||||
Year	18–21	22–44	45–64	65 and over	18–21	22–44	45–64	65 and over
1950	8.5	50.3	29.4	11.9	8.7	50.3	29.8	11.3
1960	8.2	46.2	31.2	14.4	8.5	46.8	31.3	13.3
1970	10.9	43.2	31.1	14.9	11.5	44.5	31.0	13.0
1974	11.1	43.8	29.9	15.1	11.8	45.3	30.0	13.0
1980	10.7	46.5	27.4	15.4	11.4	48.2	27.5	13.0
1985	9.1	49.3	25.9	16.3	9.7	51.1	26.0	13.2
1990	8.2	49.7	25.8	16.3	8.7	51.7	26.0	13.6
2000	8.4	45.0	30.7	16.0	8.9	46.7	31.1	13.2

SOURCE: *Statistical Abstract of the United States,* various editions. The projection for the eighteen to twenty-one age group assumes a lifetime fertility rate of 2.1 children per woman.

and 1985, an increase in the proportion of individual assets held in common stocks seems likely, assuming a similar or greater propensity to hold stock by age groups as currently observed.

The proportion of individual assets invested in stock is only one variable in the determination of the proportion of total stock held by individuals. If individuals were to maintain or decrease their share of all assets in the economy, and the proportion of total assets financed by stock were to remain constant or increase, it can be shown mathematically that this expected decline in the proportion of individual assets invested in stock over the next several years would lead to a further decline in the ownership of stock by individuals.[14] The amount of stock held by individuals may continue to decline over the next several years, although at a considerably more modest pace than in the recent past. Given the plans of stockholders (revealed in the survey reported in Chapter 3) to increase on balance the amount of stock in their portfolios, any further decline would probably be moderate.

Stocks Held by Individuals

Combined with characteristics of the specific stocks held, the 1971 special sample of individual income tax returns provides a unique data base for assessing the types of stocks held by individuals. As mentioned previously, the reporting bias is negligible. Except for a small degree of misreporting, the dividend amounts and the names of the associated companies may be assumed to be accurate. The following report on some analyses of this data base is designed to give some insight into the characteristics of stocks held as a function of income, occupation, and region. The returns realized on individual portfolios as well as the distribution of the individual portfolios are also examined.

Characteristics of Stocks Held, by Income. The investment practices of individuals tend to vary according by income. For instance, the proportion of their stock in NYSE issues held in their own name, as distinct from stock held in a trust as a nominee, tends to decrease as income increases. In 1971 households with incomes below $5,000 held 42 percent of their portfolios in such NYSE stock,[15] households with incomes between $50,000 and $99,999 had 34.5 percent in NYSE stocks, and households with incomes in excess of $500,000 invested only 25.7 percent of their portfolios in these holdings (Chart 2–2). This negative relationship of income to proportion invested in NYSE stock is particularly apparent for issues with market values both in excess of $500 million and below $100 million. For the issues between $100 and $500 million, the relationship is reversed and becomes positive, but it is not statistically significant at the 5-percent level (see Chart 2–3).[16]

These percentages were derived from estimates of the total value of each issue held by all stockholders within each of nine income classes. Each issue was then classified into one of several broadly defined stock categories according to the market type of the issuing firm and the total market value within each category summed.

The estimate of the total OTC stock held by individuals was given by the sum of issues traded over the counter and two categories of unidentified stock. The first unidentified category, banks and insurance companies, was composed of companies whose names, as listed on individual tax forms, were clearly those of a bank or an insurance company (e.g., First National Bank) but could not be identified further. In 1971, most of these unidentified banks and insurance companies would have been traded over the counter. The second category contained those stocks whose names could not be matched to listed companies or to the more actively traded OTC issues. Stocks in this category would thus represent closely held OTC stock with limited markets or OTC stock with a small number of shares outstanding.

Whereas the proportion invested in NYSE issues decreased with

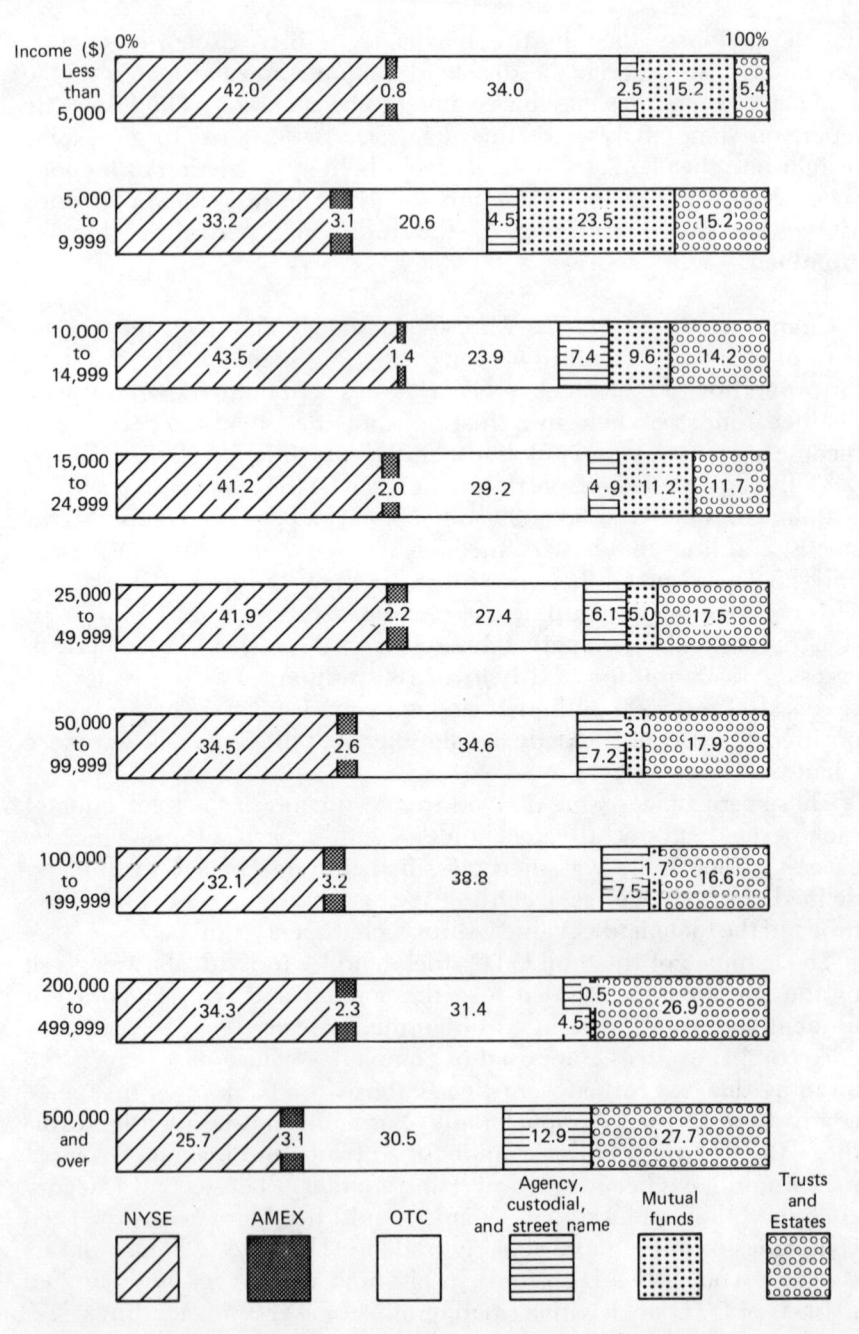

Chart 2–2. Percentage distribution of market value of individual stockholdings income and type of security, June 1971.

Income ($)	NYSE	AMEX	OTC	Agency, custodial, and street name	Mutual funds	Trusts and Estates
Less than 5,000	42.0	0.8	34.0	2.5	15.2	5.4
5,000 to 9,999	33.2	3.1	20.6	4.5	23.5	15.2
10,000 to 14,999	43.5	1.4	23.9	7.4	9.6	14.2
15,000 to 24,999	41.2	2.0	29.2	4.9	11.2	11.7
25,000 to 49,999	41.9	2.2	27.4	6.1	5.0	17.5
50,000 to 99,999	34.5	2.6	34.6	7.2	3.0	17.9
100,000 to 199,999	32.1	3.2	38.8	7.5	1.7	16.6
200,000 to 499,999	34.3	2.3	31.4	4.5	0.5	26.9
500,000 and over	25.7	3.1	30.5	12.9	—	27.7

Income ($)	500 or more	100 to 499	Under 100
Less than 5,000	30.5	7.6	3.9
5,000 to 9,999	24.9	4.6	3.7
10,000 to 14,999	32.0	9.5	2.0
15,000 to 24,999	29.9	9.1	2.2
25,000 to 49,999	28.3	10.9	2.7
50,000 to 99,999	24.0	8.0	2.5
100,000 to 199,999	24.1	6.4	1.6
200,000 to 499,999	26.0	6.2	2.1
500,000 and over	10.9	12.1	2.7

Market value of NYSE issues (millions $)

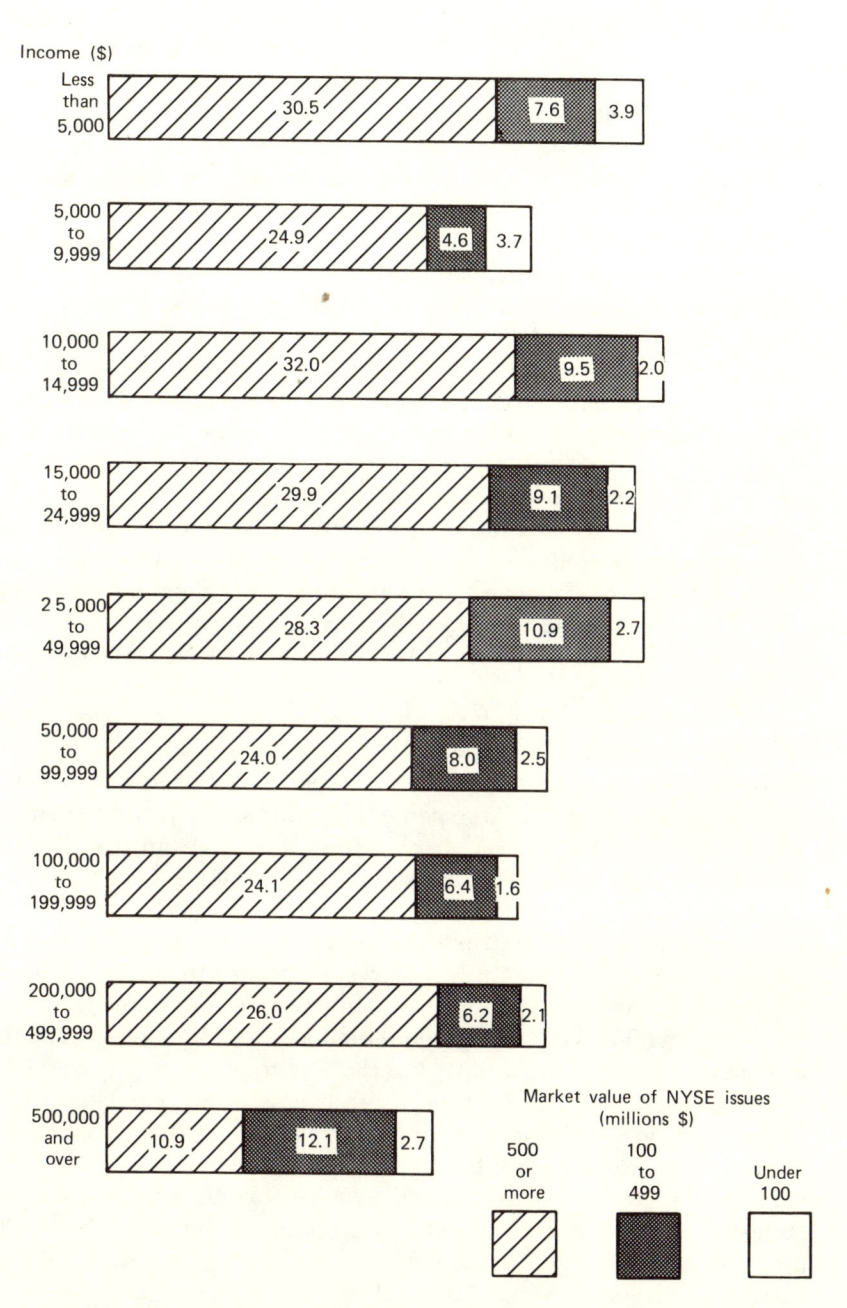

Chart 2–3. Breakdown of NYSE issues by income levels, June 1971.

income, the proportion invested in OTC stock generally tended to increase with income. This conclusion follows from an examination of the identified OTC stocks. The relationship of the rankings is positive and statistically significant at the 5-percent level for the identified OTC stocks, and positive but not significant at the same level for the expanded definition of OTC stocks, including the unidentified issues.[17] Only for unidentified banks and insurance companies is the relationship negative. If, however, households with incomes of less than $5,000 are excluded, this relationship virtually vanishes.

There are some valid reasons for excluding this $5,000 and under group. First, some of the "dividends" reported on individual tax forms were not dividends but more probably interest on savings accounts and dividends from insurance policies, which are actually refunds of premiums.[18] Such misreporting was more likely in the lower income ranges. Second, reported income is only an approximation of economic income, and some very wealthy people with closely held and hence unidentified corporations probably are able to use the tax laws and regulations to reduce their reported income to close to zero. Such persons should really have been subsumed in higher income categories. This phenomenon would help to explain the blip in the miscellaneous unidentified stocks held by individuals with incomes below $5,000.

There was little relation between income and the proportion held in agency, custodial, or "street-name" accounts for any income level up to $500,000. Above that level, the percentage increased to 12.9. If not a statistical aberration, the large percentage of stock in agency, custodial, and street-name for these households may stem from the desire of individuals with extremely large portfolios to delegate the custodial function.

The proportion held in trusts and estates was positively and significantly related to income, although this relationship was not linear.[19] There was a considerable increase in this proportion as income moved above the $5,000 level and a gradual increase until it reached $200,000, followed by another big jump. For those with incomes over $200,000, the proportion in trust was slightly in excess of 27 percent. Mutual funds, however, were held primarily by those in the lower income ranges. The largest proportion of stock invested in mutual funds, 23.5 percent, was found in the $5,000 to $9,999 category, with the next largest in the $15,000 to $24,999 group. Above the $25,000 level the proportion in mutual funds never exceeded 5 percent, and above $100,000 it never exceeded 2 percent.

A similar type of analysis was carried out based on the industry

Characteristics and Overall Trends in Assets 39

instead of the market type of the issuing firm. The percentages of each industry held across income classes showed a remarkable similarity. The principal differences occurred in the telephone and communications industry and in the utilities. Both of these tended to make up a much larger part of the portfolios of lower-income than those of upper-income households.

For households with incomes of less than $25,000, the percentages in utilities ranged from 4.7 to 6.5; with incomes of $200,000 or above, the percentages declined to less than 1. Although the 1960 study found a similar pattern, the percentages of individual portfolios held in utilities at all levels of income were larger in 1960 than in 1971.

For households with incomes under $25,000, the percentage invested in the telephone and communications industry ranged from 5 to 10.5; for households with incomes of $200,000 or over, it ranged from 0.6 to 3.6. In 1960, the comparative importance of such holdings in the portfolios of persons in the lower-versus upper-income classes was even more pronounced.

Risk Characteristics, by Occupation and Income. The 1971 special survey of income-tax forms showed that managers tended to hold riskier portfolios than did other occupational groups, including the retired, not gainfully employed, and unknown categories. The retired and not gainfully employed in turn tended to hold less risky stocks than did other groups. Finally, there was a strong tendency for the riskiness of portfolios to increase with increase in income.

These conclusions follow from an analysis of two different but objective measures of risk. One measure is the so-called beta coefficient, which measures how a stock tends to respond to general market movements. Since fluctuations in the returns of individual securities other than those due to general market movements can be eliminated or greatly reduced through appropriate diversification, theoretically the most important factor in judging the risk of a security is how it tends or is expected to react to changes in the overall level of the market. A beta coefficient greater than 1 means that a stock tends to increase in value faster than the market when it is rising and to decline faster when it is falling. A positive beta coefficient of less than 1 means that a stock tends to rise less rapidly in a rising market and also fall less rapidly in a falling market. The market portfolio of all risky assets has a beta coefficient of 1.

Another measure of risk is the weighted average of the standard deviations of the returns on the individual stocks in the portfolio (the sigma coefficient), weighted in proportion to their market values. This

40   The Changing Role of the Individual Investor

average would be the appropriate measure of risk, at least as subjectively viewed by investors, if they thought that diversification would not reduce the level of risk.[20]

Subsequent analyses revealed that many investors hold highly undiversified portfolios. For this group, the average standard deviation of returns might be a more appropriate measure of their subjective view of risk than the beta coefficient since the beta coefficient is a valid measure of risk only for a fully diversified portfolio. Since both measures yield roughly the same conclusions, it is unncessary to discuss their relative merits. The only minor difference is at the highest income levels.

Each of these risk measures was calculated for each portfolio in the special sample of income-tax forms. Specifically, the beta coefficient and standard deviations were estimated for each NYSE stock from monthly returns for the five years prior to 1971.[21] These monthly returns measure both capital gains and dividend yields. In calculating the beta coefficient, the market return was measured by the NYSE Composite Index adjusted for dividends.[22]

To obtain the portfolio risk measures, the individual stocks in each portfolio were matched to their risk measures, and these were then averaged, giving each a weight proportional to the value of the stock in the portfolio. Finally, these measures were combined by income and occupation by averaging the measures of all the portfolios in a category, giving each a weight proportional to its contribution to the estimate of the total stock outstanding. Only NYSE issues were used, so that the risk measures apply only to the NYSE portion of the portfolio.

Characteristics of Stock Held, by Region. The 1971 individual income-tax forms were also grouped by region (Table 2-7). Several characteristics were estimated for each region, each of which is examined in turn.

Households in New York and New England, with the exception of Massachusetts, owned more stock per houshold of those reporting dividends than did the national average. New Yorkers, for instance, owned 16 percent of all stock held by individuals but filed only 12.6 percent of individual income-tax forms listing dividends. New Englanders, except for residents of Massachusetts, owned 6.1 percent of the stock but filed only 4.2 percent of tax forms with dividends. At the other extreme, persons living in California, Washington, and Oregon, the Mountain and East South Central states, and the West–North Central States accounted for smaller percentages of stock owned than of forms filed.

Some may see these regional differences as corresponding to the

Characteristics and Overall Trends in Assets 41

Table 2-7. Regional Distribution of Individually Held Stock, 1971

Region	Percentage of Households Owning Stock	Percentage[a] of Stock Held
New York	12.6	16.0
Pennsylvania or New Jersey	12.9	12.5
Massachusetts	3.6	3.8
Balance of New England	4.2	6.1
Illinois	7.3	7.4
California, Washington, and Oregon	12.5	10.3
South Atlantic and East–South Central states	15.5	16.0
Mountain and West–South Central states	10.5	9.0
East–North Central states, except Illinois	13.1	12.3
West–North Central states	7.9	6.6
All footnotes on states	100.00	100.00

[a]By "households owning stock" is meant an income-tax form that lists the receipt of dividends.

traditional stereotype of the moneyed East with its great concentration of inherited wealth. Although it is not possible to confirm this speculation solely on the basis of data from income-tax forms, it is interesting to note that 19.2 percent of households with incomes in excess of $200,000 and reporting dividends were situated in New York. Moreover, 22.6 percent of all the stock owned by this high-income group was owned by New Yorkers, implying a relatively greater concentration of stock holdings than in the nation as a whole. This upper-income group on the West Coast represented 10.8 percent of all these upper-income households reporting dividends on their tax forms but owned only 10.6 percent of the stock. Nationwide, this upper-income group owned 13.9 percent of all individually held stock.

On the basis of either of the two risk measures discussed previously, investors in the East North Central states, particularly those in Illinois, held the riskiest stocks (Table 2–8). The average beta coefficient for the NYSE issues held by investors in Illinois was 1.10, and the average standard deviation, 0.080. The average beta coefficient for the balance of these states was 1.05, and the average standard deviation, 0.079. Investors in Massachusetts held the least risky stocks. The average beta coefficient was 0.94, and the average standard deviation, 0.068. According to the average and those beta coefficients, investors in the rest of New England held less risky stocks than the average investor nationally, but according to the average standard deviation, their stocks were of about the same risk as that of the average investor. Thus, if Massachusetts is included, investors in New England tended to hold less risky stocks than the average investor nationwide.

Similarly, by either measure of risk, investors in the South Atlantic and East South Central states tended to hold stocks of lower risk than

Table 2–8. Risk Characteristics of Stock Portfolios by Region, 1971

Region	Beta Coefficient	Standard Deviation
New York	1.01	0.075
Pennsylvania or New Jersey	1.02	0.076
Massachusetts	0.94	0.068
Balance of New England	0.99	0.076
Illinois	1.10	0.080
California, Washington, and Oregon	1.04	0.075
South Atlantic and East–South Central states	0.97	0.075
Mountain and West–South Central states	0.99	0.074
East–North Central states, except Illinois	1.05	0.079
West–North Central states	1.01	0.074
All	1.01	0.076

the average. In the remaining regions there is no clear-cut ranking of the risk-taking behavior of investors.

Again it is tempting to explain these patterns of risk-taking with traditional regional stereotypes. To some, the correspondence may seem remarkably accurate, particularly with the stereotype of the conservative New Englander. However, it should be kept in mind that these estimates are subject to occasionally substantial sampling error. Nonetheless, using a different technique for assessing risk in 1960, it was found that the portfolios of investors in Massachusetts were less risky than the average.[23] Moreover, the survey evidence in Chapter 3 leads to similar conclusions for New England as a whole.

Realized Returns. The processing of the special sample of 1971 individual income-tax forms included an estimate of the returns realized by each portfolio. Returns were defined to include both dividends and capital gains.

The assumption used in estimating these returns was that the average number of shares of each issue held in 1971 was in fact the actual number of shares held over the period under consideration. If there were no turnover, this assumption would entail no approximation. To the extent that there was turnover, this assumption will introduce some error in the estimates of return. Since the average numbers of shares are estimated from the dividends received throughout 1971, these averages would be expected to approximate most closely the actual composition of the portfolio on June 30, 1971—the midpoint of the year.

On the assumption that the average number of shares held in 1971 was in fact the actual number of shares held from July 1, 1971 through June 30, 1972, the returns for each portfolio in the sample were calculated for this period. These returns were derived only for the dividend-paying portion of each portfolio, first for NYSE issues alone and then for all issues. In view of the low turnover rate of most individual portfolios, roughly 20 percent per year, these estimated returns should be highly accurate for most portfolios. Even the errors for the few portfolios with rapid turnover may tend to offset each other in averages, and what is being reported are averages by income group or region.

Returns for 1970 were also estimated on the assumption that the number of shares of each stock held at the beginning of 1970 was the same as the average number held in 1971. Again assuming no changes in portfolio composition over the year, these returns were calculated only for dividend-paying NYSE issues. They obviously entail more error than those estimated for the period July 1971 through June 1972 but are probably close enough to the mark to prove useful.

44 The Changing Role of the Individual Investor

Table 2-9. Average Realized Returns by Income

	Realized Returns (Percent)		
	NYSE Only		All Items
Income[a]	1/70–12/70	7/71–6/72	7/71–6/72
Under $5,000	2	5	10
$5,000– 9,999	3	−1	8
$10,000–$14,999	4	5	9
$15,000–$24,999	4	6	11
$25,000–$49,999	0	5	11
$50,000–$99,999	0	6	12
$100,000–$199,999	−2	7	12
$200,000–$499,999	−3	9	12
$500,000 and over	2	3	10
Total	1	5	11

[a] Income is measured by adjusted gross income as reported on tax forms.

In 1970 individuals on the average gained 1 percent on their dividend-paying NYSE issues (Table 2-9). During that year, the market basket of all dividend-paying NYSE issues returned 0.7 percent. Thus individuals fared about as well as did the market. On average, households with incomes of less than $25,000 realized somewhat greater returns than those with higher incomes. Investors in the West North Central part of the United States realized the biggest returns, while those in New York realized the smallest.

From July 1971 through June 1972, individuals realized 5 percent on their dividend-paying NYSE stock and 11 percent on all dividend-paying items. Their substantially larger overall return is due to the much better performance of OTC issues in this period. The market basket of all dividend-paying NYSE stocks returned 8.8 percent.[24] Individuals thus experienced lower returns than did the market, at least on their NYSE stocks, so that in this period institutions must have fared somewhat better in their investments on the NYSE than did individuals. In contrast to the 1970 results, individuals with higher incomes averaged returns marginally bigger than those with lower incomes. Investors in New York, who had the worst returns in 1970, realized the biggest returns on their dividend-paying NYSE issues in the year ending June 1972, whereas investors in Illinois realized the lowest returns on these issues.

Thus individuals on balance realized about the same returns as did the market over these two years. A similar result was found in 1960.[25]

Size of Portfolio. In 1971 households whose stock portfolios exceeded $1 million in value owned over 40 percent of all individually held stock, and those with portfolios in excess of $100,000 owned nearly 80 percent (Chart 2–4). These numbers of course leave only 20 percent of the stock to households with portfolios of $100,000 or less. Portfolios of less than $10,000 have only 2.4 percent of individually held stock.

The majority of stockholders almost certainly have portfolios of less than $10,000. Households with such portfolios filed 45.5 percent of all individual income-tax forms listing dividends. Since many stockholders with portfolios of this size would not be required to list their dividends, the percentage of total households with portfolios of less than $10,000 must be far greater than 50 percent. Likewise, the number of households with portfolios of more than $1 million would make up less than 1.1 percent of all households owning stock. The corresponding percentage for households with portfolios of more than $100,000 would be 14.2 percent.

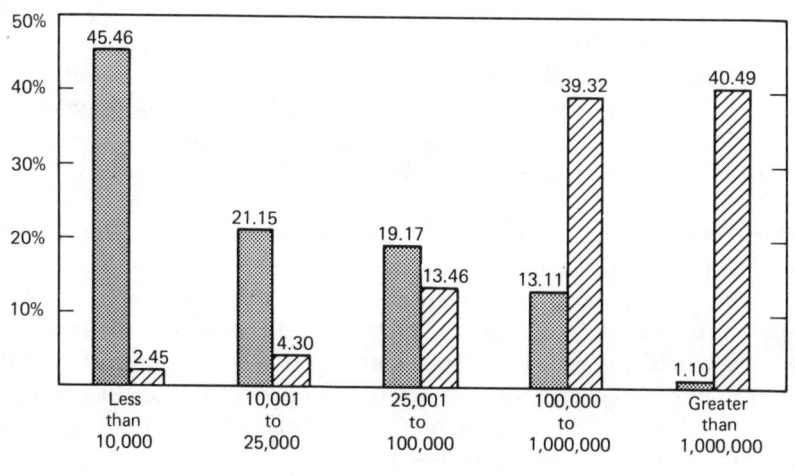

Market value per portfolio ($)	Households	Value of stock held
Less than 10,000	45.46	2.45
10,001 to 25,000	21.15	4.30
25,001 to 100,000	19.17	13.46
100,000 to 1,000,000	13.11	39.32
Greater than 1,000,000	1.10	40.49

Chart 2–4. Distributions of households and value of stock held by size of portfolio, June 1971.

Extent of Diversification

Economic theory espouses the advantages of diversification. Nonetheless, many investors do not hold diversified portfolios, including a large number with stock portfolios of over $100,000 or even of over $1 million. Such investors expose themselves to unnecessary risks, risks that could be eliminated through effective diversification. These investors may think that the potential rewards outweigh the risks, but the empirical results below do no support such a perception.

Measures of Diversification. The number of stocks in a portfolio may be used as a simple measure of its diversification. The assumption underlying this yardstick is that the number of stocks is directly related to the potential for diversification. This measure has two principal shortcomingings. First, it is insensitive to the weight given to each issue. Two portfolios with the same number of stocks may differ substantially as to the level of diversification, depending on the amount invested in each issue. Second, it assumes that all stocks offer the same potential for diversification. This obviously is not correct. A typical mutual fund is in itself already fairly well diversified.[26]

Despite these deficiencies, the number of stocks in a portfolio does provide useful information, can be readily understood, and, if attention is confined to dividend-paying issues, is easily calculated from the 1971 special sample. To the extent possible, other measures of diversification, which partially overcome some of the obvious deficiencies in a measure of diversification based solely on the number of dividend-paying issues, will be examined to verify the general nature of the results.

Over 34 percent of households listing dividends on their tax forms showed only one dividend-paying stock, and nearly 51 percent showed at most two (Chart 2–5). As might be anticipated, many of these households were in lower income ranges or had relatively small portfolios. Nearly 62 percent of those reporting only one stock, and slightly more than 60 percent of those reporting two, had incomes of less than $15,000. Roughly 70 percent of the portfolios containing only one dividend-paying security were less than $10,000 in value. The corresponding percentage for those portfolios with two dividend-paying stocks was 56.5 percent. If it were possible to include those who own stock but were not required to list their dividends, generally persons with small portfolios or low incomes, the percentage of individual portfolios with only one or two dividend-paying stocks, would be expected to be much larger than the figures based solely on the households in the 1971 special sample.

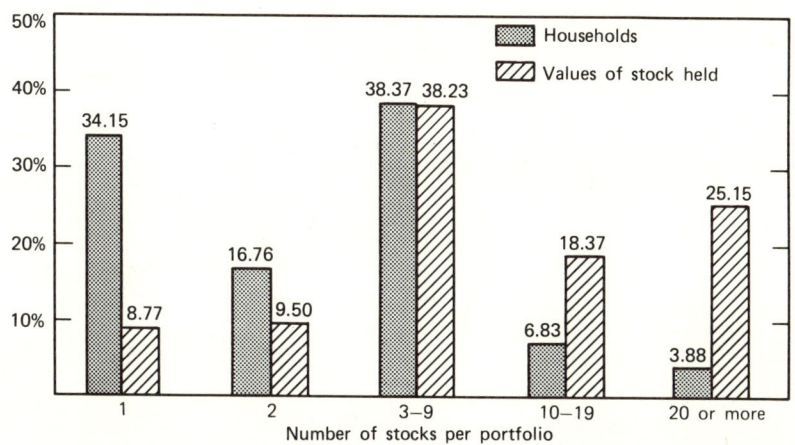

Characteristics and Overall Trends in Assets 47

Chart 2-5. *Distribution of households and value of stock held by number of stocks, June 1971.*

Although portfolios with one or two dividend-paying stocks constituted by number over 50 percent of all individual portfolios, the value of the stock held in these portfolios was slightly less than 20 percent of the value of all individually held stock. (This figure of 20 percent is adjusted to include those not covered in the 1971 special sample.) Furthermore, over half of the market value in portfolios with at most two dividend-paying stocks was held in stock portfolios of more than $100,000. Some of this stock was probably held for reasons of control, which would explain some of the lack of diversification.

Slightly over 38 percent of households listing dividends on their tax forms held three to nine dividend-paying stocks. Coincidentally, these portfolios represented roughly 38 percent of all individually held stock. Whereas the number of portfolios with 10 or more dividend-paying stocks accounted for only 10.7 percent of the portfolios of households listing dividends on their tax forms, the stock in these portfolios constituted 43.5 percent of all individually held stock. Portfolios with more than twenty dividend-paying stocks, representing less than 4 percent of all portfolios, contained over a quarter of the value of all individually held stock.

As would be expected, the percentage of portfolios with a small number of dividend-paying stocks decreased as portfolio size increased (Chart 2-6). Roughly three quarters of all portfolios under $10,000 contained no more than two issues, compared with only 12.8 percent for those in excess of $1 million. At the other extreme, portfolios with more than twenty dividend-paying stocks represented 5.8 percent of all portfolios valued between $25,000 and $100,000, 17.8

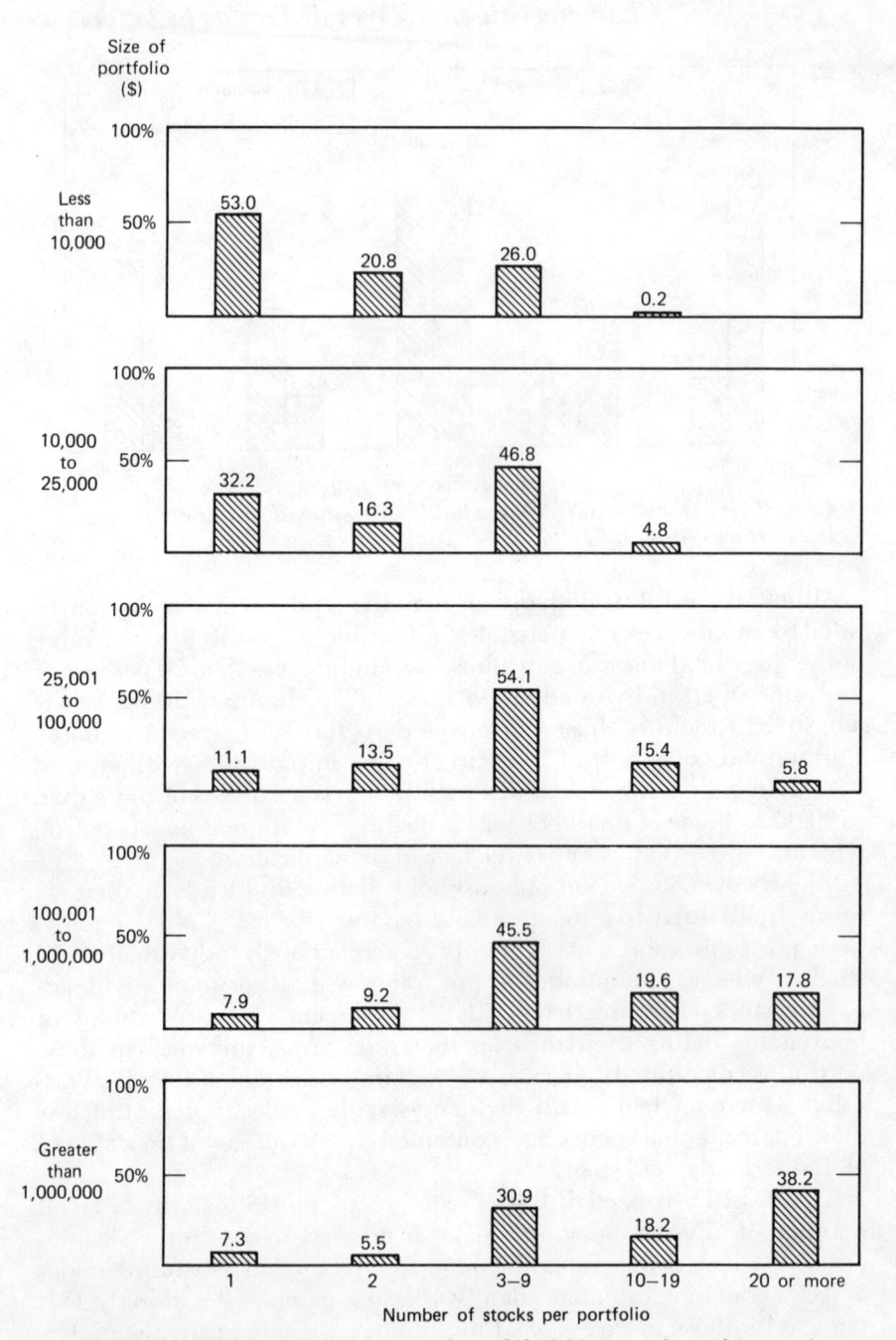

Chart 2–6. Distribution of value of stock held by number of issues by portfolio size, June 1971.

percent of those valued between $100,000 and $1 million, and 38.2 percent of all portfolios in excess of $1 million.

A principal flaw in using the number of stocks as a measure of diversification is its disregard of the differences in the weights assigned to each issue. One way of allowing for such differences is to sum the squares of the proportions invested in each dividend-paying issue. Squaring gives greater relative weight to the larger proportions in the sum. Thus a portfolio of two securities with 0.9 of the value invested in one issue and 0.1 in the second would have a diversification measure of 0.82, the sum of the squares of 0.9 and 0.1. An equally weighted portfolio of two securities, however, would have a diversification measure of 0.5, whereas a portfolio of one security would have a measure of 1.

Assuming that all issues offer the same potential for diversification, the reciprocal of these sums of squares can be interpreted as the number of stocks in an equally weighted portfolio that would yield an equivalent amount of diversification.[27] It is easily verified that this reciprocal for a portfolio of one stock is 1; for an equally weighted portfolio of two stocks, 2; for an equally weighted portfolio of three stocks, 3; and so on. A number such as 2.5 would indicate an amount of diversification somewhere between those provided by equally weighted portfolios of two and three securities.[28]

According to this measure, roughly 70 percent of the portfolios of those filers who listed dividends displayed an effective level of diversification of less than that obtainable from an equally weighted portfolio of two securities. Even for portfolios containing twenty or more items, roughly 25 percent showed a lower level of diversification than might be obtained from an equally weighted portfolio of seven securities. These figures show levels of diversification much lower than those implied by the number of dividend-paying securities per portfolio.

A Confirmation. In interpreting these results, it should be borne in mind that no adjustments have been made for non-dividend-paying issues nor for the fact that some holdings may represent highly diversified portfolios. Nonetheless, a detailed analysis of a survey undertaken in 1962 by the Federal Reserve Board suggests that adjustments[29] for these deficiencies would not substantially alter the general patterns. The evidence of that survey indicates that the large number of portfolios with limited numbers of issues is not a new phenomenon.

This 1962 survey of a stratified sample of households, entitled "The Survey of the Financial Characteristics of Consumers," listed the price and number of shares of each stock held at the end of 1962. These

50 The Changing Role of the Individual Investor

data differ conceptually from those of 1971 in three principal respects: (1) they encompass all sampled households, regardless of whether individual income-tax forms were filed; (2) they included stock held by every member of a household; and (3) they included both dividend- and non-dividend-paying stocks. Although not so reliable as tax data, the financial information collected in this survey can be used to construct various measures of diversification that are not subject to the same deficiencies as those derived from the 1971 special sample of income-tax forms. In 1962 the median number of issues per portfolio, including non-dividend-paying stocks, was two. According to the second measure, 80 percent of the portfolios displayed a level of diversification less than an equally weighted portfolio containing two to three securities. These numbers are similar to those obtained from the 1971 special sample.

The measures derived for 1971 make the explicit assumption that all issues provided the same potential for diversification. The most glaring exceptions were mutual funds, which for the most part represent highly diversified portfolios.[30] One measure that avoids this obviously incorrect assumption is the ratio of the value of the largest holding, with the exception of mutual funds, to the value of all holdings including mutual funds. In 1962 the median value was 0.24 or more. Again these results are similar to those obtained from the 1971 special sample.

A special tabulation of a sample of 1963 individual tax forms by number of separate dividends listed gives further evidence that there has been little change in the levels of diversification over time.[31] The 1963 results are not exactly comparable with those of 1971 because of changes in both the tax law and the distribution and levels of income. Nonetheless, it is interesting to note that, in 1963, 41 percent of households listing dividends on their tax forms reported at most two dividends, compared to 50 percent for 1971. At the other extreme, 3.9 percent of such households reported more than twenty, the same percentage as in 1971.

Risks Inherent in an Undiversified Portfolio. The inherent risk of any portfolio of stock is the possibility that its realized return will be substantially lower than expected. No matter how diversified a portfolio, there is always some risk that it will not yield the expected returns. This is called *nondiversifiable risk*. An undiversified portfolio contains additional risk, the so-called diversifiable risk. To the extent that this can be eliminated through proper diversification, the marketplace should offer no reward for bearing this type of risk.

Characteristics and Overall Trends in Assets 51

The market basket of all assets, in short, the market portfolio, is the one portfolio that is fully diversified. Some have claimed that it is possible to approximate the diversification of this portfolio with a very limited number of securities, say eight or ten.[32] The rationale appears to be that the probability of realizing a return substantially lower than expected decreases at a very rapid rate as one goes from a portfolio of one security to two, and so on. By the time a portfolio contains eight or ten securities, the potential benefits of diversification have been largely realized.

Although this is true, it does not follow that the further benefits of complete diversification should not be realized. Abstracting from motives of control, there are two rational reasons for not seeking these further benefits. The first is the possibility of realizing the added return from superior security selection. If, for instance, one can identify eight to ten securities that promise larger returns than warranted by the underlying risks, additional diversification will only dilute these potentially larger returns. In that case, the degree of diversification warranted hinges on a trade-off between the dilution of the potentially larger returns and the potential benefits from further diversification. This rationale assumes that an investor can pick eight or ten undervalued stocks, but it is no secret that most institutional investors, despite all their resources, have been unable to do this,[33] and analyses of the 1971 special sample of tax forms presented below show that on average poorly diversified portfolios yield returns the same as well-diversified ones.

The second rationale for holding a limited number of securities is that the benefits of diversification are not worth the additional costs, monetary and nonmonetary, of expansion. Under this rationale, the optimal amount of diversification would in general involve a subjective trade-off between the reduction in risk and the reduction in expected returns due to the added costs. Such a trade-off would of course vary from investor to investor. However, under at least one set of assumptions, it turns out that this trade-off will be approximately the same for all investors and hence independent of a particular investor. Before analyzing this theoretical possibility, let us examine the actual distributions of returns realized by individuals with different levels of diversification to gain some perspective on the relationship of risk to diversification.

The frequency distribution of the returns realized by individual investors testifies to the importance of diversification in reducing risk. For households with portfolios containing only one dividend-paying security, 65.6 percent realized a loss on their dividend-paying NYSE stocks from July 1971 through June 1972, compared with only 30.8 percent for those portfolios with more than twenty dividend-paying securities (Chart 2–7). Moreover, there is a steady monotonic decrease in the percentage of portfolios, which showed a loss as the number of items increased. The frequency distributions of returns covering NYSE dividend-paying securities for the year 1970 tell the same story (see Chart 2–8).

The average rates of return, however, do not vary substantially with the number of securities in the portfolios; hence this monotonic decrease in the percentage of portfolios showing extremely low returns means that the distributions of returns are more skewed for the less diversified portfolios. In other words, whereas the majority, perhaps as many of 70 percent of households with portfolios of only one stock, realized below-average returns, a limited number of households realized returns substantially above the average. As the number of stocks increased, the distribution of returns showed less evidence of skewness. Thus households with undiversified portfolios experienced not only the risk of realizing greater variability in returns, but also a greater probability of realizing a below-average return.

These distributions of realized returns by number of securities illustrate the power of diversification. The difficult question is how much diversification is warranted in view of the potentially greater costs, such as increased accounting costs, increased custodial costs, or increased commission costs. If one is willing to make the following types of assumptions, it is possible to establish a framework for assessing the reduction in expected return an investor should be willing to accept in return for a corresponding reduction in risk. First, the risk of a portfolio can be measured by the standard deviation of returns. Second, there exist risk-free assets, such as savings accounts or government bills, which an investor can use, at least in the absence of uncertain inflation, to adjust the risk of his portfolio of risky assets to the overall level of risk he desires. If he wished to bear less risk, he could invest part of his wealth in risk-free assets, and if he wishes greater risk, he could borrow and lever his portfolio.

Since he could thus use a risk-free asset to adjust the risk of a portfolio to obtain the desired level of overall risk, he could proceed in two steps: (1) determine the optimal portfolio of risky assets and (2) use the risk-free asset to adjust the overall risk. In the absence of any investment costs, the resultant portfolio of risky assets would be the same for all investors who felt that risky assets are properly priced, or at least felt that they could not discriminate between the properly and improperly priced. This portfolio would be the market portfolio of all risky

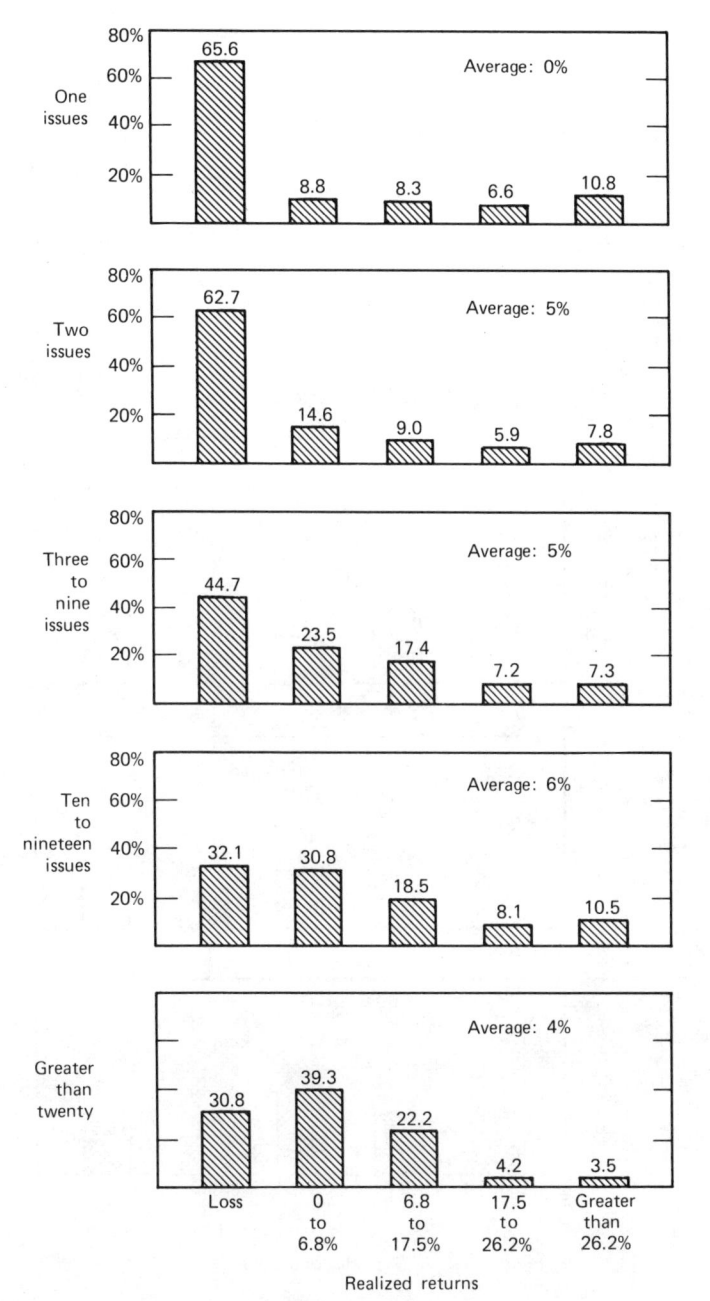

Chart 2–7. Distribution of realized returns on NYSE stocks by issues in portfolio, July 1971–June 1972.

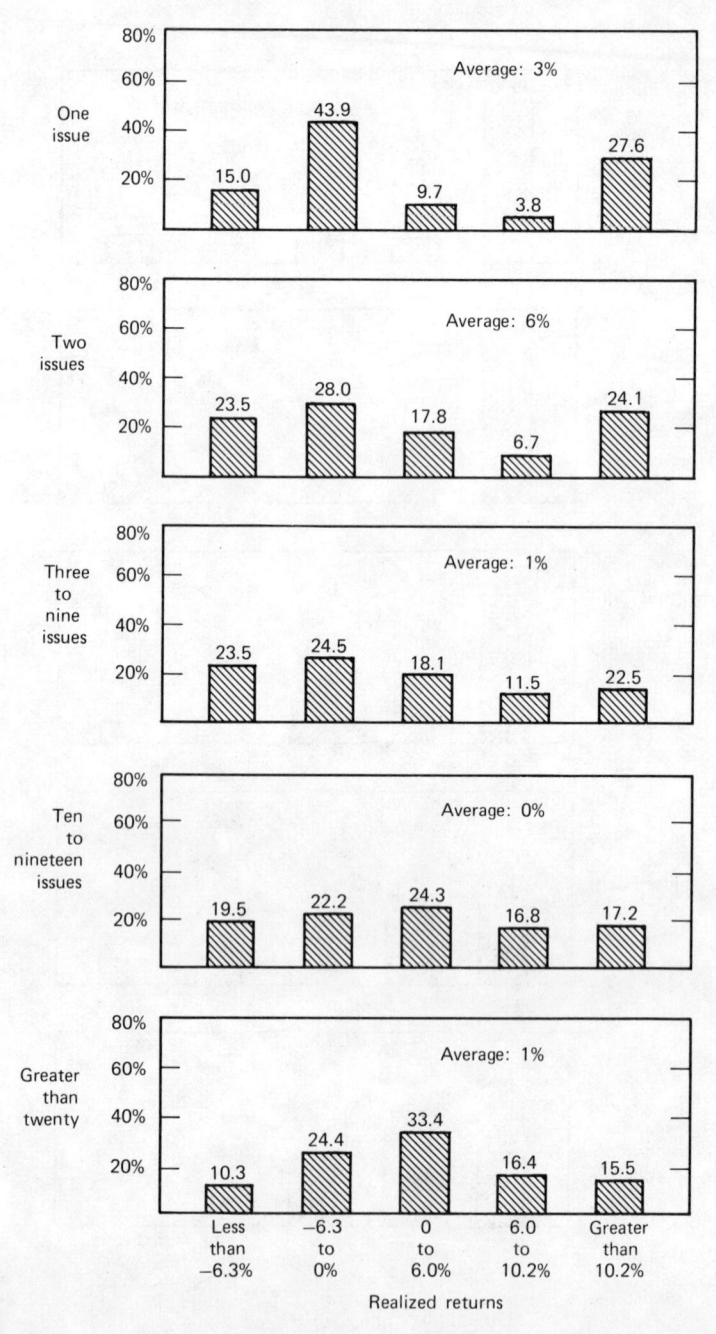

Chart 2–8. Percentage distributions of households cross-classified by realized returns, January 1970–December 1970.

assets. In this scenario, all investors who are not playing the security-selection game would hold the market portfolio of risky assets together with a position in risk-free assets. The increased costs of managing a portfolio with a growing number of issues, as well as the indivisibility of individual shares, would of course rule out the market portfolio for most investors. Yet the risk-return trade-off determined by the market portfolio is what an investor should strive to approximate as closely as possible with a portfolio of a limited number of assets. The question is how many assets offer the best approximation given the transaction costs.

The first assumption that risk can be adequately measured by standard deviation of returns is plausible, at least for short intervals in which the range of potential returns is not great. The second assumption is less adequate. In fact, investors cannot borrow and lend at the same rate to adjust the risk of their overall portfolio. Yet if the range of adjustment is limited, it may be useful to make such an assumption. Certainly in practice an investor can easily reduce his risk by investing in risk-free assets or can increase his risk over a limited range with margin accounts.[34] Moreover, for an investor whose desired overall risk level is close to the risk of the market portfolio of risky assets, this assumption probably does little harm.

Under these assumptions, the maximum increment of expected return an investor should be willing to give up for, say, a one-percentage point reduction in standard deviation hinges on the values of three factors: the risk-free rate, the expected return on the market portfolio of risky assets, and the standard deviation of return on that portfolio. For purposes of illustration, let us assume that the annual risk-free rate is 6 percent, the expected return on the market 11 percent, and its standard deviation 20 percent. Other values will produce different quantitative results but will not change the underlying logic.

Under these assumptions, the market portfolio of risky assets commands an expected risk premium of 5 percent, or stated another way, 1 percentage unit of expected return for 4 percentage points of standard deviation. Now consider an investor who wishes to hold a portfolio but with a standard deviation of only 10 percent. This investor could obtain such a portfolio by placing half of his money in the market portfolio and half in the risk-free asset that has a standard deviation of zero. Since he is bearing only half the risk, his expected risk premium is only half of 5 percent, or 2.5 percent. Added to the risk-free rate of 6 percent, his expected return is thus 8.5 percent. Now note that this investor should be equally content with this portfolio constructed of the market portfolio and the risk-free asset and a portfolio of risky assets alone, which promises the same expected return of 8.5 percent and a standard deviation of 10 percent. This second portfolio of risky assets alone differs from the market portfolio in that its expected risk premium is 2.5 percent lower and its standard deviation 10 percent, but the ratio of its expected risk premium to its standard deviation is 1:4 — the same as the market portfolio.

Without going into detail, this example illustrates a general proposition of modern theory. Any portfolio that promises the same ratio of its expected risk premium to its standard deviation as another portfolio is as desirable as the other, and one that promises a greater value of this ratio is preferable. In the previous example, if the expected return on the market portfolio exceeded the expected return of this second portfolio by less than 2.5 percent, this second portfolio in combination with the risk-free asset would be preferable to the market portfolio since it would promise a greater value of the ratio of its risk premium to its overall risk.

This discussion provides the basis for determining the maximum reduction in expected returns that an investor should be willing to accept for a specific reduction in standard deviation. Assume, for concreteness, that the investor currently holds an undiversified portfolio of risky assets with a standard deviation of 20 percent—the same as the market portfolio. Since the portfolio is assumed to be undiversified, it would have an expected return of less than the market portfolio, say, 10 percent. Assume that the expected risk premium on this undiversified portfolio is 4 percent, in contrast to 5 percent for the fully diversified market portfolio. Thus, for this undiversified portfolio, the investor can obtain 1 percentage unit of expected return for each 5 percentage points of standard deviation. Following the same logic, an investor who can reduce his standard deviation by less than a 1:5 reduction in expected return will be better off.

In the case of this particular undiversified portfolio, this 1:5 ratio is the key in determining how much further diversification is warranted. As long as the reduction in expected returns is less than one-fifth the reduction in standard deviation, additional diversification is warranted. This 1:5 ratio obviously depends on the specific numbers assumed for the market portfolio and the risk-free asset. Other numbers would of course lead to different ratios.

The use of a ratio such as 1:5 in evaluating the degree of diversification warranted requires an understanding of how diversification reduces standard deviation and the costs associated with further diversification. Part of the variability of the returns of individual securities stems from factors common to all securities, and the remainder originates from factors unique to specific securities. Since World War II, about one-third of the variability of returns of individual securities, as measured by the variance or square of the standard deviation, could be attributed to general movements in the market.[35] If it is assumed that the remaining variability is due to unique effects, that returns are normally distributed, and that the standard deviation of the market is 20 percent, the standard deviation of returns for portfolios of different numbers of securities, each equally weighted, can be calculated with standard statistical formulas.

These results, shown in Chart 2-9, indicate the rapid drop in standard deviation as one further diversifies portfolios of small numbers of securities. A portfolio of one security would have a standard deviation of 34.6 percent. Adding another two would drop it to 24.5 percent. With eight securities, the standard deviation would be 22.4 percent, which is only 2.4 percentage points greater than that of a completely diversified portfolio, or 1.8 percentage points greater than a portfolio of thirty-two securities. Although these differences are smaller than

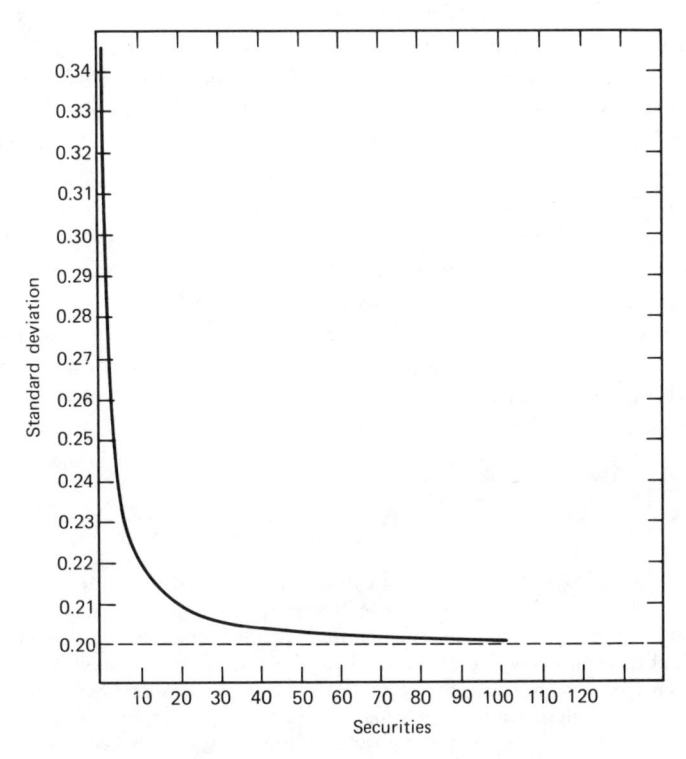

Chart 2-9. Reduction in standard deviation from diversification.

those obtained from the initial diversification, they are not unimportant. As long as it costs less than one-fifth of 1.8 percent, or 0.36 percent, per year to increase the size of the portfolio from eight to thirty-two securities, it is worth doing.

This simple statistical model of security returns probably overstates the rate of diversification. First, there is more than one effect common to two or more securities. This means that some of the variability attributable to unique effects is common to sets of securities and in portfolios of these securities would not be eliminated. Second, it is generally agreed that returns of individual stocks are better described by certain nonnormal distributions that entail a greater probability of extreme returns than implied by the normal. For such distributions, the reduction in risk would proceed at a slower pace.[36]

The remaining question is how much it really costs to increase the number of issues in a portfolio. It is clear that an investor with only $5,000 would find it difficult, in terms of both time and money, to hold, say, thirty stocks in his own name, although perhaps less expensive than the purchase of a mutual fund with a load fee. Yet such an investor could place this $5,000 in a no-load mutual fund or a closed-end investment company with little or no initial cost. Furthermore, a few investment companies holding diversified portfolios have kept their total expenses (including trading costs) very low, less than the prevailing management fee of a typical mutual fund, 0.5 percent per year. In addition to the management fee, the total expenses of a typical mutual fund would include operating expenses and trading costs.[37] Thus an individual with limited means does have the opportunity to obtain a diversified portfolio at reasonable costs.

The empirical results show, however, that many investors, particularly those of limited means, do not hold well-diversified portfolios. The analysis of the returns realized by them confirms that these investors have exposed themselves to far greater risks than necessary.

NOTES

1. These estimates of the total market value of all assets owned by individuals were derived from the detailed breakdowns of assets and liabilities of individuals used by the Federal Reserve Board in constructing its flow-of-funds statements, as well as from unpublished data on the value of personal residences, consumer durable goods, and land. Helen Tice was kind enough to provide us with these detailed breakdowns.

One of the two principal adjustments made to these data, which make the data comparable with those derived below for the richest families, was to remove 90 percent of pension-fund reserves on the assumption that about 10 percent of pension reserve funds, like Keogh plans, are under the personal control of individuals, whereas the remaining 90 percent are corporate and similar funds on which beneficiaries have no direct ownership claims. The other principal adjustment was to evaluate trusts according to their actuarial, rather than market, value. The rationale is that the individual beneficiaries of a trust benefit only from the expected cash payments and not from any residual, such as might be left to a nonprofit institution at the termination of the trust.

The specific adjustment was to reduce the value of trusts as given in the flow of funds by 25 percent. In their "New Dimensions of Economic Inequality: The Concentration of Personal Wealth, 1929-1969," *American Economic Review* (May 1974), J. D. Smith and S. D. Franklin estimate the ratio of the actuarial value of trusts over $60,000 to their market value as 54.3 percent in 1965. If valid, this estimate would suggest a reduction of 45.7 percent, not 25 percent. However, Smith and Franklin's ratio probably has a downward bias. One reason is that the set of trusts used in deriving the actuarial value is not identical to the set used in estimating the market value. The estimate of the actuarial value as well as the number of trusts of over $60,000 was based on estate-tax data. The market value of these trusts was then estimated by totaling estimates of the market values of a like number of the largest trusts from the fiduciary income-tax returns. Since a fiduciary income tax is filed for each trust independent of the number of potential beneficiaries, whereas the number of trusts estimated from the estate tax data is really an estimate of the number of beneficiaries, Smith and Franklin's estimate of the market value of trusts is probably too high.

Also, the actuarial value is perhaps too low to the extent that executors understate the expected cash flow in filing estate-tax forms. Although the error could be great measured as a percentage of all trusts, it is likely to be small when measured as a percentage of all assets. Thus 25 percent is assumed. Finally, trusts were allocated to asset types according to the distribution of assets in bank-administered personal trusts and estates for the year ending 1969.

Whereas the flow-of-funds data would permit an estimate of asset levels at periods other than mid-1962, mid-1969, and 1972, these are the only three dates from 1960 to the present for which data used in estimating the trends in the holdings of the richest families are available. (The flow-of-funds figures represent year-end values. The estimates for mid-1962 and mid-1969 were obtained by averaging the year-end figures bracketing each of these dates.) Unlike the account labeled "households" in the flow of funds, which includes nonprofit organizations, the asset holdings given here pertain only to individuals. The assets of nonprofit institutions have been excluded.

2. The appendix contains a detailed description of the estate-tax data.

3. I. Friend and M. E. Blume, "The Demand for Risky Assets," *American Economic Review* (December 1975).

4. M. E. Blume, J. Crockett, and I. Friend, "Stockownership in the United States: Characteristics and Trends," *Survey of Current Business* (November, 1974), contains a brief review of previous literature on the concentration of wealth.

5. Ibid.

6. Technically, adjusted gross income.

7. *Statistics of Income,* Internal Revenue Service, various issues. The income figure for 1969 is probably too large, but it corresponds to a break in the tables presented in *Statistics of Income.*

8. R. Ferber, "The Reliability of Consumer Surveys of Financial Holdings: Time Deposits," *Journal of the American Statistical Association* (March 1975).

9. Blume, Crockett and Friend, "Stockownership," contains a detailed technical discussion of the sample and all the adjustments made on the data.

10. The principal income item used in the stratification was adjusted gross income (AGI), defined as income before deductions and exemptions. When the text refers to family income or in short income in connection with this special sample, the technical definition is that of AGI.

11. J. Crockett and I. Friend, "Characteristics of Stock Ownership," *Proceedings of the Business and Economic Statistics Section, American Statistical Association* (1963).

12. This statement is based on the survey results reported in Chapter 3. R. C. Lease, W. G. Lewellen, and G. C. Schlarbaum, "The Individual Investor: Attributes and Attitude," *Journal of Finance* (May 1974), also reached the same conclusion.

13. In both 1960 and 1971, males sixty-five and over made up 8.4 percent of the total male population. From 1960 through 1971, the percentage of males sixty-five and over in the male age group of forty-five and over declined from 29.9 percent to 29.6 percent.

14. Specifically, the ratio of the market value of individual stockholdings (S_I) to total stockholdings (S_T) can be expressed as

$$\frac{S_I}{S_T} = \frac{S_I}{A_I} \cdot \frac{A_I}{A_T} \cdot \frac{A_T}{S_T}$$

where A_I represents individual financial assets and A_T, total financial assets.

15. To the extent that a filer listed the names and dividends of individual stocks rather than recording a single amount received through a brokerage firm, this percentage would include some "street-name" stocks.

16. The rank-order correlations for the larger issues, middle-size issues, and small issues are −0.70, 0.23, and −0.44, respectively. For all NYSE issues, the rank-order correlation is −0.67.

17. The rank-order correlations for the identified OTC stocks and the sums of the identified and unidentified OTC stocks are 0.73 and 0.33, respectively.

18. When the payer was clearly a mutual company, these improperly reported dividends were deleted. This blanket rule would be expected to introduce a slight bias, since under highly unusual circumstances it is possible to receive valid dividends through a mutual life-insurance company acting as an agent.

19. The rank-order correlation is 0.88.

20. The statistical condition for this is perfect positive correlation of the returns on all assets, which is obviously not true.

21. If less than five years but at least forty-eight months of data were available, these risk measures were still calculated.

22. Formally, the beta coefficient for a security is the slope coefficient in the regression of the monthly returns of the security on the correspondingly dated returns on the market portfolio.

23. I. Friend and J. S. deCani, "Stock Market Experience of Different Investor Groups," *Proceedings of the Business and Economic Statistics Section, American Statistical Association* (1966).

24. This number is somewhat less than that implied by the NYSE Composite Index. Blume, Crockett and Friend, "Stockownership," p. 33, footnote 65, discuss the conceptual differences between these two numbers.

25. Friend and DeCani, "Stock Market Experience."

26. Because of limitations of the tax data, it was not generally possible to identify stock held in trust or in the name of a nominee. All such stocks had to be treated as single issues. As can be seen below, this deficiency does not affect the overall results.

27. R. H. Litzenberger, "Discussion: The Allocation of Wealth to Risky Assets," *Journal of Finance* (May 1975).

Characteristics and Overall Trends in Assets   61

28. Specifically, a number of 2.5 is equivalent to 44 percent in each of two securities, and 12 percent in the third. As the number changes from 2 to 3, the proportions in the first two securities would drop from one-half to one-third, and the proportion in the third would increase.

29. M. E. Blume and I. Friend, "The Asset Structure of Individual Portfolios and Some Implications for Utility Functions," *Journal of Finance* (May 1975).

30. Another exception would be claims on trust assets. The 1962 survey separates these assets from others, and they are not included in the measures of diversification presented in the text. When households listing dividends from trust, custodial, or agency accounts are dropped from the 1971 special sample, the measures of diversification show, if anything, less evidence of diversification.

31. SOI Individual Income Tax Returns, 1963.

32. The classic study is the one by J. L. Evans and S. H. Archer, "Diversification and the Reduction of Dispersion: An Empirical Analysis," *Journal of Finance* (December 1968).

33. There is a vast literature on this subject. See, for instance, Friend, Blume, and Crockett, *Mutual Funds.*

34. To be sure, the interest rates on loaned and borrowed funds differ, which implies that the trade-off between expected return and risk, as measured by standard deviation, is nonlinear. This nonlinearity is one of the lesser problems in assessing the optimum desirable diversification, and will hence be ignored. The analysis could easily be extended to treat explicitly any such nonlinearity.

35. M. E. Blume, "On the Assessment of Risk," *Journal of Finance* (March 1971).

36. Although there is some controversy as to what type of distribution best describes security returns, it is clear that some type of distribution with fatter tails than the normal is required.

37. According to accepted accounting principles, trading costs are not shown in the income and expense statement but are treated as an adjustment to the price of the security purchased or sold. If shown, trading costs would appear in a footnote.

CHAPTER 3

The Individual Investor: Recent and Prospective Behavior

In the latter part of 1975 the NYSE conducted a survey of a large sample of individual stockholders in different socioeconomic–demographic groups. The purpose of this survey, which was planned and carried out under the auspices of the Wharton School and financed by the Twentieth Century Fund, was to obtain information about the degree and nature of stock-market participation of individual households and the reasons for recent and prospective changes in such participation. The implications of these changes for the importance of different classes of assets in the respondents' balance sheets were analyzed, particularly with regard to the relative importance of stock. The survey also was used to obtain indications of the effects that certain changes in the tax laws, the economy, and the institutional arrangements of the market itself might have on the stock market. Finally, the survey was used to analyze the relation between the stockholders' perceptions of and attitudes toward risk and the rates of return they required or expected on common stock as compared with other investments.

The Wharton Survey was conducted by the NYSE as a supplement to its own quinquennial stockholder survey, the NYSE Census of Shareholders. The purpose of the census is primarily to determine the number of individual stockholders. The NYSE 1975 Census drew a large random sample of 78,440 individual stockholders, including individuals listed as owning stock held by banks and brokers, from corporate books of record of publicly held corporations. From these books, it was possible to trace the number of stock issues of all public corporations held by each individual in the sample so that the same stockholder would not be counted more than once. Universe estimates of the number of individual stockowners were then made from the sample data. The census also obtained a limited amount of additional information (including household income) by a telephone survey of a subsample of 1500 individual stockholders.

The sample of individual shareowners for the much more detailed analysis in the Wharton Survey was drawn from the larger NYSE Census sample stratified by region and by the number of individual stocks in publicly held corporations owned by each shareholder. The Wharton Survey solicited information for the entire household or decision-making unit of which the stockholder was part, whereas the NYSE Census focused more closely on the individual stockholder. The procedures followed in the Wharton Survey, which are described in detail in a report available from the Wharton School, ensured that the sample was confined to stockholders and permitted several checks of the survey's results; for example, the number of shareholdings according to the survey was checked against the objective data obtained from the corporate books by the NYSE Census.

Of 2500 stockholders who received the Wharton Survey questionnaire, 1041 respondents submitted usable returns—an effective response rate of 41.6 percent.[1] Two questionnaire forms were used; each contained some relatively simple questions that appeared in the other questionnaire and some questions that did not.[2] This arrangement halved the number of possible replies to each nonidentical question. Even so, each of the questionnaires was ten pages long. The relatively high response rates to such lengthy and fairly complex questionnaires probably reflect interest in the material covered, the Wharton School name, and the fact that the U.S. Securities and Exchange Commission allowed us to allude to the potential usefulness of the survey results to its own work.

The terminology and phrasing of the questions were the product of extensive pretesting. These pretests consisted of in-depth interviews with ten stockholding heads of households selected on the basis of ready accessibility, followed by a mail pretest of 401 households selected from a list of 3000 relatively active clients of NYSE member firms throughout the country.[3] Of the 401 mail pretest households covered in the late spring of 1975 (May 23 through July 3), 212, or 52.8 percent, submitted usable returns. Since these 212 households included a large number of high-income, active investors, the pretest returns were used to check some of the results on the market behavior of upper-income shareowners and households with large stock portfolios obtained from the final Wharton Survey sample. Finally, a survey covering 189 of the 1459 nonrespondents of the 2500-subject Wharton sample was conducted by the NYSE to determine, for comparative purposes, the socioeconomic–demographic characteristics and elicit some simple qualitative information on the trading behavior of the stockholding households that failed to respond to the original questionnaires.

In general, a comparison of the appropriately weighted estimates of the socioeconomic–demographic characteristics of respondents in the Wharton Survey with corresponding estimates for the nonrespondents in that survey and with estimates made by the NYSE in connection with its Census of Shareowners indicates that the most important difference is the higher average income estimated from respondents in the Wharton Survey than from nonrespondents or from the special NYSE telephone survey. Corresponding differences were found in other income-related characteristics, including the amount of stock held.[4] Thus the median 1975 before-tax household income of shareowning households responding to the Wharton Survey was $22,855, compared to the NYSE estimate of $19,000.[5] The median income implied in the replies by the nonrespondents of the Wharton Survey lay between these two estimates, but closer to the Wharton figure. The difference between the Wharton and the NYSE estimates of stockholder median income may be explained by the fact that the NYSE survey responses were not weighted and by biases in both sets of data. Unfortunately, there are no completely satisfactory external data against which these different estimates can be checked. A special tabulation of the 1971 tax sample of dividend respondents discussed in Chapter 2 points to a median adjusted gross income for stockholding families of somewhat less than $18,000 in 1975, after adjusting for the trend in personal income between 1971 and 1975. However, adjusted gross income tends to understate total family income substantially.

The available external data for checking the Wharton and NYSE estimates of the median amount of stocks held are considerably more satisfactory. Thus the median stock portfolio size of shareowners was estimated at $13,405 for households in the Wharton Survey, compared with $10,050 for adult stockholders in the NYSE survey, both in the fall of 1975, and $13,225 for shareowning households as of mid-1971 according to universe estimates based on individual income-tax data presented in Chapter 2. The median value was about the same for nonrespondents in the Wharton Survey as for respondents. Assuming that from 1971 to 1975 the median value of stock held by shareowners moved at the same rate as NYSE stock prices, the universe median would have been about $12,500 in the fall of 1975, which is reasonably close to the Wharton Survey estimate and moderately higher than the NYSE estimate. In part, the difference between the two estimates is probably attributable to the fact that the Wharton study refers to households and NYSE, to individual adult stockholders.[6] While the Wharton Survey estimate of the median portfolio size seems reasonably reliable, none of the respondents to the Wharton Survey reported stock portfolios in excess of $1 million, although the Chapter 2 results seem to indicate that about 1 percent of the stockholding population and a large proportion of outstanding stock fall into this category. As a result, all important findings about the behavior of the wealthier stockholders were checked first against the findings for the somewhat more than 12 percent of surveyed families with stock portfolios between $100,000 and $1 million (close to the proportion indicated in Chapter 2), and then against the sixteen pretest respondents with stock portfolios of over $1 million.

These differences in the estimates of median income and portfolio size between the Wharton Survey and those obtained from data for nonrespondents or from other sources do not appear to be large enough to raise serious questions about the applicability of our weighted sample results on the characteristics of stockholding households to the population at large, except that care has to be taken in applying our findings to the very rich stockholders. All the results in the subsequent analysis will be weighted.

Of course, despite the absence of any substantial sampling bias in the weighted universe estimates of the socioeconomic–demographic characteristics of stockholding families, the actual detailed information on stockownership and trading reported by individual respondents, and hence the universe estimates based on these data, may still be subject to either large random or systematic errors. Generally, the only possible checks on the accuracy of the reported data were those of internal consistency and reasonableness. Yet in one instance, a more rigorous test was feasible by comparing the number of stock issues reported held in the portfolios of individual households with the number of issues collected in the NYSE Census. Since the NYSE Census collected information on individuals and the Wharton Survey on households, the Wharton figures should generally be either about the same or higher than the NYSE figures. In fact, this held true for over 86 percent of the respondents, confirming the validity of the information supplied.[7]

Still another bias that might affect the universe estimates of variables measuring investors' stock-market behavior and experience might exist in cases of systematic differences with respect to these variables between respondents and nonrespondents in the Wharton sample that were not closely correlated with the family characteristics (region and, more important, the number of shareholdings) on which the stratification was based. Thus it might be noted that, on the average, the ratio of stock to financial assets of the original respondents to the mail questionnaire was larger than that of respondents to the mail follow-up, as was the probability of their stock purchases in 1975 exceeding their sales, and they indicated a greater willingness to take risk. The respondents to the mail follow-up had larger values of these variables than did respondents to the final telephone follow-up. Nor can these differences be explained by the socioeconomic–demographic characteristics of the three groups of respondents.

In other words, the nonrespondents in the Wharton Survey may differ from respondents in ways that do not appear amenable to any completely satisfactory adjustment. As a result, the weighted aggregate estimates of the variables subject to these differential responses may be substantially biased. We have attempted to safeguard our analysis by the following procedures. First, where any aggregate estimates appear to be subject to a substantial response bias, we also present an alternative estimate based on the assumption that the respondents to the telephone follow-up are representative of the nonrespondents, once the number of stocks held by a family and the region in which it lives are held constant. Second, in regression analysis of the effects of a family's socioeconomic–demographic characteristics on its stock-market activities, the impact of sample response bias has been mitigated by explicitly differentiating among the three subsamples. As a result, this part of our analysis is not subject to the same limitations as our aggregate estimates of variables that are subject to substantially different responses in the three subsamples.

One last bias in the Wharton Survey sample for purposes of analysis of recent and prospective stock-market activity should be mentioned. Since the sample was drawn from the corporate stockholder books as of the middle of 1975, households that sold all their shareholdings before that time and those entering (or reentering) the market afterward (but not owning any stock as of mid-1975) are not covered. This bias in our results is likely to be relatively more substantial in the lower- than in the upper-income or wealthy groups.

Characteristics of Stock Trading in 1975

About two-fifths (41 percent) of the stockholding families in 1975 bought or sold some NYSE stock in 1975, 16 percent bought or sold shares of other publicly held corporations, excluding mutual funds, and 14 percent bought or sold mutual funds, excluding money funds (see Table 3-1; taken from Wharton School Stockholder Survey). Not surprisingly, only a relatively small proportion of stockholding families (15 percent) had never bought or sold NYSE stock, although even some of these may have inherited or been given such stock. As might be expected, a much higher proportion of shareowners never had any stock transactions in either mutual funds (55 percent) or other publicly held stock (54 percent).[8]

Transactions in NYSE stock in 1975, as measured by the number of market participants, seemed to be maintained considerably better than transactions in mutual funds or in other publicly held stock, with mutual funds holding up least well (see Table 3-2; from Wharton Survey). Fully half of all stockholding families that had ever bought or sold mutual funds did not engage in such transactions after 1972. A cross-classification of the transaction data by family characteristics indicates that, as might be expected, the percentage of stockholding families having transactions in stock other than mutual funds was much higher for the upper-income groups than for the rest of the population.

Of the stockholding families that either bought or sold NYSE, mutual fund, or other publicly held stock in 1975, the overwhelming majority either only bought or both bought and sold stock during the year (see Table 3-2; from Wharton Survey). A surprisingly small proportion of families with stock transactions reported sales only, which is especially surprising for mutual funds in view of the substantial redemptions of funds shares in that year. Stockholders with incomes under $10,000 were more likely than others to report sales only in 1975, particularly for NYSE stock.

If no adjustment for response bias is made, it would appear that fully one-third of the families (34 percent) had a dollar amount of stock purchase in 1975 in excess of their stock sales, 14 percent had purchases below their sales, 5 percent had purchases equal to sales, and close to half had neither purchases nor sales (see Table 3-3; from Wharton Survey). Consequently, an estimated 65 percent of the families with stock transactions had net purchases during the year. This figure would be reduced to a little more than 60 percent if a rough adjustment is made for response bias on the basis of the telephone responses to the Wharton Survey.[9] Although the survey data suggest that on balance more stockowning families bought than sold stock, the available data on aggregate net stock issues by corporations and net stock purchases by financial institutions and foreigners indicate a moderate overall level of net stock sales by individuals in the United States in 1975.[10]

Table 3-1. Recency of Stock Transactions

	Total	Since Jan. 1, 1975	Between Jan. 1, 1973 & Dec. 31, 1974	Prior to 1973	Neither Bought nor Sold	Number of Respondents	Number of Nonrespondents
		(Percent distribution of respondents)					
1. Shares of corporations listed on New York Stock Exchange	100	41.0	19.9	24.3	14.8	1013	28
2. Shares of any other publicly held corporations, excluding mutual funds	100	16.2	13.2	16.4	54.3	853	188
3. Mutual funds (excluding money funds)	100	14.3	8.1	22.7	54.8	858	183

QUESTION: When, if ever, was the *last* time you either bought or sold any of the following assets for your own account or for the account of any member of your immediate family? (Circle one number for each lettered row.)

Table 3–2. Nature of Stock Transactions in 1975[a] **(Percent Distribution of Families)**

	Total	Bought only	Sold only	Bought and Sold	Neither Bought nor Sold	Number of Respondents	Number of Nonrespondents
		(Percent distribution of respondents)					
1. Shares of corporations listed on New York Stock Exchange	100	39.8	10.0	36.6	13.6	544	9
2. Shares of any other publicly held corporations, excluding mutual funds	100	17.0	5.2	10.1	67.7	435	25
3. Mutual funds (excluding money funds)	100	23.5	3.2	3.0	70.3	449	8

QUESTION: Since January of this year, which of the following kinds of assets have you bought and/or sold for your account or the account of any member of your immediate family? (Circle one number on each line.)
[a] From beginning of year to time of survey in fall.

70 The Changing Role of the Individual Investor

Table 3–3. Comparison of Value of Stock Purchases and Sales in 1975

		Percent Distribution of Respondents
1. Purchases greater than sales		34.2
2. Purchases less than sales		14.1
3. Purchases equal to sales		4.6
4. No purchases or sales		47.1
5.	Total	100
6. Number of respondents		1,019
7. Number of nonrespondents		22

QUESTION: Since January of this year, how has the *dollar* amount of your combined family stock *purchases* (including NYSE issues, mutual funds, and other stock in publicly held corporations) compared with the value of your stock *sales*? (Circle *one* number.)

The greater frequency of net stock purchases than sales at a time when aggregate dollar sales were apparently somewhat in excess of aggregate purchases can be explained if it is assumed that net sales of stock in 1975 by households liquidating part or all of their portfolios typically were larger than net purchases by households accumulating stock. Such an assumption seems plausible since accumulation of stock seems more likely to take place than does liquidation over a protracted period and since net purchases will frequently represent relatively small amounts of stock acquired through employee stock purchase or monthly investment plans. It also is possible that this result reflects the fact that for families not owning stock in mid-1975, when the Wharton sample was drawn, but who were shareowners earlier or later in the year, net sales in the first half of 1975 may have exceeded net purchases in the second half. As noted below, there is little evidence that the richer families in 1975 were more or less likely to have net purchases or sales than were the rest of the stockholding population, although they were more likely to be net purchasers in 1973 and 1974 and, according to the estate-tax data presented in Chapter 2, in earlier years were selling off stock at a faster rate than were lower-income shareowners.

Over one-sixth of the value of all stock transactions executed by a stockowning household in the first ten or so months of 1975 was below $1,000, and another one-sixth between $1,000 and $2,500, with the median value a little under $4,500 (see Table 3–4; from Wharton Survey).[11] During this period, fewer than 2 percent of the shareowning households engaged in transactions with an aggregate value in excess

Table 3-4. Value of Stock Transactions in 1975

	Percent Distribution of Respondents
1. Under $1,000	18.4
2. $1,000–$2,499	17.9
3. $2,500–$4,999	18.3
4. $5,000–$9,999	19.2
5. $10,000–$24,999	15.5
6. $25,000–$99,999	8.8
7. $100,000–$499,999	1.6
8. $500,000 or more	0.3
9. Total	100
10. Number of respondents	538
11. Number of nonrespondents	23

QUESTION: Approximately what has been the total dollar value of stock and mutual funds made by you and your family since January 1st of this year? (Circle *one* number.)

of $100,000, but 9 percent had aggregate transactions valued between $25,000 and $100,000. There was, of course, a strong positive correlation between the value of stock transactions and both family income and the size of its stock portfolio (see Chart 3-1).

Only a relatively small proportion of individual investors made use of such speculative investments as margin accounts, stock options, or short sales in their 1975 stock transactions (see Table 3-5; from Wharton Survey). Short sales were least common and were resorted to by less than 4 percent of the shareowning families. The purchase of stock options, reported by 8 percent of the families, was much more common than short selling and somewhat more common than margin trading, apparently reflecting the substantial recent growth in speculative interest in such options associated with their exchange listing.[12]

The great majority of heads of shareowning households (72 percent) spent less than ten hours a month on investment analysis and financial decisionmaking. Of this group, 18 percent reported spending less than one hour a month. At the other extreme, fewer than 1 percent reported spending one hundred hours or more each month, and fewer than 3 percent spent fifty to one hundred hours. Obviously, the upper-income stockholders spent more time than others did on investment analysis and financial decisions, but even of those with incomes of $50,000 and over, close to 89 percent devoted less than twenty hours per month to this.

72 The Changing Role of the Individual Investor

Most stockholding families (74 percent) had accounts with brokerage firms with whom they could place an order without filling out an application. About 50 percent had an account with only one firm, 26 percent had none, 17 percent had accounts with two different firms, and 5 percent with three. Stockholders with annual incomes below $10,000 typically had no regular account with a brokerage firm, whereas those with incomes of $100,000 or more generally had accounts with two or three firms.

If no adjustment is made for response bias, it is estimated that close to 16 percent of the stockholding families switched brokerage houses in the 1975 period covered or stopped doing business with a particular brokerage firm. With the rough bias adjustment previously described, this proportion is reduced to somewhat over 11 percent. The most

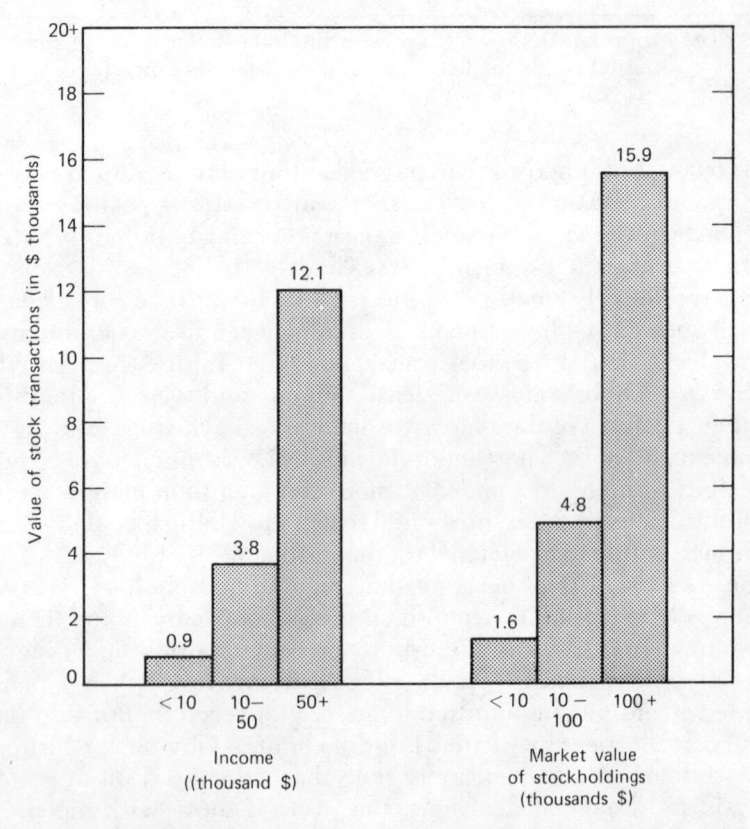

Chart 3–1. *Median values of stock transactions by income and market value of stockholdings.*

Table 3–5. Use of Margin, Option, or Short Sales

	Total	Yes	No	No. of Respondents	No. of Nonrespondents
	(Percent distribution of respondents)				
1. Used a margin account?	100	6.3	93.7	982	59
2. Written a stock option?	100	5.7	94.3	978	63
3. Bought a stock option?	100	8.1	91.9	983	58
4. Sold a stock short?	100	3.7	96.3	966	75

QUESTION: Since the beginning of 1975, have you or any member of your family done any of the following? (Please circle appropriate answer for each item.)

important reasons for these switches were the feelings that better brokerage services were available elsewhere (41 percent), that they had been getting poor advice (27 percent) and the fact that the broker they had been using had moved (26 percent). Only 2 percent switched to take advantage of lower commissions. The richer investors, in particular those with large stock portfolios, were less likely than others to switch, suggesting that smaller investors were less satisfied with brokerage services received.

Although the Wharton Survey did not compile data on the actual investment performance of the stock portfolios owned by households, it did collect information on investors' perceptions of their market performance during 1975, as compared with the actual performance of the Dow Jones Industrial Averages. Previously available data indicate little difference in investment performance between individual and ionstitutional investors and the market generally for the postwar period as a whole,[13] or among investors in different income and other socioeconomic–demographic groups in either 1960 or 1970–1972.[14] As a result, although no information was collected that would allow calculation of the average investment performance of individual investors in 1975, their *average* performance would be expected to be the same as the market assuming no unusual differential price movements among different classes of stock. In view of the asymmetry of stock returns and the lack of diversification in many portfolios, it is not surprising that the greatest *number* of investors perceived the performance on their stock portfolio to be less than the market; 26 percent of the shareowning families believed they did better than the Dow, 40 percent worse, and 34 percent about the same. This pattern of perceived performance may also be explained by the somewhat above-average performance of the Dow–Jones Industrials over the period covered,[15] transaction costs, and the psychological aftermath of several years of weak markets.

To determine how these characteristics of stock trading in 1975 were related to the socioeconomic–demographic and other characteristics of the shareowning families, two different types of analyses were carried out. First, the trading characteristics were cross-classified by the household's individual characteristics, one at a time. Second, the more interesting trading characteristics were expressed in a multiple regression analysis as a function of a wide variety of family characteristics. The first type of analysis has the advantage of treating qualitative factors more easily and does not assume simple linearity in the relationships among variables, whereas the second analysis, unlike the first, is able to handle a large number of explanatory variables simultaneously. In view of the extremely large number of cross-classifications involved in the first type of analysis, only a selected group is presented in this study, but all of the regressions are available to the interested reader.[16]

The net stock purchases by shareowning families in 1975 seemed to be widely dispersed among socioeconomic–demographic classes, with no indication from the statistical regressions that families with different incomes, value of stock portfolio, age of household head, occupation, or education behaved substantially differently in this respect from the rest of the population, although there were some sizable regional differences. However, when the two-way cross-classification results are examined rather than the regressions, the $10,000 to $50,000 income class and the thirty-five to forty-four and forty-five to sixty-four age groups clearly had a greater proportion of stockholders with net stock purchases exceeding net sales than did the other income and age groups, a result that is probably obscured by the assumption of linearity made in statistical regressions (see Chart 3–2). Similarly, stockholders with portfolios between $10,000 and $100,000 were net purchasers relatively more frequently than were investors with either smaller or larger portfolios. According to the cross-classifications, the self-employed, the professionals (doctors, lawyers, accountants, etc.), and the stockholders in the East North Central, East South Central, and Mountain states were more likely, and corporate officials less likely, to be net

Recent and Prospective Behavior 75

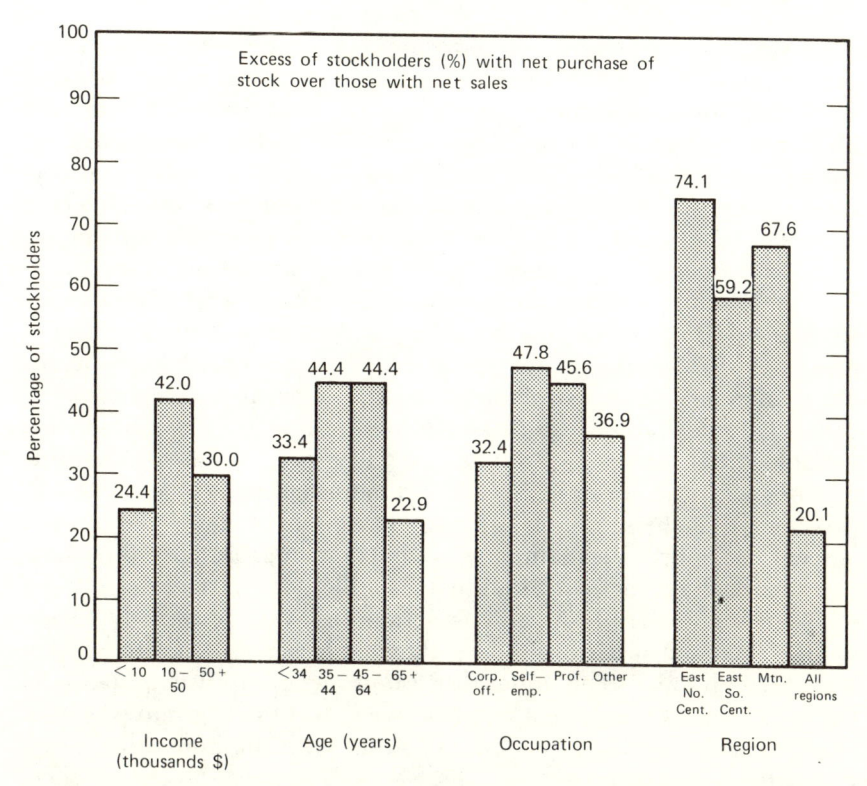

Chart 3–2. *Net percentage of stockholders with net purchases over those with net sales of stock in 1975 by income, age, occupation, and region.*

purchasers of stock than were other occupational and regional groups.

Net stock purchases in 1975 did not appear to be strongly related to the year in which a family made its first stock purchase; expected rate of change in cost of living; percentage of financial assets in stock; willingness to take financial risks; use of such speculative trading mechanisms as margin, stock options, or short sales; portfolio performance in 1975; or expected rate of return over the next five years. However, there is some evidence that those families that had bought their first stock in the 1965–1969 period, when stock prices were at a peak, were less likely to be net purchasers of stock in 1975 than were other families. Furthermore, in the most multivariate analysis carried out, where portfolio performance in 1975 and expected rate of future returns are kept constant, corporate officials are transformed from below-average into above-average net purchasers of stock.

No single socioeconomic–demographic group accounted for a major proportion of the public's use of speculative mechanisms for trading in stock, but some differences among groups did exist (see Chart 3–3). Shareowning families in the upper-income brackets or those with large stockholdings (with all other objective family characteristics held constant) did make greater use of margin accounts and were more likely to write and buy stock options than were other stockholders, but were no more likely to make short sales. When two additional subjective variables—the family's perception of the comparative performance of its stock portfolio with the market as a whole and its expected rate of return on stock over the next five years—were also held constant, the upper-income group's use of margin and options was no longer statistically distinguishable from that of other groups. Disregarding other variables, it is interesting to note that 11 percent of the stockholding families with incomes of $50,000 and more had margin accounts, 16 percent wrote stock options, 16 percent bought stock options, and 4 percent had short sales, compared with 2 percent, 1 percent, 6 percent, and 4 percent, respectively, for incomes under $10,000 (see Chart 3–3).

The older heads of shareowning families were less likely to use margin accounts and exhibited a somewhat lesser tendency to write or buy stock options. The under-thirty-four age group was particularly likely to use margin, while the thirty-five to forty-four group was most likely to write stock options and, together with the under-thirty-four group, to buy such options (see Chart 3–3). The most interesting effect of education on use of speculative mechanisms for trading in stock, once income and other subjective as well as objective factors were held constant, was a significant decrease in a family's tendency to buy stock options. However, disregarding other variables, the level of education was positively correlated with the stockholder's use of speculative mechanisms, including purchase of stock options.

Corporate officials and self-employed shareowners, like the upper-income groups, did tend to make above-average use of some speculative mechanisms, with both more likely than other families to buy stock on margin, the corporate officials more likely to write stock options, and the self-employed to sell short (see Chart 3–3). It is interesting, however, that neither group was especially active in the purchase of stock options. The fact that the frequency of short sales by corporate officials was no greater than that of other stockholders may reflect the legal constraints on such activity. Professional groups tended to have above-average activity in both writing and, especially, buying stock options.

There do not appear to be consistent or clear regional differences in

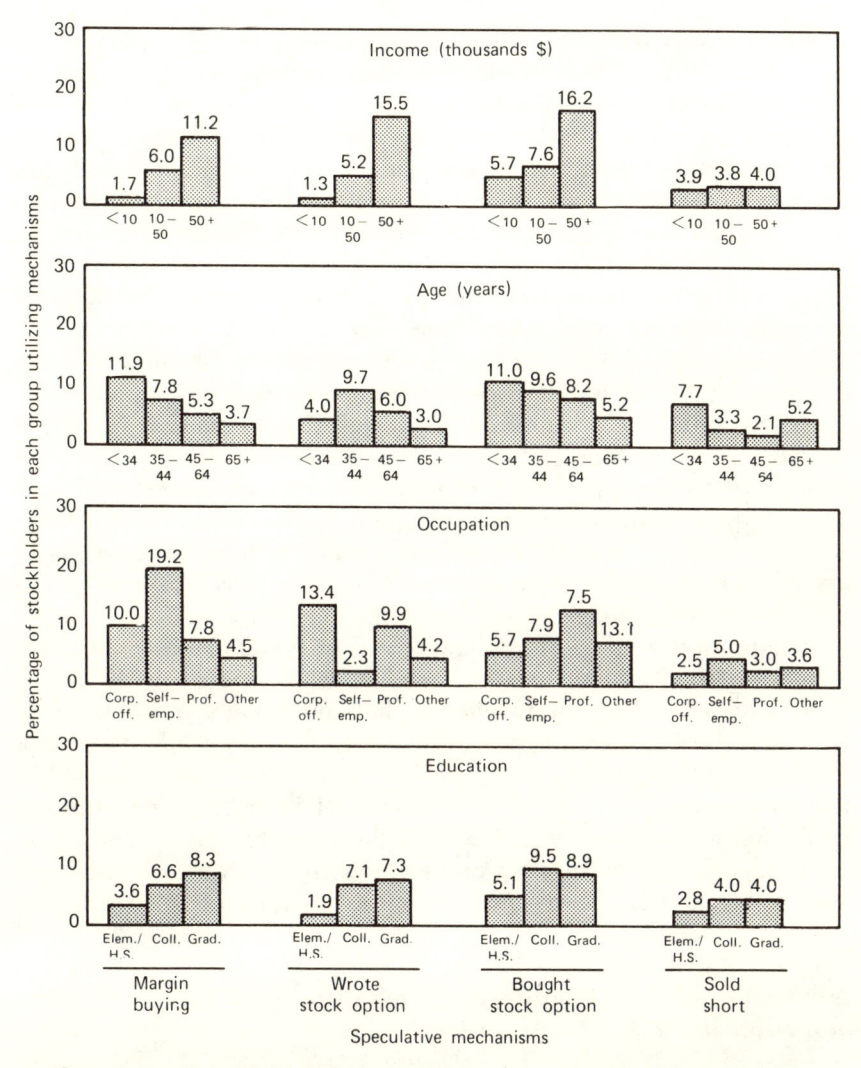

Chart 3-3. *Use of speculative mechanisms in 1975 by income, age, occupation, and education.*

the use of these speculative mechanisms, with the results of the analysis depending not only on the mechanisms used but also on whether comparative portfolio performance and expected stock return are held constant. Not unexpectedly, male heads of households were found to engage in margin trading with relatively greater frequency than their female counterparts. Sex differences did not affect other speculative mechanisms as strongly, with males appearing to write and buy options, and females to sell short, with relatively greater frequency.

A household's expected rate of return on stock investment over the next five years was positively related to its use of margin in 1975, which is consistent with what one would expect, and to its use of short sales, which is rather surprising, since an investor would seem more likely to associate high expected returns with increases rather than decreases in stock prices.

Interestingly enough, a household's perception of the 1975 investment performance of its stock portfolio relative to the market as a whole was not closely correlated with most socioeconomic–demographic or other characteristics that we were able to measure. However, upper-income stockholders believed that theirs was an above-average investment performance, whereas those with the lowest income believed their performance to be below average (see Chart 3–4). The young stockholders considered their performance less favorably than did the older ones.[17] There is also some evidence that stockholders who first acquired stock prior to 1970 were less likely to believe they had below-average performance.

Stockholders who had margin accounts or bought stock options believed they had done somewhat better than the market in 1975, and those who sold stock short believed they had done somewhat worse. Although these last results pertaining to the use of speculative mechanisms are not generally statistically significant, they are supported by two-way classifications of the perception of investment performance by income and age for users of each of these mechanisms. The results are also consistent with what one would expect in a market that rose fairly substantially between the beginning and the end of the year.

Sources and Uses of Funds for Stock Purchases and Sales in 1975

As noted previously, over three-fifths of the stockholding families that bought or sold stock during the year are estimated to have had net stock purchases in 1975. The most common source of these purchases was current income, which accounted for 44 percent of the responses on sources of funds by stockholding families. Next were withdrawals from savings accounts (17 percent), profits from earlier stock transactions (11 percent), withdrawals from checking accounts (7 percent), loans from either bankers or brokers (6 percent combined), and sales of other assets (5 percent). More than one source of funds may, of course,

Recent and Prospective Behavior 79

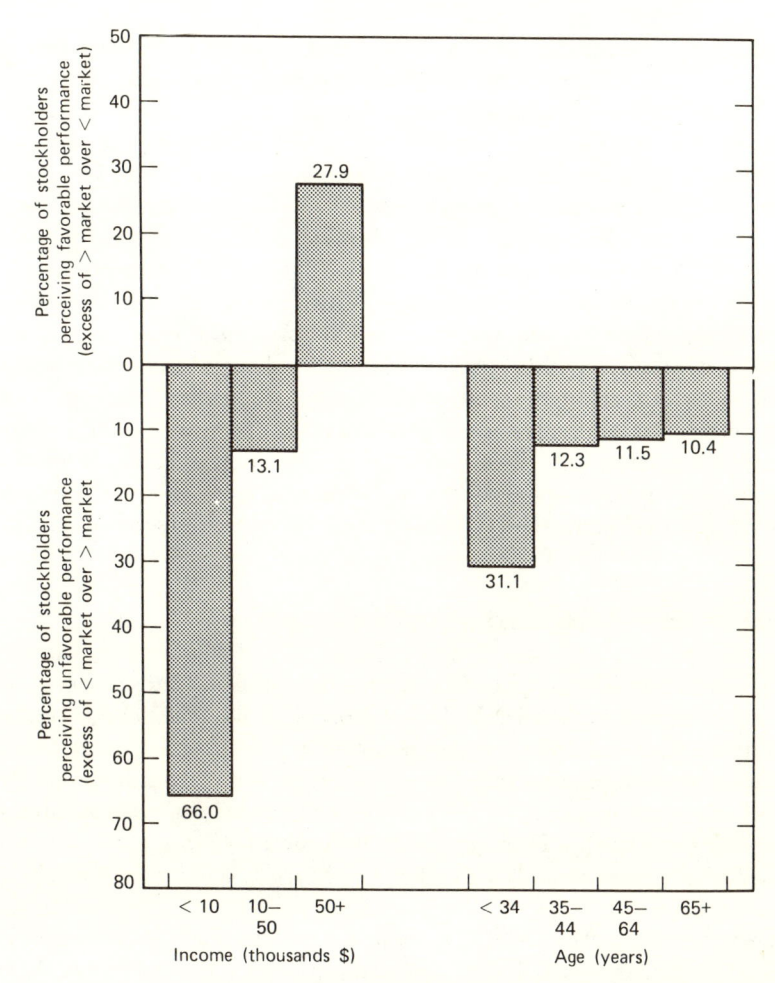

Chart 3–4. Perceived 1975 stock portfolio performance by income and age.

have been used by the same investor. The substantially greater resort to savings than to checking accounts as a source for stock purchases may reflect the recent tendency to monetize savings deposits—that is, to earn interest on balances designed for transactional purposes.

The most common use of funds from net stock sales in 1975 was to increase bank deposits (25 percent). Next in importance was diversification of previous holdings (15 percent); debt repayment (10 percent); and expenditures for education, illness, or emergencies (over 8 percent). The number of families using the proceeds from stock sales to acquire tax-exempt bonds (close to 8 percent) was of particular interest. Of far less importance were purchases of short-term fixed-interest obligations and of corporate and U.S. government bonds. It is noteworthy that although short-term fixed-interest obligations and corporate and U.S. government bonds were about as common a source of funds as a use of funds, tax-exempt bonds were much more frequently reported as a use than as a source of funds for stock transactions.[18] The use of funds from stock sales for home purchases or improvements (7 percent), other real-estate investments (7 percent), and purchases of durable goods (6 percent) and of nondurable goods and services (6 percent) was also of some interest. Not surprisingly, funds from stock sales were more frequently used to acquire real assets than the reverse.

The distribution of the sources and uses of funds associated with stock purchases and sales in 1975 was similar for most groups. One not too surprising exception was the greater deployment of current income, and liquidation of other investments, as sources of funds for the under- and the over-thirty-five-year-old stockholders, respectively.

Comparison of 1975 Trading with Earlier Years

Of the shareowning families, 31 percent reported an increase in average monthly purchases of NYSE stock in 1975 over the corresponding months of 1974 and 27 percent reported a decrease. The excess of increases over decreases in reported average monthly sales over this period was somewhat greater (29 percent reporting an increase and 18 percent a decrease). The aggregate volume of NYSE stock transactions increased moderately from 1974 to 1975, and again in 1976 (SEC *Statistical Bulletin*).

The proportion of mid-1975 stockholders who made their first stock transaction between 1970 and 1975 (16 percent), a period of nearly six years, was lower than in correponding periods in the preceding decade. This decline may reflect the same forces, most notably a weak stock market, responsible for the decrease in the number of shareowners in the 1970–1975 period shown by the NYSE Census.

As in 1975, more families owning stock as of mid-1975 reported net stock purchases in 1973 and 1974 than net stock sales, although again a high proportion (43 percent) showed no transactions or no net balances (see Table 3–6; from Wharton Survey). The predominance of families with net purchases over those with net sales was relatively higher in 1973–1974 than in 1975. Since aggregate net stock sales by individuals in 1973–1974 were larger than in 1975,[19] the frequency of net purchases in these years is rather surprising and may, as noted earlier

Table 3-6. Comparison of Value of Stock Purchases and Sales in 1973 and 1974

		Percent Distribution of Respondents
1. Purchases greater than sales		41.1
2. Purchases less than sales		15.8
3. Purchases equal to sales		8.1
4. No purchases or sales		34.9
5.	Total	100
6. Number of respondents		491
7. Number of nonrespondents		23

QUESTION: During the years 1973 and 1974, considering the *dollar* value of *all* of your stock transactions and those of your immediate family during this period, would you say that your stock purchases were:
More than sales.. 1
Less than sales.. 2
Equal to sales 3
Had no purchases or sales... 4

for 1975, reflect relatively small stock-purchase balances. An additional explanation may lie in the fact that families that sold all their stockholdings between 1973 to the middle of 1975 would not be included in the 1975 Census of Shareholders and hence would not be in the Wharton sample.

Regression analysis suggests that the characteristics of a stockholder's family had little bearing on whether he bought or sold stock on balance in 1973 and 1974. Unlike 1975, when no consistent trend by income or size of portfolio could be established, the richer families and those with large stock portfolios were more likely to buy stock on balance in 1973 and 1974 than were other shareowners (see Chart 3-5). As a result, there is evidence for the entire 1973-1975 period that the earlier decline in the degree of concentration of stockownership discussed in Chapter 2 may have been arrested. In the perspective of the mid-1977 level of stock prices, 1973 was a relatively unfavorable time for the acquisition of stock, whereas 1974 and 1975 were relatively favorable periods.

In 1973 and 1974 professionals seemed somewhat more likely than other occupational groups, and corporate officials less so, to be net purchasers of stock. Stockholding families living in the East South Central, West South Central, and Mountain states were somewhat more likely to sell on balance than were those living elsewhere.[20] The

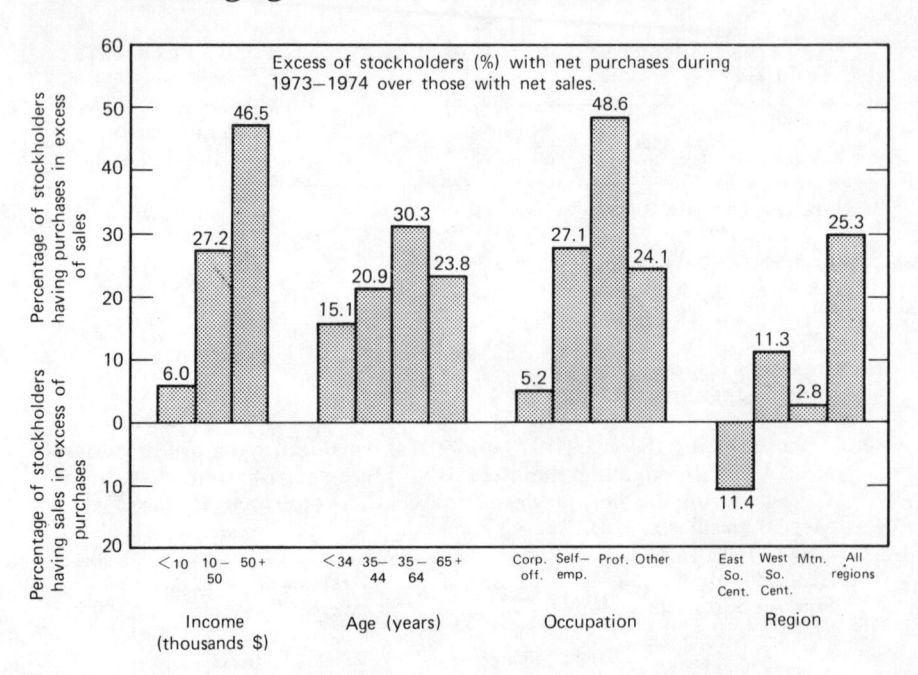

82 The Changing Role of the Individual Investor

Chart 3–5. Net percentage of stockholders with purchases over sales of stock in 1973–1974 by income, age, occupation, and region.

occupational differences in the propensity to be net purchasers of stock in these years paralleled the 1975 differences, but this did not hold true for some of the regions.

Reasons for Recent Trading Activity

The reasons most frequently cited by stockholding families for net stock purchases in 1975 included access to surplus funds from profits or cash resources (18 percent), the expectation of higher return (including price appreciation) on stock than on other investments over the next two to five years (14 percent), expected improvement in the general economy or investment climate (13 percent), participation in employee stock-purchase or monthly investment plans (13 percent), expected higher return over the next year (8 percent), purchase of stock as a hedge against inflation (8 percent), and the technical condition of the stock market (7 percent) (see Table 3–7; from Wharton Survey). The

Table 3–7. Reasons for Net Stock Purchases in 1975

	Percent Distribution of Responses
1. Had additional capital from former profits or extra cash from other sources to invest/reinvest	17.5
2. Expected a higher return, including price appreciation, on stocks or mutual funds than on other investments during the next year	8.2
3. Expected a higher return, including price appreciation, on stocks or mutual funds than on other investments over the next two to five years	13.8
4. Expected improvement in the general economy/investment climate	13.4
5. General increase in stock prices during this period	4.3
6. Believed stocks/mutual funds better/less risky than other investments	3.7
7. Bought stocks/mutual funds as a hedge against inflation	7.8
8. Technical condition of the stock market made stocks/mutual funds seem more attractive	7.4
9. Technical situation or new information obtained concerning specific stocks purchased	4.1
10. Seeking diversification of holdings to broaden stock portfolio	4.9
11. Participation in employee stock purchase plan or monthly investment plan	13.0
12. Other	1.9
13. Total	100
14. Number of respondents	173
15. Number of nonrespondents	1

QUESTION: (If stock purchases were *greater* than sales.) Since January of this year, what reasons did you and your immediate family have for *buying* more stocks or mutual funds than you sold (excluding money funds) against other possible uses of these assets? (Please circle *all* that apply.)

84 The Changing Role of the Individual Investor

greater importance placed on two-to-five-year as against one-year returns suggests that most stockholders are long-term investors rather than short-term speculators, supporting the evidence from the aggregate NYSE portfolio turnover statistics, which indicate a turnover ratio of less than 20 percent for individual domestic public stockholders—stockholders other than financial institutions, foreigners, and exchange members. The number of shareowners purchasing stock as a hedge against inflation probably declined since in recent years stocks have proved a poor hedge. Of particular interest is the relatively sizable number of families that acquired stock in 1975 through employee stock-purchase or periodic investment plans. As observed earlier, such plans would help to explain the larger number of families with stock purchases than sales at a time that saw liquidation of stockholdings on balance. As might be expected, the survey shows that such plans were much more important for stockholders under sixty-five years of age than for those over sixty-five.

Table 3–8. Reasons for Net Stock Sales in 1975

	Percent Distribution of Responses
1. Poor investment performance of stocks in portfolio	17.1
2. Concern about adverse effect on my stock investments	9.8
3. Needed the funds to help keep up with inflation	8.1
4. Needed the funds to cover margin calls	0.0
5. Needed the funds for specific purpose or emergency	10.1
6. Reinvestment of stock sale proceeds in other securities	8.9
7. Concern about business recession or unemployment	5.4
8. Concern about technical conditions in the stock market	9.9
9. To realize capital gains-profits on earlier stock purchases	12.4
10. Obtained new information about stocks	2.4
11. Sold stock for tax purposes to establish a tax loss	9.6
12. Started or increased investment in own business	0.0
13. To invest in real estate[a]	.7
14. To increase savings deposit[a]	1.6
15. To take advantage of tender offer or co. offer to buy back stock[a]	1.1
16. Other[a]	2.9
17. Total	100
18. Number of respondents	69
19. Number of nonrespondents	6

QUESTION: Since January 1, 1975, what were the main reasons you and your family sold more stock than you bought? (Please circle *all* that apply.)

[a]These replies were elicited from "Other (specify)."

The only other noteworthy difference in the reasons of groups of stockholders for buying stock on balance in 1975 was the greater tendency of the upper-income groups and corporate officials to emphasize longer-term returns, while the self-employed emphasized extra funds and short-term returns. The lesser importance of the inflation-hedge incentive in stock purchases in the New England and Middle Atlantic regions also was of some interest.

The most frequent reasons for net stock sales in 1975 were poor investment performance of stock in the family's portfolio (17 percent), realization of capital gains on earlier stock purchases (12 percent), the need of funds for a specific purpose or emergency (10 percent), concern about technical conditions of the stock market (10 percent), concern about adverse effects on portfolio stock (10 percent), establishment of a tax loss (10 percent), reinvestment of stock sale proceeds in other securities (9 percent), the need for funds to keep up with inflation (8 percent), and concern about business recession or unemployment (5 percent) (see Table 3-8; from Wharton Survey). Generally, the reasons for net stock sales of most groups of families were similar, except that the upper-income groups were less likely to sell because of poor investment performance or for technical market considerations. Reactions to the business climate and prospects seemed to be more important on the purchase than the sales side, whereas inflationary influences and technical conditions in the stock market had approximately the same impact on the households motivated to buy as on those motivated to sell. Finally, poor investment performance of portfolio stocks, presumably associated with a decline in stock prices, appeared to have a far greater effect on stock sales than the increases in stock prices during the year had on purchases.

The reasons given for changes in trading activity during 1975, as distinguished from reasons for net purchases or sales, included in order of importance: change in stock prices (27 percent), increased concern about inflation (15 percent), recession bottoming out (13 percent) historically high yield on stock (12 percent), and changes in interest rates (9 percent). It is interesting, though somewhat surprising, that as contrasted with the 15 percent of stockholding families that reported changes in their trading activity because of increased concern about inflation, only 1 percent were similarly affected by decreased concern about inflation.

For 1973 and 1974, the relative order of importance of the reasons given by stockholding families for their net stock purchases was quite close to that of 1975, with several noteworthy exceptions. In 1973 and 1974, only 6 percent of the families registered net stock purchases through employee stock purchase or monthly investment plans as compared with 13 percent in 1975. Both availability of surplus funds and acquisition of stock as a hedge against inflation were somewhat more important reasons for stock purchases in 1973 and 1974 than in 1975. With the onset of recession and the continuation of inflation, presumably fewer free funds were available in 1975, and with the inverse relationship between inflation and stock price movements in recent years, investors in 1975 may no longer have considered stocks a satisfactory hedge against inflation. Finally, there was no substantial increase in the stock market in 1973 and 1974 so that this possible motivation for net stock purchases was not covered, but even in 1975, it appeared to affect only 4 percent of the families.

The major single difference in the reasons for net stock sales in 1973 and 1974, as compared with 1975, is the general decline in stock prices in the former two years, cited by 11 percent of the families as the reason for their sales, which had no counterpart in 1975. Other economywide or marketwide psychological effects also seemed more important in encouraging stock sales in the previous two years. There was a slightly higher proportion of shareholding families with net sales to cover margin calls during 1973 and 1974, but the percentage (less than 2 percent) was still very small. On the other hand, technical conditions in the stock market and realization of capital gains were less frequently cited as reasons for selling in 1973 and 1974 than in 1975.

Current and Prospective Importance of Stock in Balance Sheet

If no adjustment for response bias is made, the mean percentage of financial assets invested in the stock of publicly held corporations by stockholding families is estimated at somewhat over 39 percent (see Table 3–9; from Wharton Survey), but with a rough adjustment for response bias, the mean is reduced to a little more than 33 percent.[21] In contrast to the substantial proportion of stockholding families with more than half of their financial assets in publicly held stock, only a very small proportion held more than half of their financial assets in bonds and other fixed-income securities. Both deposits and other financial assets ranked between stocks and fixed-income securities as predominant shares of financial assets.

There is no clear evidence that shareowning families in the fall of 1975 generally planned a change in the relative importance of stock in their portfolios during the next five years; yet what evidence there is points to a small reduction in the portfolio share of stock, although not

Table 3-9. Composition of Family's Financial Assets

Asset Category	Mean Percent of Financial Assets	Percent of Respondents with Less than 10 percent of Financial Assets in Asset Category	Percent of Respondents with 50 percent or More of Financial Assets in Asset Category	Number of Respondents	Number of Nonrespondents
1. Stocks of publicly held corporations, including mutual funds other than money funds	39.5	19.9	34.7	970	71
2. Bonds, short-term and other fixed-income issues	9.4	65.9	4.2	970	71
3. Savings, time and demand (checking) deposits	30.6	21.1	26.5	970	71
4. Other (including closely held corporations, farms, and real-estate investments other than own home)	20.5	53.4	20.9	970	71
5. Total	100				

QUESTION: What percentage of your total financial assets, excluding your and your immediate family's own home(s) or investment in a private business, is in each of the following four categories? (Please make sure the figures total 100 percent.)

necessarily in the absolute amount of stock held given the likely increase in total assets.[22] During this period more of these families expected that the largest proportionate increase in their financial assets would occur in the stock portfolio than in any other major class of assets (see Table 3-10; from Wharton Survey); however only 27 percent of responding families held this expectation, a substantially greater percentage than the corresponding proportion for bonds and other fixed-income securities but not much greater than that for deposits or other assets, and shareholding families might be expected to be biased in favor of shareownership.

Moreover, when the proportions of financial assets expected to be held in stock in five years are compared with the current percentages, the mean expected change over this period was a decrease of 1.7 percent (see Table 3-11; from Wharton Survey).[23] As might be expected, the largest percentage decreases were anticipated by stockholders having the highest proportion of their assets in stock at the beginning of the period. There also was a fairly substantial anticipated increase (from 4 to 12 percent) in the proportion of families with virtually no investment in stock. However, these data do not reflect purchases of stock by those families that did not hold stock at the beginning of the period. Even for families that did own stock, the maintenance of their beginning period stock ratio would require net purchases of stock as their total financial assets increased.

As a result, in terms of dollars the expected 1.7 percent decrease in the ratio of stock to financial assets of stockholding families in late

Table 3-10. Categories of Financial Assets Expected to Increase Most

	Percent Distribution of Respondents
1. Stocks of publicly held corporations, including mutual funds other than money funds	26.5
2. Bonds, short-term and other fixed income issues	10.5
3. Savings, time and demand (checking) deposits	20.4
4. Other	20.1
5. Expected no change	22.5
6. Total	100
7. Number of respondents	968
8. Number of nonrespondents	73

QUESTION: If you expect those percentages in question 20 to change over the next five years, which category do you expect to increase the most?

Table 3–11. Trends in Proportions of Financial Assets Expected to be in Stock during 1975–1980

Percent of Financial Assets in Stock	Percent Distribution of Respondents in 1975	Mean Expected Change in Stock Percent in 1975–1980	Percent Distribution of Respondents in 1980
1. 90–100	7.1	−19.6	4.9
2. 80–89	4.3	−17.2	5.0
3. 70–79	6.8	−10.3	5.7
4. 60–69	6.3	−7.5	5.5
5. 50–59	10.2	−6.0	12.5
6. 40–49	6.4	2.0	5.4
7. 30–39	9.3	0.0	7.5
8. 20–29	14.2	4.2	16.3
9. 10–19	15.4	3.2	13.5
10. 5–9	7.6	3.1	5.5
11. 1–4	8.6	3.1	6.1
12. 0	3.7	3.9	12.0
13. Total	100		100
14. Number of respondents	970	919	941
15. Number of nonrespondents	71	122	98

QUESTION: Five years from now, what percent of these financial assets held by you or your immediate family would you expect to be in stock, including mutual funds?

1975—a less than $10 billion decrease in the amount of stock held if total financial assets of these families remained constant and if there were no new stockholders—may be more than offset by purchases of stock over the 1975–1980 period, both by new stockholders and by existing stockholders wishing to maintain the desired balance with new savings inflows. On the other hand, the amount of stock held by stockholding families will tend to be somewhat depressed over the next five years by the population trends discussed in Chapter 2. They also may be affected even more markedly either way by differential price movements in stocks and other financial assets, since investors do not make immediate adjustments in their portfolio structure and also since the desired structure may be affected by asset-price movements. Abstracting from price movements, whereas the proportion of individually held stock may continue to decline over the next few years (for reasons mentioned in Chapter 2), the Wharton Survey results suggest that individuals are not likely during this period to liquidate their stockholdings at the same rate as in recent years.

When the current and prospective importance of a stock in the balance sheet is related to the stockholding family's objective socioeconomic–demographic characteristics, several of the characteristics tested —income, age of household head, and education—stood in positive correlation to the family's ratio of stock to financial assets in the fall of 1975 once the other family characteristics were held constant. Professionals also seemed to have a somewhat higher stock ratio than did other investors. Whereas the income effect is not really statistically significant in the regressions, the two-way classifications show a strong positive relationship between income and stock ratio (see Chart 3–6). There also is a significant positive relationship between income (and, to a lesser extent, market value of stock portfolio) and the expected trend in the ratio of stock to financial assets,[24] but the statistical significance of this relationship is not clear once other family characteristics are held constant (see Chart 3–7).[25]

The addition to the regression analysis of the subjective variables— perceived stock portfolio performance in 1975 and expected rate of return over the next five years—does not alter appreciably the apparent impact of income and age on the current importance of stock, or of income on the prospective importance of stock. However, the effect of education on the stock ratio ceases to be significant, and the only important effects of occupation on the current and prospective roles of stock is that the self-employed had a below-average stock ratio in 1975 and were more inclined than other investors to increase this ratio over the next five years. As might be expected, stockholders who antici-

Recent and Prospective Behavior 91

pated relatively high rates of return over the next five years expected to increase their stock ratios.

Overall, the survey results suggest that the upper-income shareowners planned to increase, or at least maintain, their ratio of stock to financial assets over the 1975–1980 period, whereas the other shareowners planned to decrease or maintain this ratio, with little change

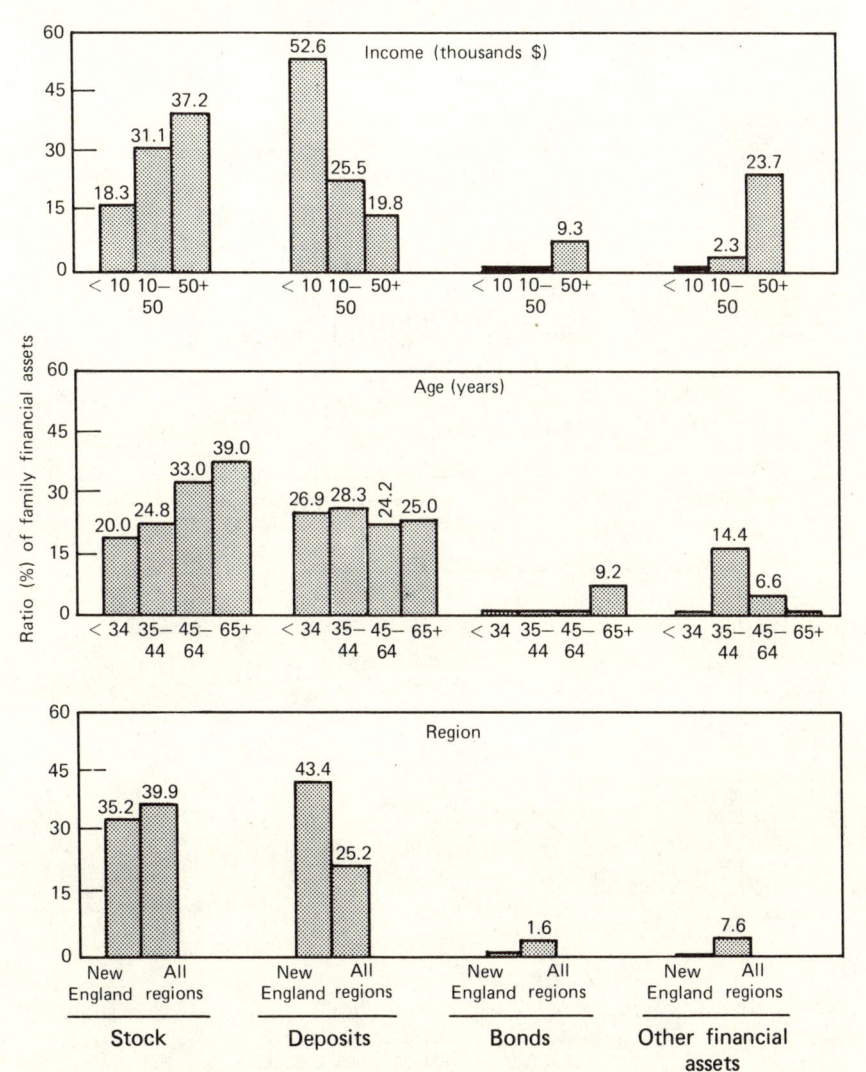

Chart 3–6. Median ratios of major classes of financial assets to total financial assets by income, age, and region.

apparent in the combined ratio weighted by market value of holdings as compared with the small reduction in the ratio indicated by the unweighted data. If these plans are realized, the decline over recent decades in the share of stock owned by all individuals, as distinguished from institutional investors, would probably be moderated.[26] Evidence that this potentially significant development may already

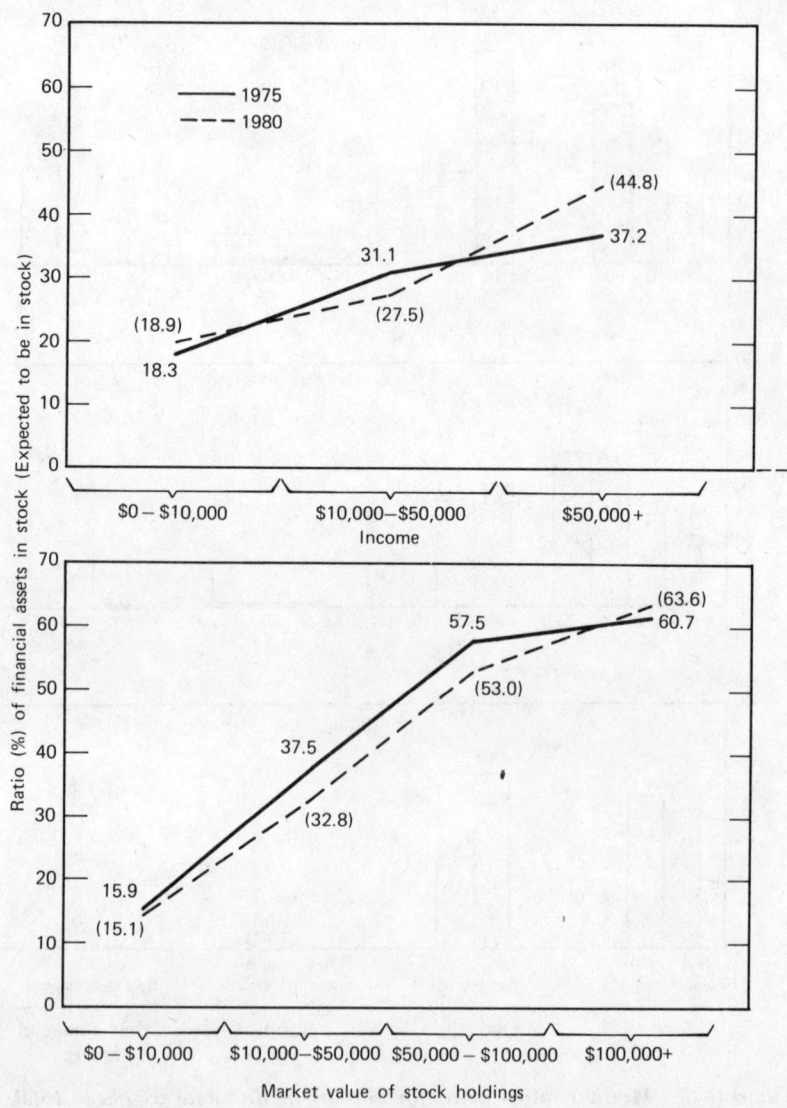

Chart 3-7. *Median ratios of financial assets held in stock in 1975 and expected in 1980 by income and market value of stockholdings.*

have begun is provided by the aggregate data indicating the small size of individuals' net sales of stock from 1974 through 1976 as compared with the preceding years.[27] However, institutional net purchases of stock in these years, though lower than in the immediately preceding years, were still substantial. The increase in stock prices after the Wharton Survey was conducted served to raise the actual, and probably the desired, stock ratios in the portfolios of both individuals and institutions, but it is not possible to tell which group was affected more.[28]

Realization of the survey plans would seem to point to a somewhat increased importance of the wealthier stockholders at the expense of smaller shareowners, or at least a stabilization of their relative position. The 1973–1975 stock purchases data discussed earlier also gives evidence that the long-term decline in the relative importance of the wealthier stockholders may have leveled off in recent years. The trend in the relative importance of the two groups of individual investors is important not only for its social implications but also because of the relatively greater propensity of the upper-income group to hold non-NYSE stocks. It is generally believed that the decline in the relative importance of the upper-income groups in stockownership has compounded the problems of the smaller and less seasoned corporations in raising capital. Although this decline may be moderated over the next five years as the upper-income groups better maintain their position *vis-à-vis* the lower-income groups and individual investors as a whole no longer have substantial net stock sales, institutions are likely to continue to increase their share of the market, though at a more moderate rate than in the last two decades.

In addition to providing insights into the family characteristics that determine the relative importance of stock in a family's total financial assets, the survey provided similar information for other classes of assets (see Chart 3–6). For bonds (and other fixed-income securities) as well as for other financial assets,[29] an increase in income was associated with a disproportionately greater increase in the ratio of the holdings of that class of assets to total financial assets. For deposits, the relationship was reversed; that is, an increase in income was associated with a disproportionately greater decrease in the relative importance of deposits to other financial assets. Stocks occupied a position intermediate between these other groups of assets, with an increase in income associated with a disproportionately greater increase in the stock-financial asset ratio, until it reached a peak in the $50,000 to $100,000 income range. Although the different relations with income do not always appear to be statistically significant in the regression analysis, they are strongly supported by the evidence in Chart 3–6.

These results imply that holdings of bonds and other financial assets are more highly concentrated among the upper-income groups than stockholdings and are much more highly concentrated than deposits.[30]

There is some tendency for the ratio of bonds to financial assets to increase with age, but the relationship, although uniformly statistically significant in the regression analysis, seems to be largely attributable to the sixty-five-and-over age group (see Chart 3–6). Both the oldest and the youngest age groups had very little of their wealth invested in other financial assets—investments that are not as marketable and require more personal attention than stocks, bonds, or deposits.

Of the regional differences, the most striking seem to be those between stockholders in New England and the rest of the country. Stockholders in New England invested a greater proportion of their financial assets in deposits and less in bonds and other assets than did stockholders in other regions (see Chart 3–6). Once other family characteristics are held constant, they also tended to invest somewhat more in stock. It should be noted that, as pointed out in Chapter 2, the asset preferences of investors in Massachusetts were somewhat different from those in the rest of New England.

Stockholdings in general apparently served as substitutes for holdings of deposits and other financial assets, but not for holdings of bonds and other fixed-income securities. In other words, families with large stock portfolios held relatively small amounts of deposits and other financial assets.

Impact of Institutional and Tax Changes on Market Behavior

In the Wharton Survey the respondents were asked a series of questions about the likely impact on stock market behavior of a number of possible changes in the tax laws and other institutional arrangements affecting the financial markets. The replies to some of the questions about the effects of these changes, particularly those relating to taxes, may be biased if respondents thought that their answers could affect legislative or institutional behavior. To guard against such possible bias, the survey results were checked for consistency and reasonableness and, whenever possible, against external sources of information. Even if such bias remains, the answers should, at the very least, provide valuable insights into the direction and the relative magnitudes of the potential effects of such changes.

In view of Wall Street's strong support for a reduction in the capital gains tax, more detailed information was requested on the effect of such a revision than on the effect of other changes. Since at the time of the survey no serious consideration was being given to taxing capital gains at the higher rates applicable to other income, the survey did not inquire into the effect of an increase in capital gains taxation. Such an increase may be part of the Carter administration's tax package. This package also may possibly recommend a reduction in the effective tax rates paid by individuals on dividend income and perhaps may also include a 50-percent ceiling on marginal individual tax rates for all sources of income. If one makes the probably reasonable assumption that the impact of an increase in capital gains taxation will roughly approximate in magnitude (but differ in direction from) the effect of an equivalent decrease in capital gains taxation, one can make some rough estimates of the possible effects of the conjectured Carter proposal. Thus it is assumed that a rise in capital gains taxes from 25 percent to 37.5 percent would possibly discourage stock purchases by the same amount that a reduction from 25 percent to 12.5 percent would stimulate such purchases.

A 50-percent reduction in the capital gains tax would, according to the survey replies, substantially affect the proportion of shareowning families' financial assets expected to be in stock in the next five years. Such a change in the tax laws would lead to an estimated mean increase of 5.5 percentage points in their stock ratio by 1980 from what it would be under present tax laws (see Tables 3–11 and 3–12; both from Wharton Survey).[31] This 5.5 figure is a mean that is weighted by the market value of stock held by the shareowners but is very close to the unweighted mean of 5.3. The pretest survey data, which are heavily weighted by rich and active stockholders, point to a higher figure. Combining both samples and using the estimates of the total value of stock held in each of the market-value per stockholder classes presented in Chapter 2 would lead to a weighted mean effect somewhat above 5.5, but this estimate would give a disproportionate weight to active stockholders.

If this difference of 5.5 percentage points in the estimate of individuals' mean demand for stock as a result of a 50-percent reduction in capital gains tax is applied to their total stockholdings in 1975, it would be about as large as the total net stock issues by corporations to the public in any three-year period. The most pronounced change in the percentage of stock asset holdings as a result of this reduction in the capital gains tax occurs in the proportion of current stockholding families that would have virtually no investment in stock five years hence. This proportion is estimated at 12 percent without the tax change and zero with the change.

96 The Changing Role of the Individual Investor

The other possible changes in the tax law that were covered also would increase the proportion of household assets in stock (see Table 3-13; from Wharton Survey). The effect of each of these changes was determined by asking respondents whether it would have any effect on their stock portfolios and, if so, whether it would increase or decrease the stock ratios by more or less than 10 percent.[32] Not surprisingly, in view of the amounts of money involved, the two changes held most effective were the exclusion of dividend income from personal income tax and the elimination of corporate taxes on income distributed as dividends. The exclusion of dividend income from personal income tax would induce 34 percent of the shareholding families to increase their percentage of assets in stock by more than 10 percent, and 23 percent by 1 to 10 percent. Only a small number indicated that they would decrease their stockholdings, whereas the elimination of corporate taxes on dividend income would not, according to respondents, be as effective.[33] The small number who indicated a decrease in stockholdings could theoretically be seen as rational, but it more likely represents respondents who did not fully understand the question.

It is interesting that the exclusion of dividend income from personal

Table 3-12. Proportion of Financial Assets Expected to be in Stock with 50 percent Reduction in Capital Gains Tax

Percent of Financial Assets	Percent Distribution of Respondents
1. 90–100	7.5
2. 80–89	6.2
3. 70–79	10.0
4. 60–69	7.1
5. 50–59	15.3
6. 40–49	5.4
7. 30–39	7.4
8. 20–29	18.1
9. 10–19	13.5
10. 5–9	4.8
11. 1–4	4.6
12. 0	0.0
13. Total	100
14. Number of respondents	848
15. Number of nonrespondents	121

QUESTION: What percent of these financial assets would you or your immediate family want to hold in stocks five years from now if there were a reduction of 50 percent in the capital gains tax?

income tax was thought to be the more effective of these two measures even though it involves a potentially smaller revenue loss to the federal government.[34] The lower tax cost of the elimination of dividend income from personal than from corporate income taxes is due to (1) the lower average income tax rate paid by individual stockholders than by corporations and (2) the fact that the tax status of dividends paid by corporations to institutions would not be changed by the elimination of dividend income from personal taxes. The apparent preference of individual stockholders for the exclusion of dividends from personal income taxes contrasts with the lower direct and indirect income to stockholders[35] generated by this tax change as compared with the elimination of dividends from corporate income taxes, providing some evidence of a preference for current dividends over savings in the form of retained earnings.

The survey results can be used to cast light on the relative impact on the stock market of the two, at least partly offsetting, potential changes in the tax laws currently under consideration in Washington, namely, the elimination of both the payment of personal income taxes on dividends received by individuals and the preferential tax rates now paid on capital gains. Since more quantitative detail was collected on the effect of a change in the taxation of capital gains than of a change in the taxation of dividend income, the capital gains responses can be recast in a form that allows a rough direct comparison of these two proposals.

According to the survey responses, a 50-percent reduction in capital gains taxes would induce 20.4 percent of the stockholding families to increase their stock ratio over the next five years by more than 10.0 percent, and 23.4 percent by 10 percent or less, with 3.7 percent of the families decreasing their stock ratio by 10 percent or less, and 5.6 percent by more than 10.0 percent. Because of the noncomparability of the wording of the capital gains and other impact questions, the impact of other tax and institutional changes may be somewhat overstated in comparison with that of the 50-percent reduction in capital gains taxes. The decrease in stock ratios that the survey respondents stated would be consistent with a reduction in capital gains taxes presumably reflects, at least in part, sales of stock "locked" into investors' portfolios as a result of substantial unrealized capital gains. Netting out stockholders with expected percentage increases in their stock portfolios against those with decreases, almost as many stated that a 50-percent reduction in capital gains taxes would lead them to increase the proportion of their financial assets in stock by up to 10 percentage points, as stated that the elimination of dividend income from personal taxes would have this effect. Yet fewer than half as many reported that

Table 3–13. Effect of Other Tax Developments on Percentage of Assets Expected to be in Stock

| Development | Total | Size of Effect ||||| No Opinion | Number of Respondents | Number of Nonrespondents |
		Decrease over 10 Percent	Decrease 1–10 Percent	Increase 1–10 Percent	Increase over 10 Percent	No Effect			
		(Percent distribution of respondents)							
1. Elimination of dividend income from personal income tax	100	1.6	3.1	23.1	34.1	25.1	13.0	488	39
2. Elimination of corporate taxation on income distributed as dividends	100	2.1	1.5	24.5	24.8	26.9	20.1	477	37
3. Doubling of dividend exclusion on individual tax forms	100	2.3	1.8	26.1	12.3	35.8	21.6	476	38
4. Reduction from six- to three-month holding period for long-term capital gains	100	1.1	2.7	13.6	13.0	48.1	21.5	475	39

5. Increase from $1,000 to $2,000 in allowable maximum tax deduction for losses from ordinary income	100	1.8	1.2	18.1	10.7	43.7	24.5	475	39
6. Reduction of 10 percent in personal income tax	100	5.0	2.6	25.5	9.7	44.8	12.4	485	42

QUESTION: Likewise, how would each of the following developments alter the percentage of assets that you and your immediate family would expect to hold in stocks five years from now? For each of the events listed below, would the occurrence of that event cause you to:
  A. Decrease your stock portfolio by more than 10 percent;
  B. Decrease your stock portfolio by 1 to 10 percent;
  C. Increase your stock portfolio by 1 to 10 percent;
  D. Increase your stock portfolio by more than 10 percent;
  E. Have no effect on the size of your stock portfolio;
  F. No opinion.

they would be induced to increase their stock ratio by over 10 percentage points by the change in the treatment of capital gains as by the change in the treatment of dividend income.

If the admittedly tenuous assumption is made that the means of the class intervals (viz., increases over 10 percent, increases up to 10 percent, etc.) are the same for the effect of the elimination of dividend income from personal taxes as for a 50-percent reduction in capital gains taxes, the dividend tax change would be estimated to lead to a mean increase of about 10 percentage points in the stock ratio over a five-year period, as compared with a 5.5 percentage-point increase for the capital gains change. However, the 10 percentage-point figure is an unweighted mean. The corresponding weighted figure is likely to be higher since, as noted later in this chapter, the survey responses indicate that the dividend tax change would have a greater relative effect on the stock investment of the rich than of other stockholders. These results are not at all conclusive, but they do suggest that the complete elimination of the preferential tax treatment of capital gains —which would entail a greater cost to stockholders than the savings associated with a 50-percent reduction in capital gains[36]—might offset a large part of the stimulating effect on stock purchases of the elimination of personal taxes on dividend income.

A doubling of the dividend exclusion on individual tax forms would be the next most effective stimulant for stock investment, although as might be expected, not nearly so effective as the first two dividend measures and not as effective as the 50 percent reduction in the capital gains tax. Two other changes rank close in potential importance to doubling the dividend exclusion: reduction of the holding period for long-term capital gains from six to three months and an increase in the maximum tax deduction for losses from ordinary income from $1,000 to $2,000.

A reduction of 10 percent in personal income taxes would be somewhat less effective in stimulating stock investment than the other tax changes that directly affect the relative yields on stocks and other investments. A comparatively large number of respondents stated they would decrease their percentage of assets in stock by over 10 percent, perhaps reflecting the implicitly smaller tax advantage of capital gains as a result of lower income-tax rates.[37] However, in view of the comparatively small size of new corporate stock issues compared with the large amount of stock held by individuals, even this 10-percent reduction in personal income taxes might on balance significantly stimulate stock investment.

Of the nontax developments covered in Table 3–14 (from Wharton Survey), the three with the most potentially favorable effect on stockholdership are a 25-percent reduction in interest rates, a substantial increase in the proportion of corporate earnings paid out as dividends (with a corresponding reduction in retained earnings), and a 50-percent decrease in the rate of inflation. The developments with least potential impact are the liberalization of margin requirements and short-selling regulations, which would stimulate stock investments only slightly, and limiting the percentage of daily movement in stock price, which would have a slight retarding effect.

Both the establishment of an Investor Protection Office by the SEC to process investor complaints on trade executions and related problems and new securities regulation limiting the role of institutional investors would moderately increase stock investment by individual investors. The Investor Protection Office would induce 15 percent of shareowners to increase their relative stockownership, in contrast to 2 percent who would decrease their investment, whereas the corresponding percentages for constraints on institutional investment are 13 percent and 5 percent, respectively. It is interesting that the pretest sample of active customers of NYSE member firms generally indicated that government regulation of the stock market or of the economy would have a more negative effect on their stock investment and that deregulation would have a more positive one. The one exception was their reaction to new securities legislation limiting the role of institutional investors, to which they responded somewhat more favorably than other investors.[38]

It is interesting to observe, though not too surprising in view of the historical inverse correlation between the short-run return on stock and the rate of inflation and interest rates, that a substantial reduction in inflation and interest rates, perhaps along the lines characterizing the early months of 1976, would greatly increase the demand for stock. More surprising, in view of the belief of many economists that dividend payout policy does not have a significant effect on stock prices,[39] is the finding that, at least in 1975, most stockholders apparently preferred increased payout to increased retention of earnings. It is possible, of course, that stockholders do not correctly assess their subsequent returns realized from corporate reinvestment of retained earnings, particularly in view of the more favorable personal tax rates applicable to capital gains. The survey results suggest, however, either that investors are dubious about the payoff from retained earnings or, because of risk aversion and securities transaction costs,[40] have a strong preference for dividends. Presumably, that preference would be even stronger if dividend income and capital gains were taxed equally.

Investors' attitudes toward government regulation or deregulation of

Table 3-14. **Effect of Indicated Economic and Regulatory Developments on Percentage of Assets Expected to Be in Stock**

| Development | Total | Size of Effect ||||| No Opinion | Number of Respondents | Number of Nonrespondents |
		Decrease over 10 Percent	Decrease 1–10 Percent	Increase 1–10 Percent	Increase over 10 Percent	No Effect			
		(Percent distribution of respondents)							
1. Reduction of 25 percent in interest rates	100	3.9	3.9	27.1	15.6	32.5	17.1	481	46
2. Substantial increase in proportion of corporate earnings paid out as dividends, with corresponding reduction in retained earnings	100	5.2	5.3	26.3	15.5	25.0	22.7	473	41
3. Reduction of 50 percent in rate of inflation	100	6.0	4.6	25.1	15.8	30.3	18.3	478	36
4. Increase of 25 percent in stock market prices	100	4.0	10.9	18.4	13.6	38.7	14.4	481	46
5. Investor Protection Office set up by SEC to process trade execution and related problems	100	1.2	0.5	9.3	5.3	58.5	25.2	476	38

		A	B	C	D	E	F		
6.	New securities legislation limiting role of institutional investors	100	1.5	3.3	7.8	4.8	47.2	35.4	478	49
7.	Liberalized margin trading and short-selling regulations	100	0.9	0.8	3.9	1.8	66.6	26.0	483	44
8.	Maximum limit placed on percentage movement in any stock during a single day	100	4.3	3.2	2.5	2.5	53.5	34.0	479	48
9.	Establishment of price and wage controls	100	11.6	8.9	7.1	4.6	42.9	25.0	484	43

QUESTION: Likewise, how would each of the following developments alter the percentage of assets that you and your immediate family would expect to hold in stocks five years from now? For each of the events listed here, would the occurrence of that event cause you to:
  A. Decrease your stock portfolio by more than 10 percent;
  B. Decrease your stock portfolio by 1 to 10 percent;
  C. Increase your stock portfolio by 1 to 10 percent;
  D. Increase your stock portfolio by more than 10 percent;
  E. Have no effect on the size of your stock portfolio;
  F. No opinion.

the stock market and economy are more mixed. Price and wage controls are considered rather undesirable, and liberalizing margin trading and short selling are seen as slightly favorable to stock investment. Limiting percentage stock-price movements apparently would also reduce somewhat the demand for stock investment. On the other hand, additional protection to investors in the form of an Investor Protection Office or legislative limits on the role of institutional investors is considered moderately desirable.

It should be noted that individual investors state that an increase of 25 percent in stock-market prices would have a favorable effect on the proportion of stock investment to total assets. This may reflect, at least in part, the effect of a higher market valuation on existing stock and investors' inertia in maintaining what they consider to be a balanced portfolio.

Finally, the accelerated growth in recent years of retirement and profit-sharing plans, especially of employer-sponsored pensions and Keogh plans, does not appear to have affected appreciably the direct investment in stock of the families covered in the survey (see Table 3–15; from Wharton Survey). However, if indirect as well as direct investment were included, these plans would appear to have substantially increased the demand for stock.

In analyzing the impact of institutional and tax changes on market behavior of the different socioeconomic–demographic groups, it may be recalled that one of these changes—the effect of a 50-percent reduction in the capital gains tax—was treated somewhat differently from the others. In this instance, the respondents were asked what influence this development would have on the actual percentage of the financial assets the family expected to hold in stock five years hence, whereas the respondents were asked for only a rough indication of the impact of the other institutional and tax changes. Stock investment of all groups would be stimulated by a 50-percent reduction in capital gains taxes; however, it is interesting to note that the effect would be somewhat above average for corporate officials, the self-employed, and families living in New England. As noted earlier in this chapter, the results by income and wealth classes are not clear since they depend on the sample used. Stockholders relatively optimistic about future rates of return on their stock investment reported somewhat stronger effects than did other investors.

The impact of other institutional and tax changes on market behavior of the different population groups was assessed through multiple-regression analysis by relating two variables to the socioeconomic–demographic characteristics of these groups. These two variables take

Table 3-15. Effect of Participation in Profit-Sharing or Retirement Plan

	Percent Distribution of Respondents
1. Profit-sharing plan	12.0
2. Keogh plan	6.4
3. Employer-sponsored retirement or pension plan	48.0
4. None of these	33.6
5. Total	100
6. Number of respondents	491
7. Number of nonrespondents	23

QUESTION: Excluding social security, do you or anyone in your immediate family participate in any of the following plans?

	Percent Distribution of Respondents
1. Increased amount	18.2
2. No effect	65.0
3. Decreased amount	16.7
4. Total	100
5. Number of respondents	306
6. Number of nonrespondents	3

QUESTION: How has this participation or coverage caused the amount you would have invested directly in the stock market to differ from what you would have invested if you had not been in any of these plans?

on the value zero or one, depending on whether a family would increase or, in the case of the second variable, decrease its stock ratio by more than 10 percent over the next five years as a result of the indicated change. The impact of different population characteristics also was analyzed through a number of simple charts. Charts 3-8 to 3-14 show the percentage of stockholders in different groups who would on balance increase their stock ratios by up to 10 percent, as well as the percentage that would increase their ratios by more than 10 percent. Again, several interesting differences emerged among these groups. The aged would apparently be less inclined than other investors to increase their stock ratio by moderate amounts (up to 10 percent) if there was a 50-percent decline in the rate of inflation, whereas stockholders with high incomes and large stock portfolios would be more

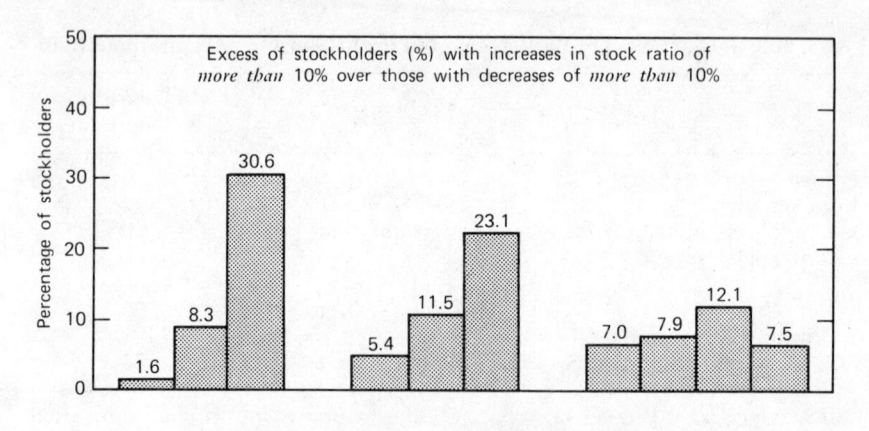

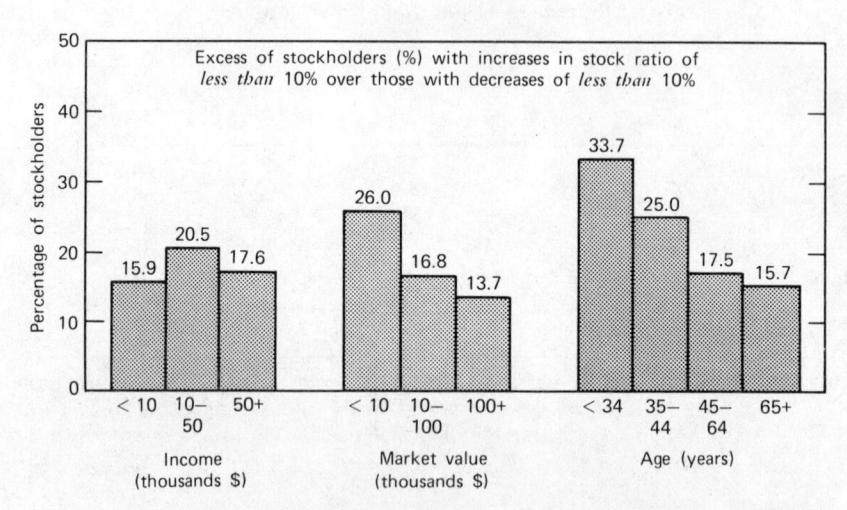

Chart 3-8. Effect of 50 percent reduction in inflation rate on percentage of stock in financial assets by income, market value of stockholdings, and age.

inclined to increase their stock ratios by large amounts (see Chart 3-8). A 25-percent reduction in interest rates would have a greater positive impact on the investments of the younger stockholders and the self-employed than of other groups in the population (see Chart 3-9).

Surprisingly, Chart 3-10 indicates that families with high incomes and large stock portfolios had a higher-than-average preference for dividend income over retained earnings. However, when other family characteristics are held constant, this preference disappears for the upper-income families. Also surprising is the apparent preference of

Recent and Prospective Behavior 107

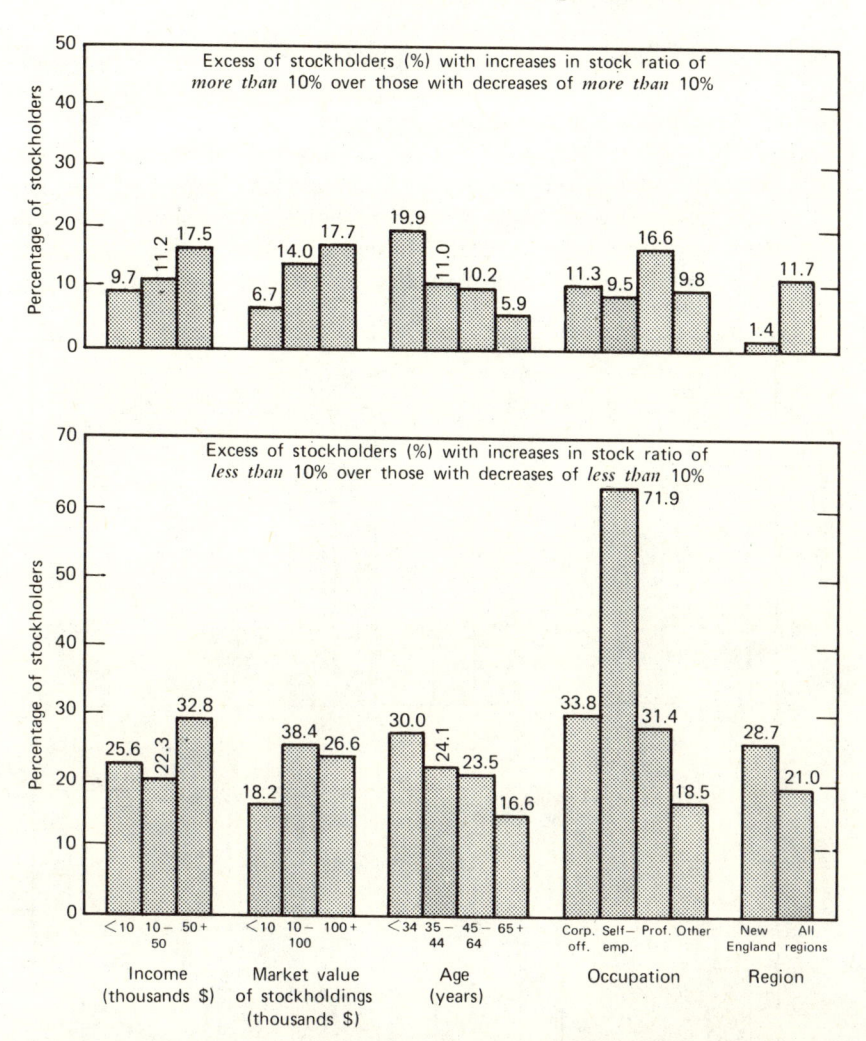

Chart 3-9. *Effect of reduced dividend rates on percentage of stock in financial assets by income, market value of stockholdings, age, occupation, and region.*

corporate officials and the self-employed for dividend income. New England stockholders had a somewhat lower affinity for dividend income, whereas that of the educated was somewhat greater. The richer stockholders and corporate officials would be affected more than other stockholders by the elimination of corporate taxes on income distributed as dividends (see Chart 3-11). Investors living in New England

108 *The Changing Role of the Individual Investor*

would be affected least. However, only the results for the richer stockholders and corporate officials are statistically significant when other family characteristics are held constant.

The exclusion of dividends from personal income taxes would act as a greater than average stimulus on the stock investment of families with high incomes and large portfolios, corporate officials, the self-employed, and stockholders with higher education (see Chart 3–12). The doubling of the dividend exclusion on individual income-tax

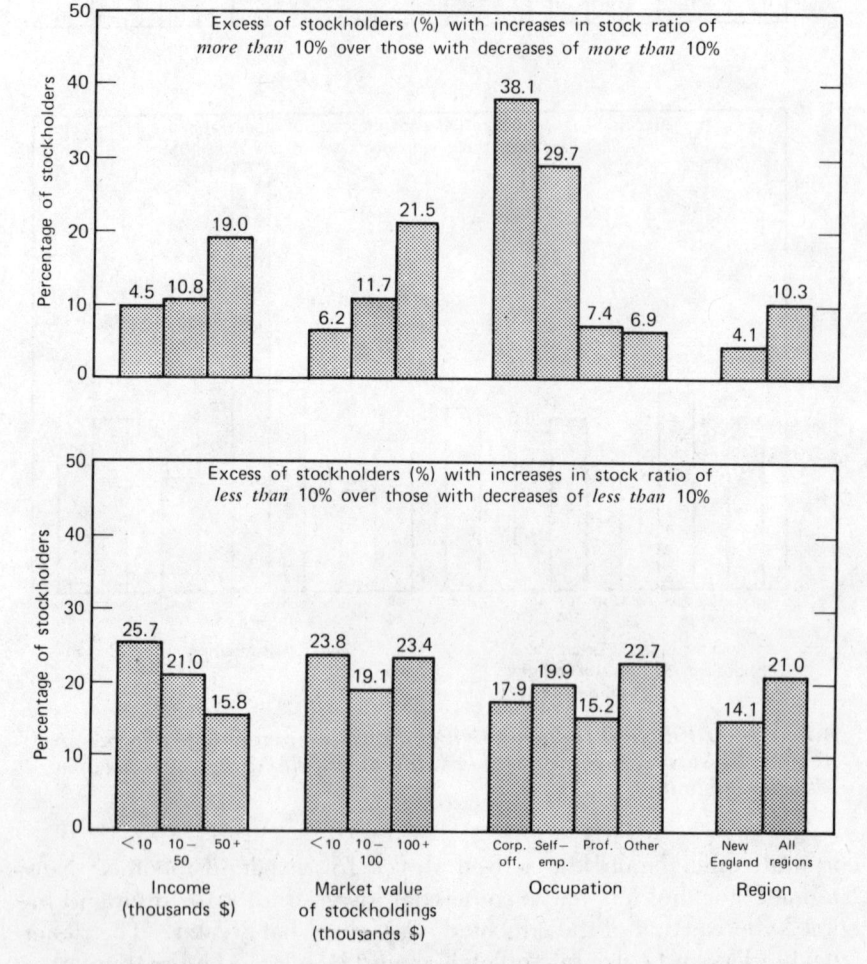

Chart 3–10. Effect of increased dividend payout ratio on percentage of stock in financial assets by income, market value of stockholdings, occupation, and region.

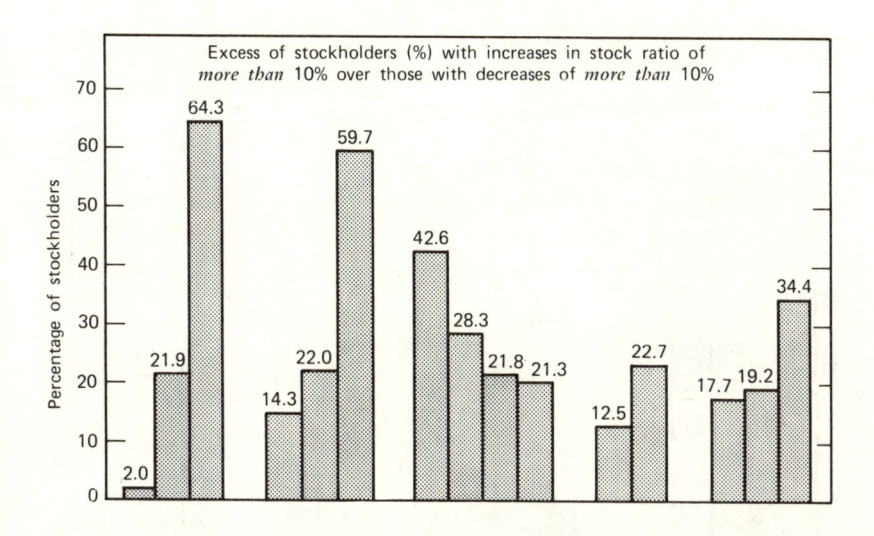

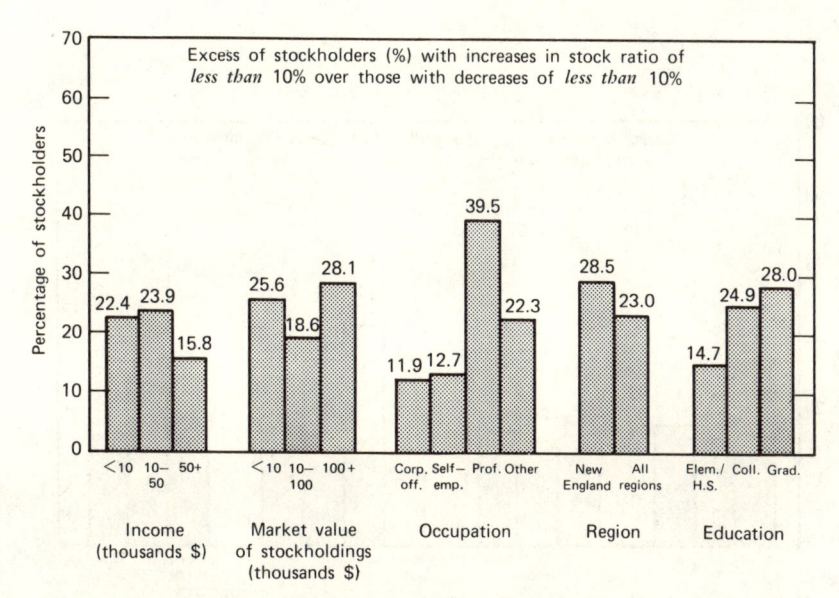

Chart 3-11. Effect of elimination of corporate dividend tax on percentage of stock in financial assets by income, market value of stock holdings, occupation, region, and education.[a]

[a] That is, elimination of tax now paid by corporations on that part of their income distributed as dividends. Currently there is no distinction between the corporate tax on dividends distributed and retained earnings.

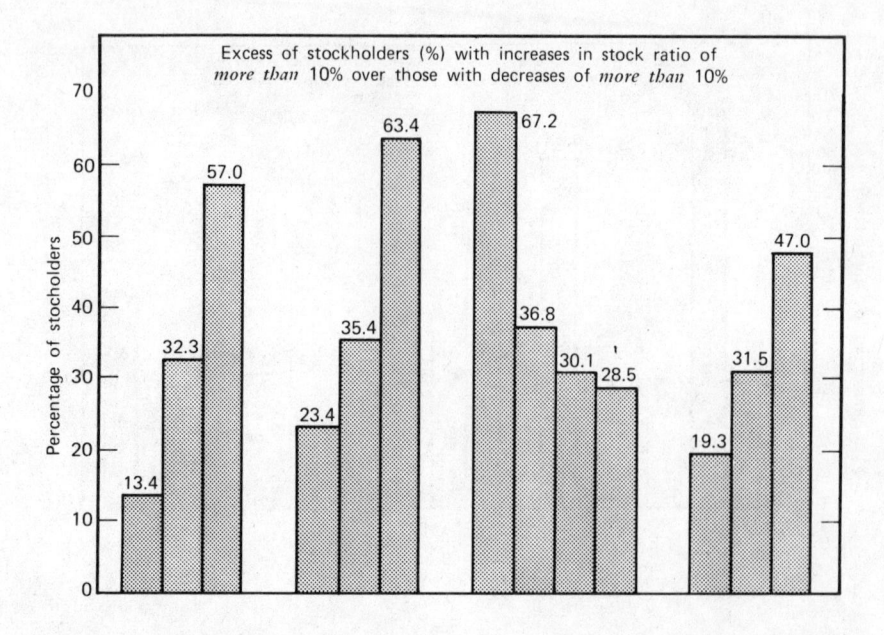

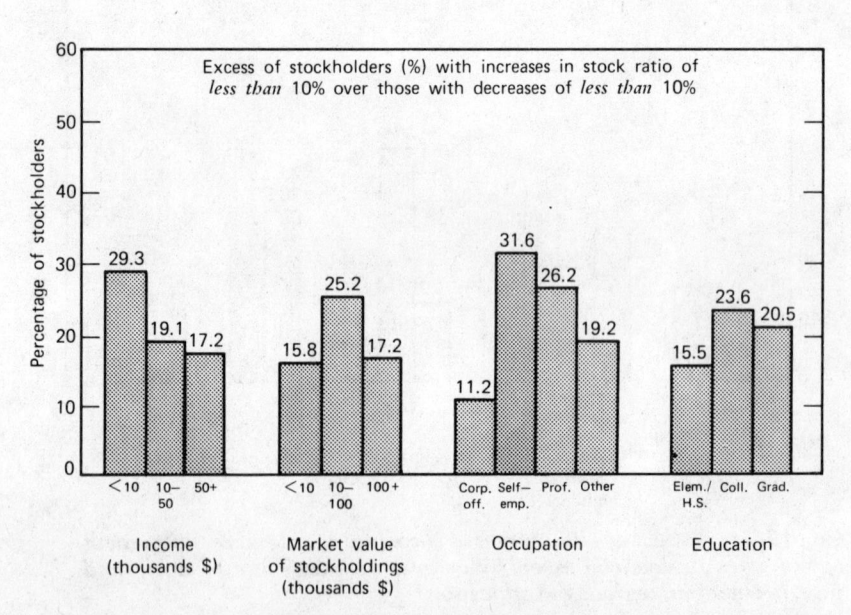

Chart 3–12. Effect of eliminating dividend income from personal income taxes on percentage of stock in financial assets by income, market value of stockholdings, occupation, and education.

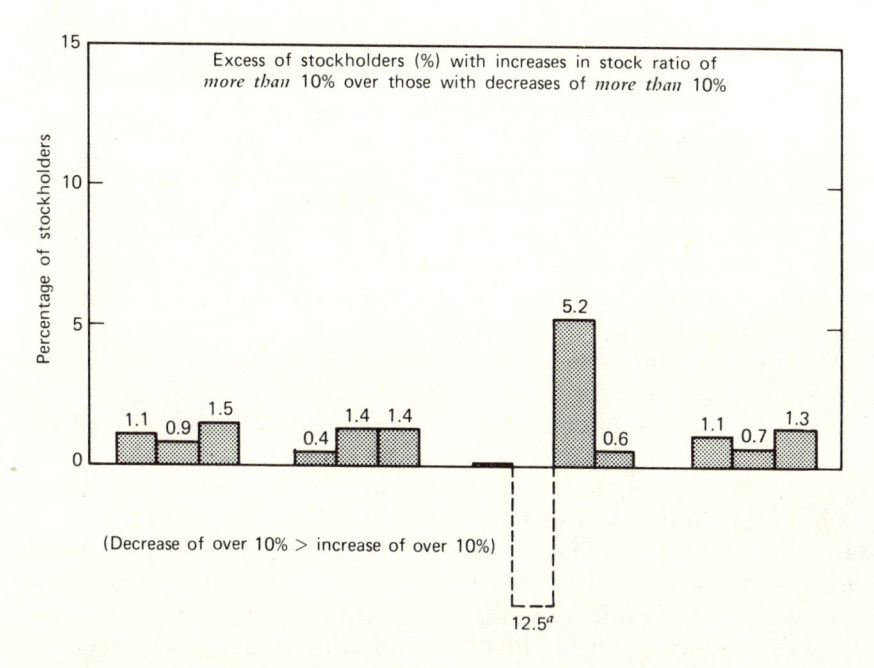

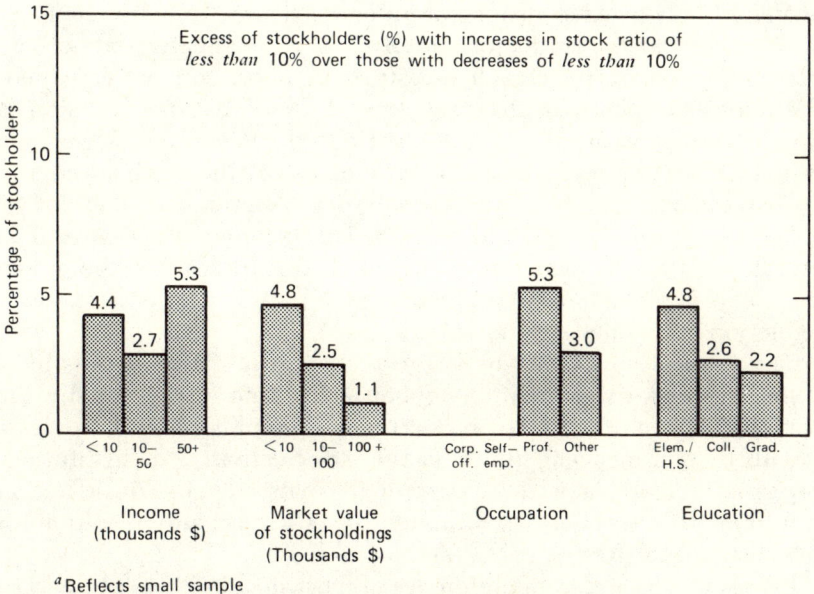

Excess of stockholders (%) with increases in stock ratio of *more than* 10% over those with decreases of *more than* 10%

1.1 0.9 1.5   0.4 1.4 1.4   5.2 0.6   1.1 0.7 1.3

(Decrease of over 10% > increase of over 10%)

12.5[a]

Excess of stockholders (%) with increases in stock ratio of *less than* 10% over those with decreases of *less than* 10%

4.4 2.7 5.3   4.8 2.5 1.1   5.3 3.0   4.8 2.6 2.2

| <10 10–50 50+ | <10 10–100 100+ | Corp. off. Self-emp. Prof. Other | Elem./H.S. Coll. Grad. |
| Income (thousands $) | Market value of stockholdings (Thousands $) | Occupation | Education |

[a] Reflects small sample

Chart 3–13. Effect of liberalizing margin trading and short-selling regulations on percentage of stock in financial assets by income, market value of stockholdings, occupation, and education.

forms also would have a greater than average stimulating effect on the stock investment of the richer families, although as would be expected, the income and size of portfolio effects are not nearly so pronounced as for the exclusion of dividends from personal income taxes. The doubling of the dividend exclusion would affect stockholders living in New England less favorably than other groups.

Professional heads of households were more likely than other investors, and the self-employed less likely, to increase their stock portfolios by more than 10 percent if margin trading and short-selling regulations were liberalized (see Chart 3–13). Price and wage controls would affect the stock investments of corporate officials, professionals, and to a lesser extent, the self-employed more adversely than those of other investors. And the effects of such controls also would be more adverse on stockholders living in New England than on those in the rest of the country,[41] whereas the effect of new securities legislation limiting the role of institutional investors would be more favorable. An SEC Investor Protection Office appeared to appeal more to corporate officials and less to professionals than to other stockholders, with not much difference evident among income groups (see Chart 3–14).

These results suggest that the only legislative and regulatory changes likely to act as major stimuli on stock investment by individuals are those that would substantially lower the effective rate of taxation on the return from such investment. If tax cuts are considered desirable as impetus for stock investment, those that increase after-tax dividend income are likely to be particularly effective. However, as explained in Chapter 5, the question remains whether such tax cuts can be justified on grounds of either economics or equity. Smaller but still substantial stimulation could be achieved by large reduction in interest rates or the rate of inflation or by a sizable increase in the proportion of corporate earnings paid out as dividends, with a corresponding reduction in retained earnings.

The responses by investors suggest that it would also be possible to stimulate stock investment moderately by setting up an Investor Protection Office in the SEC to process investor complaints and, to a lesser extent, by setting legal limits on the stock activities of institutional investors. Again, it is not clear whether cost-benefit considerations would justify these actions, although the costs probably would not be so substantial as for any of the tax cuts discussed.

In view of the apparent preference of most stockholders for dividend payout, at least in a period when stock prices are relatively depressed, one acceptable approach to stimulating stock investment by individuals might be a tax policy that encourages dividend payout by granting corporations a partial tax reduction approximately equal in aggregate

Recent and Prospective Behavior

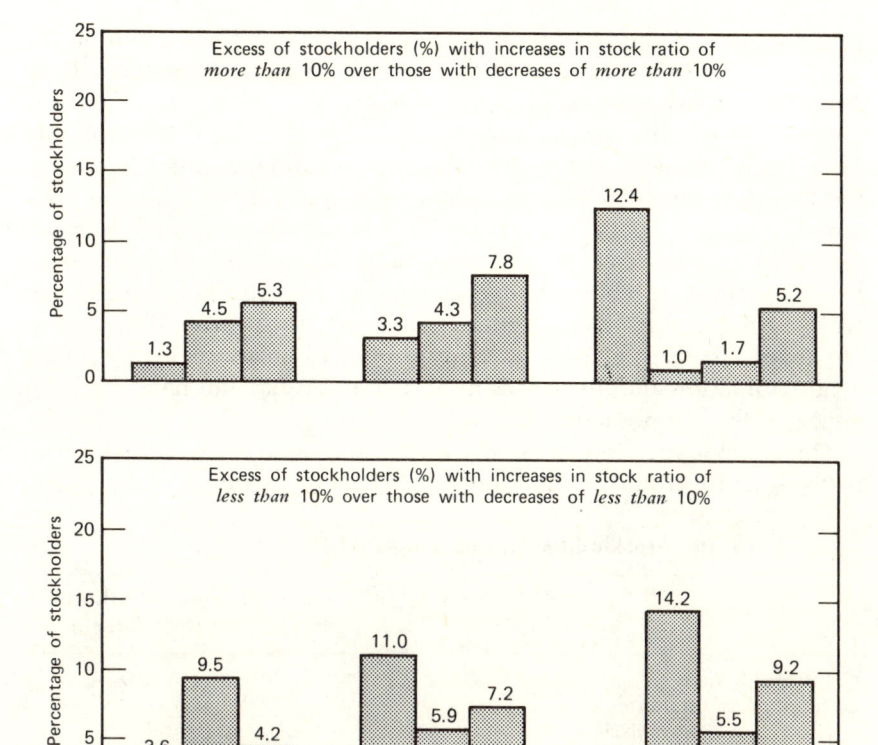

Chart 3–14. Effect of establishment of an office of investor protection on percentage of stock in financial assets by income, market value of stockholdings, and age.

amount to the additional taxes paid by individuals on their increased dividend income. The details of such a tax policy are discussed in Chapter 5.

Stockholders' Reactions to Risk

Risk should play a key role in the pricing of stock issues and in the rate of return required by investors in such issues. Investors are commonly believed to be risk averse and thus to require a positive risk

114 The Changing Role of the Individual Investor

premium or a higher return on risky assets such as stocks than on the rate they could earn on a relatively risk-free investment such as a Treasury bill or a savings account. Historically, over long periods of time common stocks have fairly consistently tended to yield considerably higher rates of market return (dividends plus capital appreciation) than the less risky investments, including high-grade, short-term, fixed-interest-bearing obligations. It is true that in highly inflationary periods no readily available asset is risk free, and that in such periods stocks might in theory be a better hedge against inflation and thus less risky in terms of real return than long-term, fixed-interest-bearing obligations. However, stocks in general have not proved to be a satisfactory hedge against inflation and, in fact, as a short-term investment have not been appreciably superior to bonds.[42]

That stockholders are generally risk averse is confirmed by the data in Table 3–16 (from Wharton Survey). Only 3 percent of the respond-

Table 3–16. Stockholder Attitudes toward Risk

		Percent Distribution of Respondents
1. I prefer to take *substantial* financial risks hoping to realize substantial gains from investments.		2.9
2. I am willing to take *moderate* financial risks hoping to achieve above average financial gains from investments.		33.3
3. I am willing to take a *small amount* of financial risk hoping to realize a fair return on my investment.		30.6
4. I wish to reduce financial risks to the *barest minimum*.		33.1
5.	Total	100
6. Number of respondents		1015
7. Number of nonrespondents		26

QUESTION: Which *one* of these statements best describes the degree of risk you are willing to take to achieve a certain level of financial gain from your investments? (Please circle *one* number.)

ing families were willing to take substantial risk on their investments in the hope of realizing substantial gains, 33 percent were willing to take moderate financial risks in the hope of achieving above-average gains, 31 percent were willing to take a small amount of financial risk in the hope of realizing a fair return, whereas 33 percent wanted to reduce risk to the barest minimum.[43] An overwhelming proportion (82 percent) of stockholders said that in purchasing a stock they customarily evaluated the degree of risk involved as well as the amount of profit they expected to receive [see Table 3-17 (from Wharton Survey), first part].

Table 3-17. Stockholder Evaluation of Risk

		Percent Distribution of Respondents
1. Yes		82.2
2. No		17.8
3.	Total	100
4. Number of respondents		500
5. Number of nonrespondents		27

QUESTION: When you purchase a stock, do you customarily evaluate the degree of risk involved as well as the amount or percent of profit you expect to receive?

		Percent Distribution of Responses
1. Earnings volatility		45.2
2. Price volatility		30.0
3. Published beta		17.3
4. Statis. performance; history of firm[a]		2.4
5. Quality of management[a]		0.9
6. Professional advice and recommendation[a]		0.8
7. Political/social/economic factors[a]		0.8
8. Dividend payment performance[a]		0.4
9. Other[a]		2.2
10.	Total	100
11. Number of respondents		386
12. Number of nonrespondents		33

QUESTION: Which of these measures of risk do you use in your evaluation of stock? Circle appropriate number(s). If other method is used, please describe.

[a]These replies were elicited from "Other (please describe)."

Stockholders use a number of different measures of risk in their investment evaluations (see Table 3-17, second part). It is interesting that 17 percent stated that they used the relatively sophisticated beta coefficient as a measure of stock risk.[44] (This measure of risk in a comparatively short span of time has become the predominant measure used in the academic literature and in recent years has been made available for publicly traded stocks by a number of brokerage and financial services.[45]) Even more interesting is the great importance placed on earnings volatility as a measure of stock risk, with 45 percent of the respondents stating they used such a measure, as compared with the 30 percent using price volatility. This result suggests that there are probably better measures of risk as perceived by investors than past price fluctuations (or market return), which many academic studies have used to measure risk.[46] Theoretically, of course, the appropriate measure of risk is that associated with future return, but whereas much of the academic literature has typically relied on past price fluctuations or on market returns to measure such risk, investors seemed to rely more heavily on past earnings volatility for this purpose. The other specific measures seem much less frequently used in assessing the risk of an investment, with evaluation of the quality of management cited by a surprisingly small proportion (1 percent) of the stockholding families and dividend payout by still fewer.

To focus more clearly on stockholders' reactions to fluctuations in stock earnings and price, they were asked which of the two they considered a more important indication of the risk of future monetary loss. Again, past fluctuations in earnings were cited more commonly than were past price fluctuations (see Table 3-18; from Wharton Survey). As would seem logical for risk-averse investors, when expected return is held constant, stocks with narrower price variations were generally preferred to those with wider variations.

More evidence that investors do not like fluctuations is provided in Table 3-19 (from Wharton Survey), with 65 percent of the respondents stating that they would be less likely to buy or hold stock that fluctuated a great deal for no discernible reason. An upward movement in the price of a stock, again for no apparent reason, would have much less net effect on investors' behavior but would also tend somewhat to reduce holdings of that stock. A downward movement in the price of a stock for no apparent reason would have a much stronger negative effect than an upward movement on the likelihood of buying or holding the stock. Apparently, stockholders generally consider unanticipated downward movements in stock price as an indication of a more risky market condition than corresponding upward movements. On

Recent and Prospective Behavior 117

Table 3-18. Stockholder Reactions to Different Market Developments

		Percent Distribution of Respondents
1. Past fluctuations in price of stock		23.9
2. Past earnings fluctuations		40.9
3. Both about the same		35.2
4.	Total	100
5. Number of respondents		421
6. Number of nonrespondents		106

QUESTION: Which do you consider a more important indication of the risk of losing money on a stock in the future? (Please circle *one* number.)

		Percent Distribution of Respondents
1. Stock A: The stock with the wider price variations		35.9
2. Stock B: The stock with the narrower price variation		64.1
3.	Total	100
4. Number of respondents		492
5. Number of nonrespondents		35

QUESTION: Suppose the expected rates of return of two stocks, A and B, are about the same and:
  Stock A had a much wider price variation both upward and downward;
  Stock B had a narrower price variation both upward and downward.
Would you prefer to invest in *Stock A* or *Stock B*? (Please circle *one* number.)

the other hand, when a large institutional investor is known to buy a stock, even though there is no apparent reason, more investors are likely to buy the stock than to liquidate it.

Still other evidence on investors' reactions to risk is provided by data on diversification of their stock portfolios. The median number of stocks held by a stockholding family, exclusive of mutual funds and personal trusts, was fewer than four, with 20 percent of the families owning one, 14 percent two, 16 percent three to four, 20 percent five to nine, 10 percent ten to fourteen, 4 percent fifteen to nineteen, 5 percent

Table 3-19. Effect of Price Fluctuations and Institutional Buying on Stock Holdings

	Total	Making Buying or Holding More Likely	No Significant Effect	Make Buying or Holding Less Likely	Number of respondents	Number of nonrespondents
		(Percent distribution of respondents)				
1. Stock that fluctuates a great deal for no apparent reason you can discern	100	12.4	22.8	64.8	488	26
2. Upward movement in the price of a stock for no apparent reason	100	29.1	37.0	33.9	486	28
3. Downward movement in the price of a stock for no apparent reason	100	16.0	30.6	53.4	485	29
4. A large institutional investor buying a stock for no apparent reason	100	34.2	46.1	19.8	485	29

QUESTION: What effect, if any, would each of these events have on your willingness to buy or hold a particular stock? (Please circle *one* number for each item.)

Recent and Prospective Behavior 119

twenty to twenty-nine, and 4 percent thirty or more stocks (see Table 3–20; from Wharton Survey).[47] Nearly half of the stockholding families had neither mutual funds nor personal trust accounts, although for 21 percent of the families such assets accounted for more than 50 percent of their entire stock portfolio (see Table 3–21; from Wharton Survey). As might be expected, mutual funds or personal trusts loomed larger in importance for female, widowed, or older stockholders than for other investors. A large single holding other than mutual funds or trusts accounted for 90 to 100 percent of the portfolio in 29 percent of the families, for 50 to 90 percent in another 18 percent of the families, and for 20 to 50 percent in 25 percent. The relative importance of this single holding was lowest for the upper income and portfolio size groups and for the older and more educated stockholders (see Chart 3–15). These results point to a rather low level of stock diversification for most respondents despite investors' aversion to risk. The degree of diversification indicated by those survey results, however, seems somewhat higher than that presented in Chapter 2, at least in part because of the non-dividend-paying stock and more inclusive household unit covered by the survey as compared with the income-tax data.[48]

Table 3–20. Number of Stocks Held

	Number of stocks	Percent Distribution of Respondents
1.	0	7.3
2.	1	20.1
3.	2	13.6
4.	3–4	15.9
5.	5–9	19.5
6.	10–14	9.7
7.	15–19	4.3
8.	20–29	5.4
9.	30–39	2.1
10.	40–49	1.6
11.	50–99	0.4
12.	100 and over	0.0
13.	Total	100
14.	Number of respondents	999
15.	Number of nonrespondents	42

QUESTION: In how many different corporations, excluding mutual funds and personal trusts, do you now own stock?

Table 3-21. Diversification of Stock Portfolios

Percent of Portfolios	Percent Distribution of Respondents
1. 90–100	10.7
2. 80–89	1.7
3. 70–79	2.6
4. 60–69	2.4
5. 50–59	3.5
6. 40–49	2.4
7. 30–39	2.5
8. 20–29	6.0
9. 10–19	10.0
10. 5–9	4.3
11. 0.1–4	6.3
12. 0	47.7
13. Total	100
14. Number of respondents	801
15. Number of nonrespondents	240

QUESTION: Of your total stock portfolio, what percent is represented by all mutual funds and personal trust accounts?

Percent of Portfolio	Percent Distribution of Respondents
1. 90–100	29.0
2. 80–89	2.6
3. 70–79	3.2
4. 60–69	4.4
5. 50–59	7.7
6. 40–49	4.8
7. 30–39	6.5
8. 20–29	13.5
9. 10–19	13.9
10. 5–9	4.4
11. 0.1–4	1.8
12. 0	8.2
13. Total	100
14. Number of respondents	890
15. Number of nonrespondents	151

QUESTION: Of your total stock portfolio, what percent is represented by your largest single holding other than mutual funds or trusts?

Recent and Prospective Behavior

Although the actual level of stock diversification was rather low, stockholders' attitudes toward portfolio diversification were more often favorable than not (see Table 3–22; from Wharton Survey). Over 50 percent of the respondents indicated that they would be very unlikely to add to stockholdings in an industry in which they already had a substantial investment, and 93 percent stated that they would not generally add to their holdings of a stock that, because of price appreciation, made up a high proportion of their portfolio value. Actually, 41 percent of the respondents would liquidate at least part of their holdings in a stock that (by increasing greatly in value) represented a

Table 3–22. Stockholder Attitudes toward Portfolio Diversification

		Percent Distribution of Respondents
1. Very likely		26.3
2. No effect		19.6
3. Very unlikely		54.2
4.	Total	100
5. Number of respondents		504
6. Number of nonrespondents		23

QUESTION: Suppose you held a substantial part of your portfolio in one industry. How likely would you be to add to your holdings in that industry instead of another industry when you purchase additional stock?

		Percent Distribution of Respondents
1. Buy more of the stock which has increased in value		6.8
2. Hold		52.5
3. Sell at least part		36.8
4. Sell all of the stock		3.9
5.	Total	100
6. Number of respondents		501
7. Number of nonrespondents		26

QUESTION: Suppose one of your stocks increases to such an extent that it constitutes a high proportion of the value of your portfolio, but its expected rate of return remains fully as high as your other stocks. What would you generally do? (Please circle *one* number).

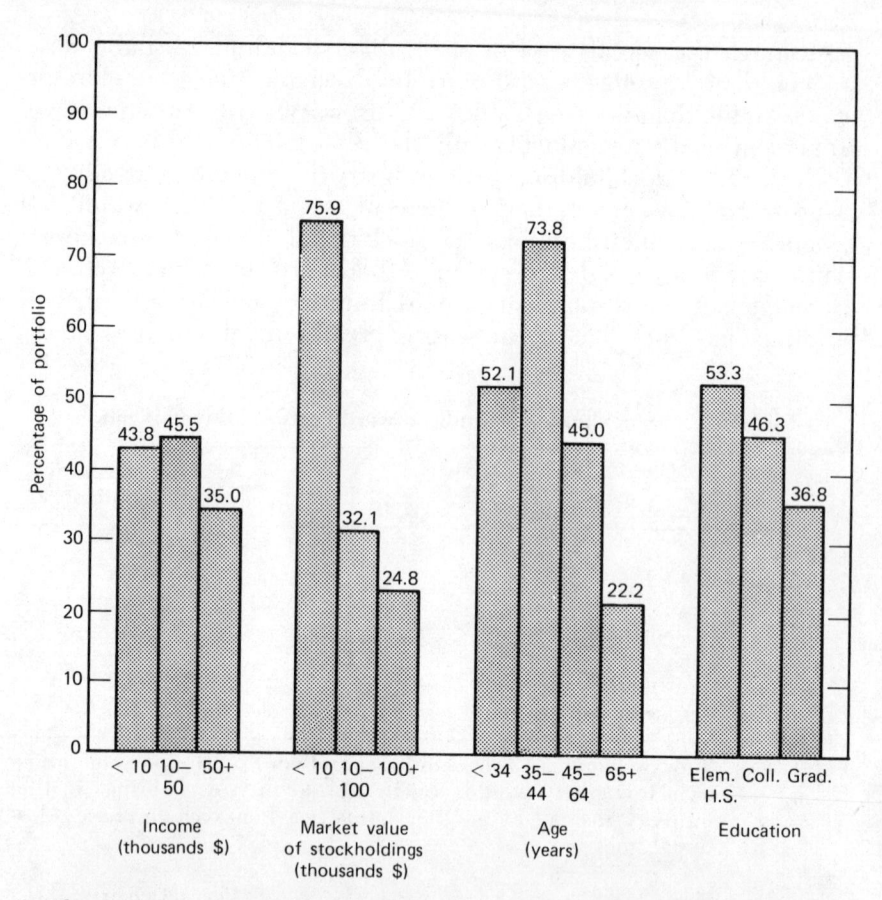

Chart 3–15. *Median percentages of portfolio in largest single holdings of stock other than mutual funds or trusts by income, market value of stockholdings, age, and education.*

high proportion of the portfolio, whereas only 7 percent would add to their holdings. The low level of stock diversification in the face of favorable attitudes toward diversification is probably attributable in part to transaction and information costs (including capital gains taxes), failure to understand how to achieve effective diversification, and, perhaps most importantly, heterogeneity of investor expectations about future returns on different stocks. Securities disclosure has, of course, been the primary policy instrument designed to reduce heterogeneity based on the inaccessibility of relevant information.

Although all socioeconomic or demographic groups of investors seemed risk averse, the richer and younger shareowning families were

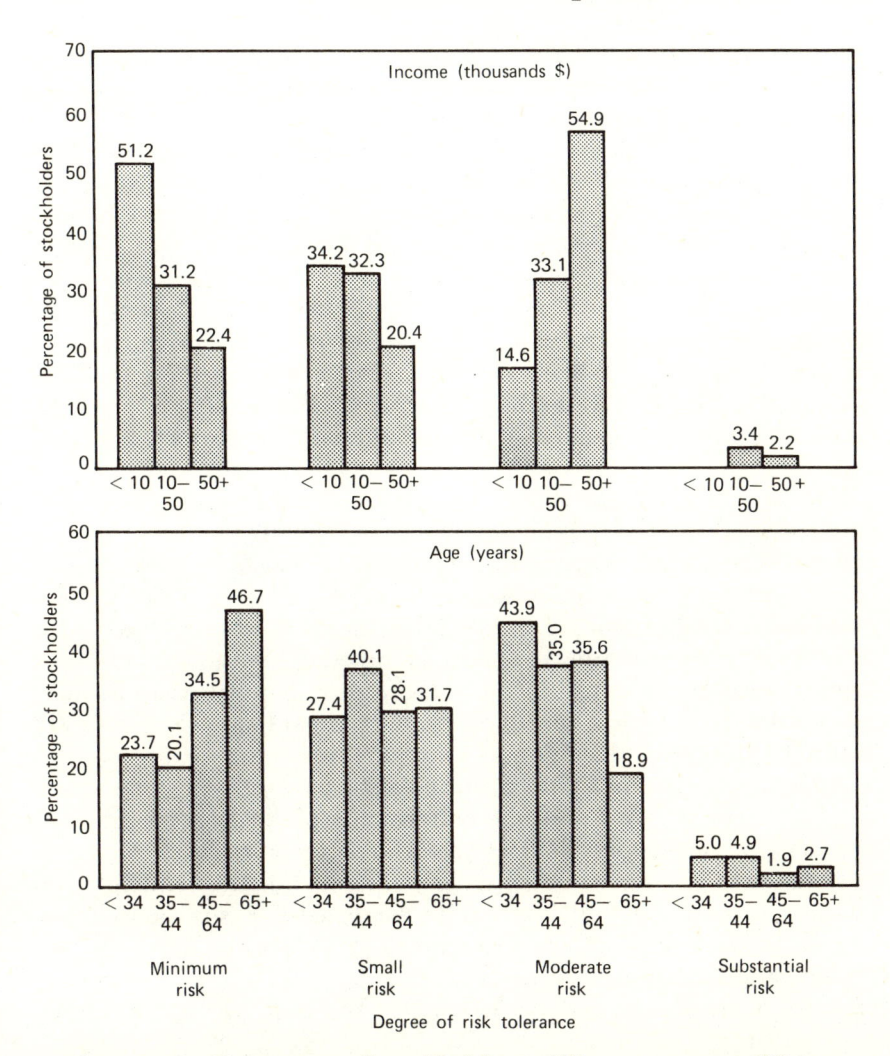

Chart 3–16. Percentage of stockholders willing to assume different degrees of risk by income and age.

less so as judged by their reported willingness to take risks. In fact, Chart 3–16 clearly shows the strong direct relationship between income and the willingness to assume risk and the strong inverse relationship between age and willingness to assume risk, tendencies that persist even when other family characteristics are held constant. It should be pointed out, however, that no group showed much willingness to assume substantial risks in the hope of realizing substantial gains from investment. Yet 55 percent of stockholders with annual incomes of $50,000 or more were willing to take moderate risks, as compared with 33 percent of those with incomes between $10,000 and $50,000, and only 15 percent with incomes below $10,000. The greater willingness of the wealthier families to assume risk is, of course, consistent with the higher measures of risk for the stock portfolios of the upper-income investors reported in Chapter 2.

Region and sex of the stockholders were also associated with willingness to assume risk. Stockholders in the East South Central states were more risk averse than those in other regions, whereas stockholders in the Pacific region were less risk averse, but these differences are not statistically significant when other family characteristics are held constant. Not surprisingly, male stockholders were much less risk averse than females.

Educated heads of households were somewhat less willing than others to take substantial risks, but at the same time, they reported a less-than-average propensity for reducing financial risks to the barest minimum, preferring some intermediate trade-off between risk and expected return. Professionals in particular and the self-employed had a lower propensity to minimize risks than did other investors and were at least as willing as the rest of the stockholding population to assume substantial risks. Corporate officials, on the other hand, were the least willing of all occupational groups to assume substantial risks.

If the expected annual rate of return on stock over the next five years and the perceived stock-portfolio performance of the past year are kept constant, the self-employed stockholders again seemed less risk averse than the rest of the shareowning population, but the reported risk behavior of corporate officials and the educated heads of households was closer to that of other stockholders. Not surprisingly, the expected rate of return on a given stock was positively related to the amount of risk the stockholder was willing to assume on that investment.[49]

Stockholders who used margin accounts, wrote or bought stock options, or sold stock short were less risk averse (i.e., more willing to assume risk) than were other investors (see Chart 3-17). This result, which is not affected when other family characteristics (notably income) are held constant, is of particular interest since it is frequently asserted that one major use of such speculative mechanisms is to reduce risk.

The relation of socioeconomic–demographic groups to other measures of risk shows some interesting differences among those groups, as well as among the different measures, when the reported willingness to

Used margin account

Yes: Minimum risk 8.7, Small risk 23.7, Moderate risk 53.8, Substancial risk 13.8

No: Minimum risk 29.6, Small risk 34.0, Moderate risk 33.6, Substantial risk 2.7

Wrote stock options

Yes: Minimum risk 17.9, Small risk 16.4, Moderate risk 58.2, Substantial risk 7.5

No: Minimum risk 29.0, Small risk 34.3, Moderate risk 33.4, Substantial risk 3.3

Bought stock options

Yes: Minimum risk 18.3, Small risk 28.0, Moderate risk 48.4, Substantial risk 5.4

No: Minimum risk 29.2, Small risk 33.9, Moderate risk 33.7, Substantial risk 3.2

Sold stock short

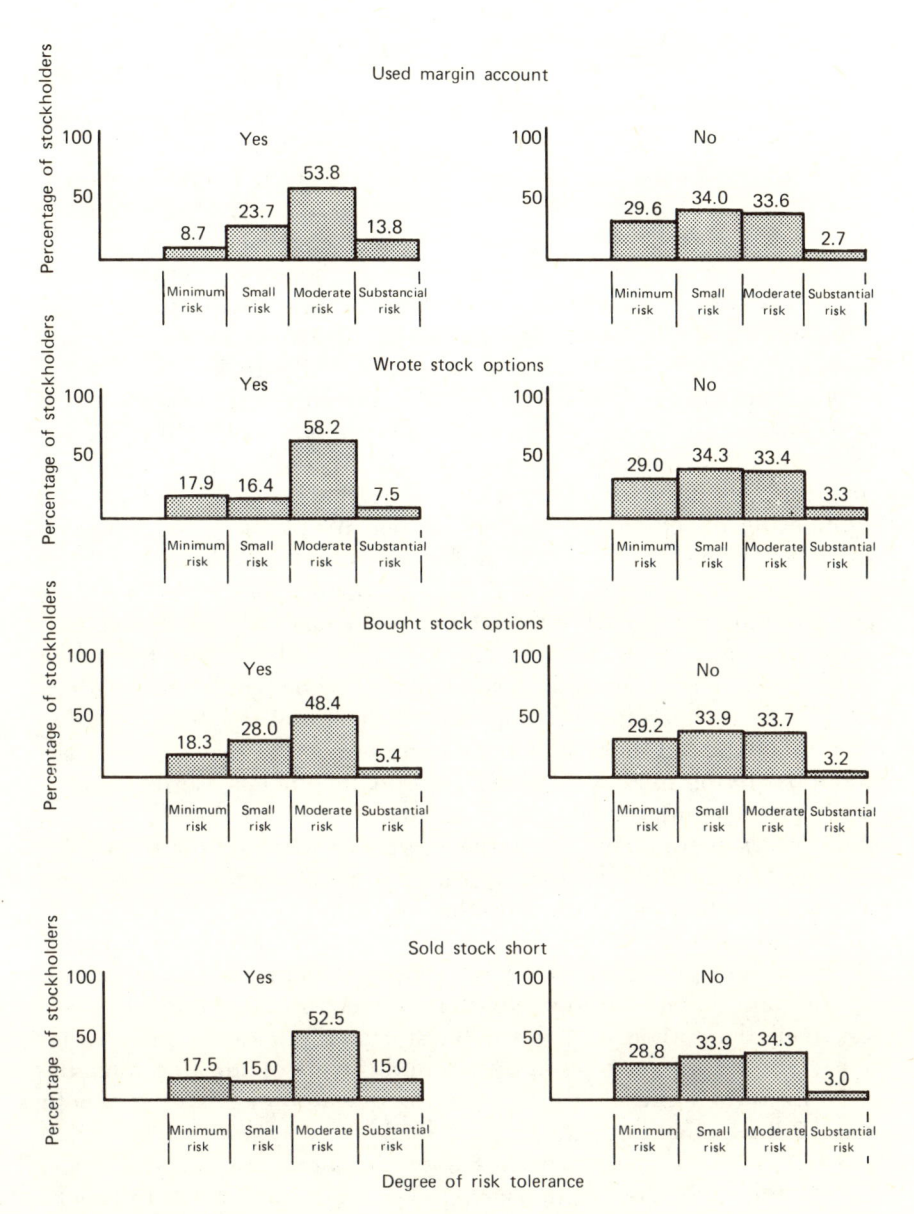

Yes: Minimum risk 17.5, Small risk 15.0, Moderate risk 52.5, Substantial risk 15.0

No: Minimum risk 28.8, Small risk 33.9, Moderate risk 34.3, Substantial risk 3.0

Degree of risk tolerance

Chart 3–17. Percentage of stockholders willing to assume different degrees of risk by use of different speculative mechanisms.[a]

[a] The "Yes" and "No" answers differentiate between stockholders who did and did not use the indicated mechanism in 1975

take risks is held constant. Thus when stocks fluctuate a great deal for no apparent reason that the shareowner can discern—a situation normally considered to be associated with increased risk—investors using margin accounts had a relatively low propensity to buy stock with substantial price fluctuations, whereas buyers of stock options showed a comparatively high propensity to buy such stock. Educated and upper-income stockholders tended to react somewhat more negatively to volatile stocks than did other investors, although the upper-income group had indicated a much greater than average willingness to assume moderate risk. A family's reported willingness to take risks is, of course, positively correlated to its taste for volatile stock.

When the prices of stocks move either upward or downward for no apparent reason, the upper-income shareowners were less likely to buy (or hold) stock than are other investors.[50] When a large institutional investor buys stock for no apparent reason, there is some evidence of a stimulating effect on the relative propensity of the more educated shareowners and purchasers of stock options to buy such stock.

No strong differences existed among socioeconomic–demographic groups in their appraisal of the relative importance of past fluctuations in the price of a stock and in its earnings as an indication of the risk of future loss. The two groups of shareowners who regarded fluctuations in price as a relatively more important indicator of risk than did other investors included those showing a minimum willingness to take risks and those living in New England. Corporate officials ascribed a relatively greater importance to fluctuations in earnings than to those in stock prices in appraising stock risk.[51] Rather surprisingly, stockholders who bought stock options appeared to place somewhat more emphasis on fluctuations in earnings than did other investors.

When stockholders were asked whether, for the same expected rates of return, they preferred a stock with much wider price variation both upward and downward to one with narrower variation, the aged were less likely than others to invest in the stock with the wider price variation. The results for margin traders and buyers of stock options differed from their earlier responses to the question of how they would react to stocks that fluctuated a great deal for no apparent, discernible reason,[52] with the margin traders now evidencing an above-average, and the buyers of stock options a below-average, preference for stocks with wider price variations. Presumably, these diverse results reflect the different wording of the two questions and, in particular, the uncertainty implicit in the phrase "for no apparent reason that you can discern."

It is noteworthy, though not surprising, that the more risk-averse stockholders, as measured by their reported willingness to take risk, shared a much stronger than average preference for stock with narrower price variation. Short sellers, again not unexpectedly, were also more likely than other shareowners to prefer stocks with narrower variation. The relatively high preference of shareowners who first bought stock prior to 1960 for stock with wider price variation is more difficult to explain, although it may reflect the fact that their stocks are more likely to have experienced substantial capital gains. Interestingly enough, the stockholders who first bought stock subsequent to 1969 were somewhat less likely than other investors to buy or hold stock when a large institutional investor is accumulating it without any apparent reason.

Still another test of the risk-aversion characteristics of different population groups is provided by questions relating to the willingness of stockholding families to add to holdings in an industry or in a stock when such holdings already constitute a high proportion of the families' portfolio. Shareowners with large stock portfolios were least likely to add to their concentration of stockholdings in either an industry or a single stock. Of the other groups, stockholders who first bought stock prior to 1970 were less likely than other shareowners to add to concentrated holdings in an industry but did not much differ from other investors in their willingness (or unwillingness) to add to concentrated holdings in a single stock.

Apart from the comparative distaste of shareowners with large stock portfolios for concentrated holdings in an industry or stock, probably the most interesting finding in the analysis of the reaction of different population groups to such portfolio concentration concerns the behavior of the aged. The two-way classifications show that the oldest stockholders, who report that they are (expectedly) more risk averse than shareowners generally, evidence a greater than average tendency to avoid concentration. This tendency does not show up in the regressions when other family characteristics are held constant, but this seems to be due to the nonlinear relationship between age and the desire to avoid concentration, with the sixty-five-and-over age group having a much greater dislike for concentrated holdings than investors under sixty-five.

The only interesting difference among socioeconomic–demographic groups in the frequency with which they considered the degree of risk as well as expected return in purchasing stock was the greater than average frequency with which investors with large stock portfolios considered risk, but this difference is not as large as might have been expected. Stockholders who reported a willingness to take substantial

128 The Changing Role of the Individual Investor

risks in the hope of realizing substantial gains were less likely than others to use price volatility as a measure of risk. The aged used price volatility as a measure of risk less frequently than did others and earnings volatility somewhat more often (see Chart 3–18). The upper-income groups used price volatility somewhat more frequently than did other stockholders and earnings volatility somewhat less frequently, but the differences among income classes were not statisti-

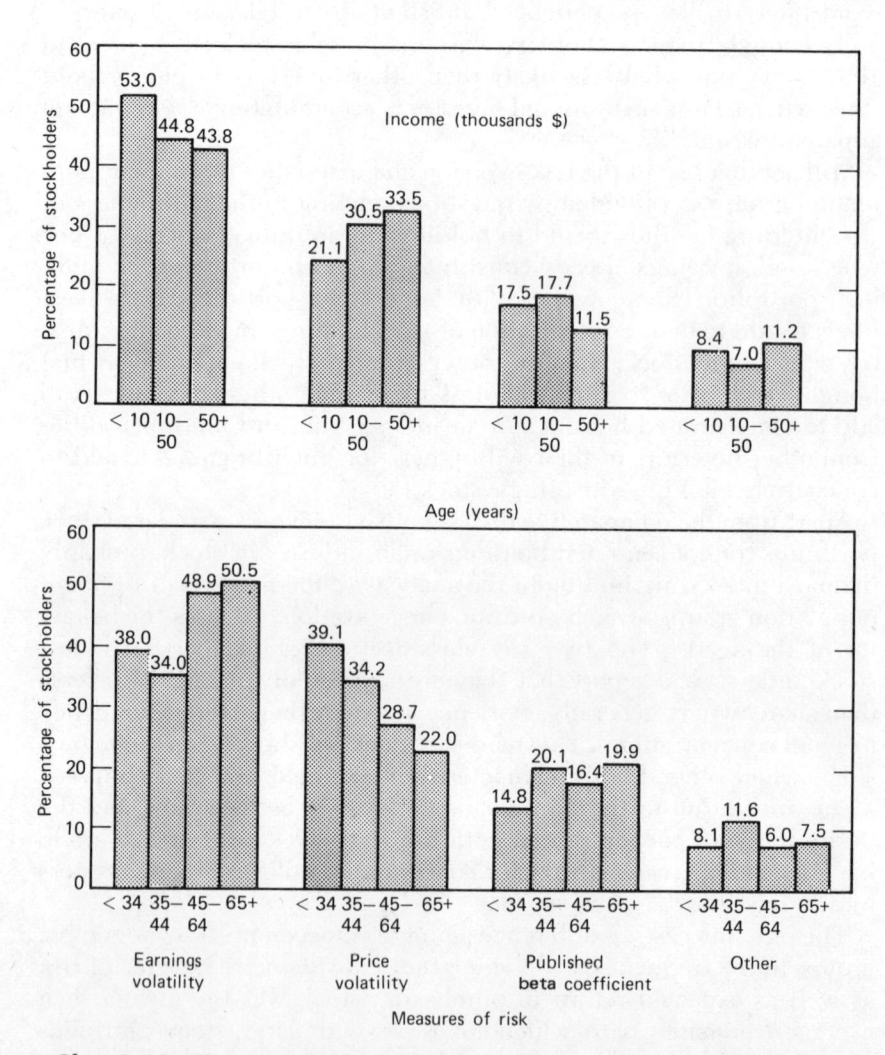

Chart 3–18. *Percentage of stockholders utilizing different measures of risk by income and age.*

cally significant when other family characteristics were held constant. Investors with large portfolios used both price and earnings volatility somewhat more often than did other stockholders, probably reflecting the greater frequency with which they customarily evaluated risk. The self-employed overwhelmingly relied on earnings volatility and shunned the beta coefficient as a measure of risk, whereas the better-educated stockholders were more concerned with price volatility than other investors and, somewhat surprisingly, less concerned with the beta coefficient. Margin traders, not unexpectedly, paid more attention than did other investors to price fluctuations rather than earnings as a measure of risk. Short sellers were somewhat more likely and stock option buyers somewhat less likely to use the beta measure.

Objective evidence on the differences in risk exposure of the various socioeconomic–demographic groups is provided by the data on the diversification of their stock portfolios, as measured by the number of stocks owned. Several groups—those with high incomes, large stock investments, older heads of households, and more education—typically had a larger number of stock issues in their portfolios than did other stockholding families. [The richer, older, and more educated investors also had a smaller than average proportion of their stock portfolio in their largest single holding other than mutual funds or personal trusts (see Chart 3–5).] The larger number of stock issues owned by the richer stockholders, despite their owners' greater willingness to assume risk, probably reflects the greater importance of their (nonhuman) wealth relative to earned income, readier access to information, and ability to cut down on relevant transaction and information costs. However, even stockholders with incomes of $50,000 and over had a median holding of only about eleven stocks, excluding mutual funds and personal trusts. Corporate officials and the self-employed also held more stock issues than did other heads of households of comparable means, but this ceases to be true when the expected rate of return is held constant.

Required and Expected Rates of Return on Stock

As noted in the preceding discussion of investors' reactions to risk, the required rate of return on stock would expectedly be equal to the risk-free rate plus a risk differential. Since a U.S. government bond is subject only to liquidity risks, the differential between the required rates of return on stocks and such bonds should normally be somewhat narrower than between risk-free instruments and stocks.

130 *The Changing Role of the Individual Investor*

Although it is relatively easy to determine the required rate of return on a risk-free rate or a U.S. government bond over the term to maturity by simply looking at market data, this is not possible for stocks, in view of the major potential difference between required and realized rates of return over any specific investment horizon. Another approach to estimating the required rate of return on stock is to elicit the necessary data from a sample of investors, and such information was requested in the Wharton Survey from half of the entire sample contracted.[53] In theory, the required rate of return most relevant to stock prices is the rate over the relevant investment horizon, and since the annual turnover rate of NYSE stock by public individual investors has been somewhat less than 20 percent, the required rate was rather arbitrarily taken to be the minimum expected (before-tax) annual rate of return (dividends and capital gains) over the next five years that would induce the respondent to buy stock at the time of the survey (i.e., in the fall of 1975).

This simple mean expected rate of return required by investors at the time of the survey to induce them to buy stock was close to 12.9 percent,[54] with 49 percent of stockholding families in the 10 to 15 percentage range, 19 percent in the 5 to 10 percentage range, 17 percent in the 15 to 20 percentage range, and 12 percent in the 20 to 30 percentage range. In view of the fact that investors differ in their expectations about future returns and their willingenss to assume risk and, partly as a consequence, do not generally hold well-diversified portfolios, the Wharton Survey requested that half of the sample of stockholding families that had not been asked for data on required rates of return to indicate the (before-tax) annual rate of return the respondent would expect over the next five years from an average market investment at the time of the survey. It was not considered feasible in the final survey to inquire into required and expected rates of return on stock from the same families, although such information would have added to the usefulness of our results.[55] The expected rates of return on an average stock investment in the market as a whole tended to be lower than the rates required by stockholders on their own investments.[56] This difference presumably reflects the fact that the stock market as a whole includes a number of issues whose rate of return many investors would regard as inadequate to warrant a financial commitment.

Some perspective on the 12.9-percent mean required rate of return on stock can be obtained by examining comparable data for bonds. The families covered in the Wharton Survey were asked to indicate the annual rate of return they would require to invest in a new fifteen-year U.S. government bond. The mean required rate of return on such bonds was 10.1 percent.[57] This rate was appreciably above the actual market rate that would have been charged on a new long-term U.S. government offering in the October–December 1975 period, when the full yield to maturity of the U.S. government 8-3/8 percent issue (maturing in the year 2000) averaged somewhat below 8.4 percent. The explanation for this disparity probably lies at least in part in the nature of the sample of the Wharton Survey. The families covered were all stockholders and represented an adequate selection of individual investors in the stock market, but only a small fraction owned U.S. government bonds (other than savings bonds), hardly a representative sample. Moreover, despite their importance as stockholders, individual generally accounted for only a minor share of bond ownership and trading.[58]

The risk differential implied by a comparison of the mean rate of return on stock required by stockholding families and the yield to maturity on a new long-term U.S. government bond was somewhat below 5 percent. This figure, it should be noted, was reasonably close to the average difference between the realized rate of return on NYSE stock and on high-grade bonds, since the latter part of the nineteenth century.[59]

In view of the potential importance of the expected rate of inflation in determining the required rate of return on stocks and bonds as well as on other types of assets, the families covered in the Wharton Survey were asked what annual rates of change in the cost of living they expected both over the next five years and over the next twelve months. Presumably the higher the expected rate of inflation for a given period, the higher the rate of return required by investors for that period. The median and mean expected rates of inflation over the next five years for those respondents who anticipated a rise or no change in prices were 6.3 percent and 7.4 percent, respectively, but, surprisingly, over 11 percent of the respondents stated that they expected a decrease in prices. The corresponding expected rates of inflation over the next twelve months were not much different (6.5 percent and 7.5 percent), although there were fewer families at both extremes of the distribution and less than 4 percent of the respondents expected a decrease in prices in 1976. Most families stated they would not be surprised if prices continued to rise considerably more over the next twelve months than indicated in their responses, but would be surprised if they rose only slightly. It is interesting but not surprising that the distribution of stockholders' views about inflationary pressures was more widely dispersed for the longer run than for the short run. The longer-run perspective is, of course, more relevant to the rates of return investors

132   The Changing Role of the Individual Investor

require on long-term financial instruments, such as stocks and bonds. Of the different groups in the population, those with incomes of $50,000 and over expected somewhat less inflation than did other stockholders.

There were few important differences in the required and expected rates of return on stock among the different groups of shareowners (see Chart 3-19). The upper-income families seemed to both expect and require somewhat larger rates of return than did other stockholders.[60] Older heads of families seemed to look for somewhat lower rates of return than did the younger investors. Those willing to assume only minimal risks expected lower returns on the average, although their required returns may not have differed from those of other families. Margin traders and families in the West North Central region required higher rates of return than other shareowners, whereas families in the

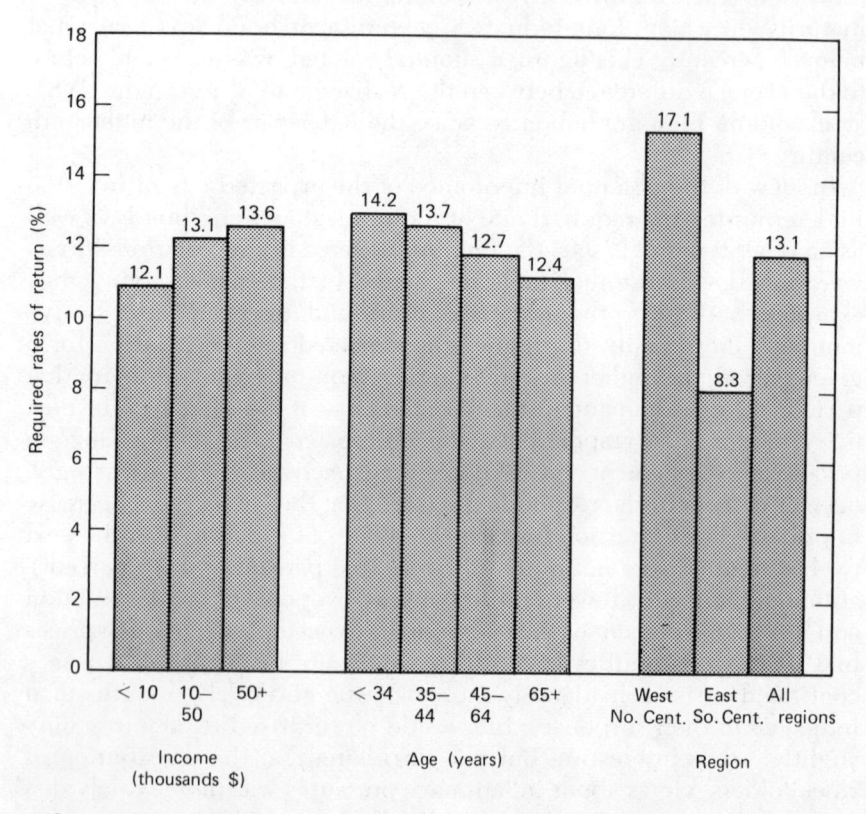

Chart 3-19. *Median required rates of return on stock investment by income, age, and region.*

East South Central region required lower rates. When other family characteristics are held constant, stockholders in New England also required higher rates of return.

Not surprisingly, the required and expected rates of return on stock were positively correlated with the expected annual rate of inflation in the cost of living over the next five years. However, the degree of correlation was not at all strong, although it was statistically significant.[61] The correlation between the required rate of return on stock and that on U.S. government bonds was somewhat stronger. Generally, stockholders of different socioeconomic–demographic characteristics anticipated about the same annual rate of inflation both over the five years and over the twelve months following the fall of 1975. However, there is some indication that when other family characteristics are held constant, corporate officials and the more educated stockholders expected a lower rate of inflation over the next five years than did other investors. The expected twelve-month and five-year inflation rates were, of course, positively correlated.

Characteristics of Stockholding Families

In connection with the analysis of trends in stock trading and holdings by households in 1975, the preceding sections of this chapter have referred to differences in behavior of specific socioeconomic–demographic groups. The distributions of stockholding families by their socioeconomic–demographic characteristics are presented in the subsequent tables (see Tables 3–23 through 3–27; all from Wharton Survey). Somewhat less-detailed information on stockholder characteristics for this same period has also been published as part of the NYSE 1975 Shareholder Census, which on the whole is based on a sample of about the same size as the Wharton Survey sample referred to in this chapter.[62] Although there are other minor divergences between the NYSE and Wharton estimates, the main differences concern the fact that the Wharton estimates are weighted and focus on shareowning families while the NYSE estimates are unweighted and focus on individual shareowners.

The median shareowning family in the fall of 1975, according to the Wharton Survey, had a stock portfolio with a market value of $13,405, an income of $22,855, and had 1.9 persons in a household whose family head was male, fully employed, 53.2 years old, and with at least three years of college education. Close to 30 percent of the shareowning families had less than $5,000 in stockholdings, whereas over 12

Table 3-23. Market Value of Stockholdings

Amount of Stockholdings	Percent Distribution of Respondents
1. Under $2,499	19.2
2. $2,500–4,999	10.5
3. $5,000–9,999	13.9
4. $10,000–14,999	9.4
5. $15,000–24,999	9.0
6. $25,000–49,999	15.5
7. $50,000–99,999	10.3
8. $100,000–499,999	11.0
9. $500,000–999,999	1.2
10. $1,000,000 or more	0.0
11. Total	100
12. Number of respondents	972
13. Number of nonrespondents	69

QUESTION: What would you say is the current market value of your total investments in common and preferred stock and mutual funds (excluding money funds)?

Table 3-24. Family Income in 1975

Income	Percent Distribution of Respondents
1. Under $5,000	3.0
2. $5,000–9,999	9.2
3. $10,000–24,999	44.1
4. $25,000–49,999	33.5
5. $50,000–99,999	8.8
6. $100,000–499,999	1.4
7. $500,000 and over	0.0
8. Total	100
9. Number of respondents	990
10. Number of nonrespondents	51

QUESTION: What do you expect your total family income will be for this year (1975) *before* taxes?

Table 3-25. Age of Respondent

		Percent Distribution of Respondents
1. Under 21		0.7
2. 21-24		1.7
3. 25-34		11.0
4. 35-44		15.6
5. 45-54		25.5
6. 55-64		25.0
7. 65-74		16.0
8. 75 and older		4.5
9.	Total	100
10. Number of respondents		1036
11. Number of nonrespondents		5

Table 3-26. Sex of Respondent

Sex		Percent Distribution of Respondents
1. Male		72.3
2. Female		27.7
3.	Total	100
4. Number of respondents		1033
5. Number of nonrespondents		8

percent owned more than $100,000 in stock (see Table 3-23).[63] An appreciable number of shareowning families had relatively low income, with 12 percent receiving less than $10,000 in annual income (Table 3-24), but as might be expected, stockholding families as a whole had substantially higher incomes than did the rest of the population, with a median income roughly twice as large. Even many of the stockholding families with less than average incomes in 1975 represented families with incomes below their normal levels either because the head of the family had retired or because, for a variety of other reasons, a decline in earnings was experienced.

The median age of the heads of shareowning families (53.2 years) is

136   The Changing Role of the Individual Investor

Table 3–27.   Region of Respondent

Region	(1) Percent Distribution of Respondents	(2) Percent Distribution of All Households in Population	(3)=(1)÷(2)
1. New England	8.9	5.70	1.56
2. Middle Atlantic	18.0	18.17	0.99
3. South Atlantic	16.1	15.30	1.05
4. East North Central	19.1	19.16	1.00
5. West North Central	6.8	8.05	0.84
6. East South Central	4.0	6.12	0.65
7. West South Central	7.6	9.51	0.80
8. Mountain	4.2	4.25	0.99
9. Pacific	15.4	13.74	1.12
10. Total	100	100	
11. Number of respondents	1041		
12. Number of nonrespondents	0		

well above that of heads of households generally (47.3 years).[64] Only 29 percent of the heads of shareowning families were below forty-five years of age, and over 20 percent were over sixty-five. As might be expected, the proportion of retired heads of shareowning families, nearly 20 percent, was quite close to the proportion older than sixty-five years. Although it may not be surprising to find that the relatively aged part of the population accounts for a disproportionate share of stockholders, it is of interest to note that the median age of stockholders in 1975 was approximately five years above that of 1970, whereas the median age in the population as a whole probably increased by only about one year over this period.[65] The change in the age distribution of stockholders over this period is consistent with the change in the relative size of the stock portfolios held by employed and retired investors discussed in Chapter 2.

Household heads in stockowning families are predominantly well educated, with 51 percent having at least a college degree. Another 21 percent had up to three years of college, and another 23 percent had graduated from high school.

The occupational distribution of these household heads conformed to their educational background, with a high proportion in managerial, professional, and technical positions. However, a surprisingly large proportion (35 percent) of these household heads were engaged in clerical, secretarial, and computer work whereas, as would be expected, unskilled workers were quite uncommon as shareowners.

Stockownership was well dispersed throughout all regions of the country. The East North Central states had the most stockowning families (19 percent), followed by the Middle Atlantic states (18 percent), the South Atlantic states (16 percent), and the Pacific states (15 percent). Compared to their proportion in the total U.S. population, the density of shareownership seemed highest in New England and lowest in the East South Central region.

NOTES

1. The effective response rate was probably higher, since replies were solicited only from the head of the stockholder's family unit. The Wharton Survey used two mailings and a telephone follow-up; 529 respondents replied before the second mailing, and an additional 218 before the telephone follow-up that added another 294 respondents. A few additional replies were received too late for inclusion in the tabulations.
2. The response rates for the two questionnaires were virtually identical.
3. The interviews were carried out under the direction of Professor Robert Ferber of the University of Illinois and the mail pretest under the direction of Frank Conran and Harvey Katz of the NYSE.
4. The other discrepancies between the Wharton and NYSE results seem largely attributable to the different economic units covered. Once the Wharton data are weighted to reflect the sampling design, the largest discrepancy is in the sex of respondent, with 27.7 percent females reported in the Wharton Survey and 50.3 percent in the NYSE census. But this is to be expected at least in part, since Wharton, unlike the NYSE, addressed itself to the household head rather than the individual shareowner. Probably for similar reasons, the Wharton data point to a significantly lower ratio of stockholders who are not employed than does the NYSE census. The difference in median age of shareowners, estimated at 53.2 years by Wharton and 53.0 years by the NYSE, is minimal. There are some differences between the two surveys in the regional distribution of respondents, with the Wharton Survey reflecting a significantly higher than average response rate for stockholders in the Pacific states and a lower than average response rate in the Middle Atlantic states, but these differences disappear when the Wharton data are weighted to reflect the sampling design.
5. It should be noted that the only NYSE estimates of stockholder characteristics not subject to the same potential response biases as the estimates from the Wharton sample are those relating to the distribution of stockholders by region, sex, and number of stocks held, which are based on information obtained from the corporate books. The other NYSE estimates of stockholder characteristics were derived from a special telephone survey covering a moderately larger sample than the Wharton Survey, but with potentially larger biases in the results obtained since the refusal rate was apparently at least as large, no oversampling was utilized, and no weighting procedures were followed.
6. The only other recent published estimate of stockholder median portfolio size, $40,000 as of the summer of 1972, appears in R. C. Lease, W. G. Lewellen, and G. G.

Schlarbaum, "The Individual Investor: Attributes and Attitudes," *Journal of Finance* (May 1974). However, this estimate is based on stockholders with accounts in a single brokerage firm. It might be noted that, whereas the May 1974 article makes no estimate of median income of stockholding families, the figure mplied by the sample data presented in that article is over $23,000.

7. For single or widowed stockholders, where the results from the two sources would theoretically be close, 9.6 issues on the average were reported held in the Wharton Survey, and 8.7 in the NYSE Census. The somewhat higher Wharton Survey figure presumably reflects the scattered presence of portfolios of closely held stock not covered by the NYSE Census. Other differences between the Wharton and NYSE figures on the number of stock issues held by these stockholders reflect stock purchases and sales between the middle of 1975, when the NYSE data on the number of portfolio issues were collected, and the fall of that year, when the Wharton data were collected.

8. The only one of these estimates that is likely to be substantially affected by response bias is the figure for the proportion of shareowning households buying or selling NYSE stock in 1975, which would be reduced from 41 to 33 percent by a rough adjustment for response bias. For purposes of this adjustment, it is assumed that the nonresponse group in our sample can be represented by the telephone responses once the number of shareholdings and regions are held constant.

9. The special survey of nonrespondents, which collected some selected data on household characteristics and trading behavior, pointed to a figure closer to 65 percent.

10. According to the Federal Reserve Board's *Flow of Funds* data, domestic individuals had $1 billion in aggregate net stock sales in 1975.

11. The median value was estimated at a moderately lower figure in the NYSE 1975 Census of Shareowners and would be estimated at a moderately higher figure if a rough adjustment were made for response bias. On the other hand, the Lewellen, Lease, and Schlarbaum transactions data would imply a very much higher figure for 1972. However, the latter figure is obviously strongly biased upward.

12. If a rough adjustment is made for response bias, the proportions of investors using margin accounts, writing stock options, buying stock options, and selling short would be estimated at 5 percent, 7 percent, 7 percent, and 3 percent, respectively.

13. I. Friend, M. E. Blume, and J. Crockett, *Mutual Funds and Other Institutional Investors: A New Perspective* (New York: McGraw-Hill, 1970).

14. M. E. Blume, J. Crockett, and I. Friend, "Stockownership in the United States: Characteristics and Trends," *Survey of Current Business* (November 1974).

15. Although the Dow-Jones Industrials did somewhat outperform the more comprehensive value-weighted market indexes, it did not perform quite as well as the equally weighted Value Line Composite Index.

16. The regressions are available from the Twentieth Century Fund, 41 East 70th Street, New York, New York 10021. Each observation in the regressions, as in the tables and charts, is weighted by the inverse of its sampling ratio. Unweighted regressions, where each observation is equally weighted, were also computed for comparative purposes but are not available.

17. The regressions analysis and two-way classifications point to the same results for income and age, but not for region. It may be noted that the positive relationship between a household's income and its perception of stock-portfolio performance was not substantially affected when the number of stocks held was kept constant.

18. The Federal Reserve Board *Flow of Funds* data indicated that aggregate net purchases of tax-exempt bonds by individuals in 1975 were well in excess of their combined net purchases of all other types of bonds and short-term obligations.

19. As mentioned in Chapter 2, the aggregate net stock sales by individuals in this period amounted to $8 billion in 1973, $1 billion in 1974, and $1 billion in 1975.
20. All these findings are confirmed by the two-way cross-classification results.
21. According to the *Flow of Funds* data, 27 percent of the financial assets of all U.S. individuals, including nonstockholders, was invested in stock at the end of 1975.
22. This conclusion does not appear to be significantly affected by response bias.
23. This is a simple mean that does not distinguish among investors by the size of their holdings.
24. Whereas this is also true for shareowners with a market value of stock portfolio of $100,000 and over, the largest portfolio size for which the Wharton Survey provides an adequate sample, the small number of respondents with stock portfolios in excess of $1 million included in the pretest returns from high-income investors who were active in the stock market pointed to a small decline in the stock ratio from 1975 to 1980.
25. The income effects are statistically significant at the 0.05 level in the unweighted but not in the weighted regressions.
26. The ratio of the market value of individuals' stockholdings (S_I) to total stockholdings (S_T) can be expressed as

$$\frac{S_I}{S_T} = \frac{S_I}{A_I} \cdot \frac{A_I}{A_T} \cdot \frac{A_T}{S_T}$$

where A_I represents individuals' financial assets and A_T represents total financial assets. The Wharton Survey results suggest that abstracting from the effects of differential price movements, the S_I/A_I ratio is not likely to decline as rapidly as it has over the past decade. Therefore, unless A_I/A_T is expected to decline more rapidly, or S_T/A_T to decline less rapidly, the decline in S_I/S_T should be moderated.
27. Individuals' net sales of stock averaged $1.5 billion annually from 1974 through 1976, compared with $5.0 billion annually in the preceding three years (Federal Reserve Board *Flow of Funds*).
28. The greater percentage increase from the fall of 1975 to the middle of 1976 in the equally weighted Value Line Composite index than in the Standard & Poor's Composite Index of 500 stocks, which gives proportionally greater weight to the larger stocks in which institutions tend to concentrate, suggests that in this period individuals may have fared better than institutions in their stock portfolios.
29. These include interests in closely held corporations, noncorporate businesses, real-estate investment other than own home, and so forth.
30. According to the *Flow of Funds* data, somewhat over 36 percent of individuals' bond holdings in 1975 were in tax-exempts, which are, of course, especially attractive to the upper-income groups.
31. The 5.5-percent figure represents the difference between the estimated means of stock ratios in 1980 both with and without the reduction in the capital gains tax and is derived from respondents reporting both ratios. The estimated mean stock ratio in 1975 for such respondents was somewhat lower than that for all respondents.
32. Because of possible ambiguity in the wording of the questions, a test was made of the base to which the respondents intended these percentages to apply. It was determined that respondents generally interpreted a 10-percent increase in the stock ratio from, say, a 50-percent base to mean that the ratio would become 60 percent. However, since some respondents may have interpreted these percentages to apply to the stock base rather than to the base of all financial assets, the estimated effect of changes in tax laws and institutional arrangements other than the change in capital gains taxes may be

slightly overstated. This would not be true of the change in capital gains taxes, since the expected proportion of assets in stock after the change was reported, as well as the actual proportion before the change.

33. The respondents, of course, may not have made adequate allowance for the increased dividend payout by corporations associated with the elimination of corporate taxation on dividend income, which would probably be greater than the increased payout associated with the elimination of personal taxes on such income.

34. How much smaller the revenue loss would be would depend on the effects of the indicated changes in personal and corporate tax on dividend payout. Financial institutions would obviously benefit more from (and presumably prefer) a change in corporate than in individual taxes.

35. The income referred to is the sum of personal dividend income after taxes and that portion of corporate retained earnings applicable to individual stockholders.

36. The current effective rate of capital gains taxes paid by individual stockholders is, on the average, probably well under 25 percent, with a substantial proportion of capital gains not subject to any income tax.

37. A 50-percent reduction in the capital gains tax would also be associated with a relatively large number of stockholders who state they would decrease their percentage of assets in stock by more than 10 percent.

38. They reacted somewhat more favorably than other investors to liberalization of margin trading and short selling, somewhat more negatively to a maximum limit on percentage movements in any stock during a single day, and much more negatively to price and wage controls. In addition, they reacted much more favorably to a substantial increase in the proportion of corporate earnings paid out as dividends.

39. For a recent exposition of this view, see F. Black and M. Scholes, "The Effects of Dividend Yield and Dividend Policy on Common Stock Prices and Returns," *Journal of Financial Economics* (May 1974). A recent exposition of the opposite position appears in S. Bar-Yosef and R. Kolodny, "Dividend Policy and Capital Market Theory," *Review of Economics and Statistics* (May 1976). The Wharton Survey finding that investors prefer higher dividend payout is not necessarily inconsistent with the finding in other studies (e.g., Lease, Lewellen, and Schlarbaum, "The Individual Investor") that investors prefer capital gains to dividends.

40. Transaction costs are, of course, also a reason for retention of earnings.

41. This is clearer in the two-way cross-classifications than in the regressions.

42. Actually, the historical correlations between the annual rate of inflation and the rate of return on stocks as a whole have generally been moderately negative instead of the positive effect consistent with even a partial hedge against inflation; see I. Friend, Y. Landskroner, and E. Losq, "The Demand for Risky Assets Under Uncertain Inflation," *The Journal of Finance* (December 1976). The corresponding correlation between inflation and the rate of return on bonds has on the average been somewhat more strongly negative over sufficiently long periods of time.

43. If the adjustment discussed earlier is made for response bias, both the estimated proportions of stockholders willing to take substantial risks and those willing to take only minimal risks are increased somewhat to 4 percent and 36 percent, respectively.

44. The figure would be increased to 21 percent by an adjustment for sample bias.

45. A potentially troublesome finding from the viewpoint of current financial theory is the pretest response of stockholding families asked whether they would prefer to purchase a stock whose price tends to move in the opposite direction to the stock market or one that tends to move in the same direction. Of ninety-five respondents, only eight

stated they preferred the opposite direction, as against fifty-seven who preferred the same direction and thirty with no preference. Before reaching more definitive conclusions, it would be necessary to follow up this question with in-depth interviews to ascertain whether the question was fully understood and whether the respondents assumed that the expected rate of return was held constant. However, the replies underline the need for further research on the common assumption in the academic literature that stockholders generally use the beta coefficient, or some other measure of covariance of return on a stock with return on the market as a whole, to assess stock risk.

46. M. E. Blume and I. Friend, "Risk, Investment Strategy and the Long-Run Rates of Return," *The Review of Economics and Statistics* (August 1974) find that subjective measures of risk such as quality ratings are clearly better for the smaller, less-seasoned stocks on the NYSE than are objective measures obtained from past fluctuations in market returns.

47. Seven percent of the families reported they held no stock at the time of the survey, although they had appeared on stockholders' books at a somewhat earlier date. The median number of stocks held by stockholding families indicated by the Wharton Survey (3.6) is higher than the median number of dividend-paying stocks estimated in Chapter 2 from income-tax data (2). This difference may be explained in part by holdings of non-dividend-paying stocks and by the more inclusive nature of the household unit covered by the Wharton Survey. The higher median obtained from the survey apparently cannot be explained by the sample bias discussed earlier, since adjustment for that bias would raise somewhat the estimated median number of stocks held.

48. On the other hand, it should be noted that, although the survey data are more comprehensive in coverage than the income tax data and may be more reliable for estimating that distribution of the number of stockholders and shareholdings, the income-tax data are probably more reliable for the distribution of the value of shareholdings.

49. These results are statistically significant at the 0.05 level in the unweighted but not in the weighted regressions.

50. Unlike the multivariate regressions, the two-way classifications do not show any systematic relation between income and the effect of movements in stock prices on stock investment.

51. This is shown even more clearly in a two-way classification of occupation and the relative importance of fluctuations in stock price and earnings in appraising stock risk.

52. Each of the two questions was asked of a different half of the entire Wharton sample.

53. It would be preferable to obtain these estimates for individual stocks from investors owning the stocks, but this was not feasible. Moreover, institutional investors, who regularly make such estimates for the stocks they follow as part of their investment process, were not covered in the Wharton Survey.

54. The median was somewhat higher, with the mean weighted by the amount of stock held somewhat lower. The projected mean for the pretest sample, which consisted of the larger and more active stockholders, was higher (13.7 percent).

55. Such information was requested from all the families in the pretest and obtained from a sizable number of respondents.

56. The simple mean of these expected ratios was 11.8 percent. The median was somewhat lower, whereas the mean weighted by the amount of stock held was somewhat higher. Again, the weighted mean for the pretest sample was higher (12.7 percent).

57. Both the median and weighted mean were somewhat lower.

142 The Changing Role of the Individual Investor

58. About 11 percent of such bonds was owned by individuals in 1975, according to the *Flow of Funds* data. For individuals, unlike many institutions, return on bonds is subject to a higher average rate of taxation than return on stock.

59. I. Friend and M. E. Blume, "The Demand for Risky Assets," *The American Economic Review* (December 1975).

60. This is clearer in the two-way cross-classifications than in the regressions. Although the higher taxes on upper-income families may be able to explain the differences in required rates of return in view of the availability to the rich of lesser taxed assets, such higher taxes would not seem to be the explanation for the differences in expected returns.

61. The coefficient of rank-order correlation between the required rate of return and the expected rate of inflation was 0.167.

62. The main exception is the regional distribution of stockholders, in which the NYSE sample is very much larger.

63. When allowance is made for the difference in dates, the percentage distribution of stockowning families by market value of shareholdings derived from the Wharton Survey is reasonably close to that obtained from the tax data in Chapter 2, with the notable exception of the numerically small over-$1-million portfolio-size class referred to earlier.

64. *Current Population Reports,* Series P-20, No. 291, Bureau of the Census (February 1976). The median age of 47.3 years refers to March 1975.

65. The median age of shareowners in 1970 was obtained from the NYSE 1970 Shareholder Census. The median age of the population as a whole was 28.6 years in 1974 and 27.9 years in 1970 according to the *U.S. Statistical Abstract* (1975).

CHAPTER 4

Market Efficiency and the Individual Investor

Despite the spectacular growth of institutional volume, individual investors still own more stock than do institutions. Thus individuals play a key role in the pricing of stocks. This chapter examines the effect on market efficiency of the growing role of institutions in stockownership and trading activity. The purpose of this examination is to determine what economic justification government might have for adopting a public policy encouraging the shift of stockownership from institutions to individuals, or vice versa.

The term "market" can be used in several senses. In its narrowest sense, a market is the physical place for buying and selling goods. In a broader sense, the term includes those persons who are engaged in extensive trading. In its broadest sense, a market consists not only of places and people, but also of the items that can be traded and the forms of interaction of its participants.

The term "market" is used in the broadest sense here. The market for common stocks thus consists of the communication network among participants, the participants themselves, the information available to the participants, the potential interaction among participants, particularly among buyers and sellers, and finally the stock instruments themselves. For purposes of exposition, the participants in the market are divided into investors who hold securities and firms that issue securities and make physical investments.

The Meaning of Market Efficiency

Although there is no standard definition of an efficient market, it would seem that a market should possess at least three general characteristics if it is to be called perfectly efficient. First, it should be informationally efficient; all investors and managers should perceive correctly the expected cash flows and inherent risks for all investment projects. As a result, the prices of securities traded would be expected to provide as much correct information as possible to managers of firms about the funds they use.

Second, the market must have mechanisms, such as voting rights or takeover bids, that compel the best possible utilization of the available information by managers and the most beneficial investment for the welfare of the stockholders. In short, firms should undertake allocationally efficient investments. In a competitive society, as firms attempt to maximize stockholders' welfare, society's welfare would be enhanced.

Third, the market should be operationally efficient; any investor, whatever his means, should be able to buy or sell stock with no explicit or implicit transaction costs. Explicit transaction costs comprise such factors as commissions; implicit transaction costs include such factors as the time spent by an investor to find the best market. These are attributes of a perfectly efficient market. No real market can, in fact, possess all these qualities. For example, trading securities will always involve some real costs. Nonetheless, these attributes do provide a clear and reasonably unambiguous standard.

The three characteristics listed above are primarily those of the market for existing securities, the so-called secondary market. In addition to these three characteristics, an efficient market should encourage firms and allow them freely to issue new securities in the primary market, with returns commensurate with risk as determined by the prices of other securities in the secondary markets. This last characteristic could logically be subsumed under the umbrella of informational, allocational, and operational efficiency. Since the empirical techniques and data required to analyze efficiency of the two markets are, however, different, a distinction will be drawn between efficiency in the secondary and the primary markets.

This list of efficient market characteristics does not pretend to be exhaustive; it is merely one applicable to any reasonable definition of market efficiency. Furthermore, these characteristics are the ideal and do not describe any real market. In any market, there will be some transaction costs. The prices of assets may convey incorrect information. Firms will not always make the best decisions. In practice, one can only attempt to determine whether under specific technologies, factor costs, and institutional arrangements, participants in the market make the market as efficient as possible or whether changes in technologies, factor costs, and institutional arrangements would tend to promote greater or lesser efficiency. For the purposes of this study, the important question is whether markets dominated by individuals are more efficient than markets dominated by institutions.

The substantive meaning of allocational efficiency hinges ultimately on the concept of an optimal investment strategy. In a competitive society, a common definition of an optimal investment strategy states that it is optimal if resources are allocated so that (1) each individual, given his wealth and the prices of consumption and investment goods, cannot improve his position by trading with any other individual and (2) any investment an individual would wish to finance is undertaken by himself or somebody else. Such an equilibrium has been named after Vilfredo Pareto, the Italian economist who first set down conditions of equilibrium in a competitive society.

Yet one can conceive of particular allocations of resources that, while consistent with a Pareto optimum, would be considered by many to be nonoptimal. For instance, a Pareto optimal allocation of domestic resources within the United States may well be consistent with Lockheed undertaking investments involving the bribing of foreign officials. To avoid this type of situation, an optimal allocation of resources might be defined as one that maximized the value of some social-welfare function.

Whereas maximization of some social-welfare function may be desirable as an ultimate goal, theory has not advanced sufficiently to make it a practical definition of allocational efficiency in a competitive market. If individuals acting in their own self-interest are responsible for an allocation of resources inconsistent with the maximization of the social welfare, the government in a competitive society can restrain the behavior of individuals to bring their actions in line with such maximization. Indeed, the government has responded to undesirable outcomes of the competitive process by imposing such restraints—for example, the recent controls on pollution.

In the presence of monopoly, a competitive system would not lead to a Pareto optimal allocation of resources. In the monopolized sector, production and its associated investment would be curtailed, making the potential rewards from investing in it greater than warranted. Investors would thus want to increase their share in this sector, but it is the essence of monopoly that they cannot. Thus to promote a better allocation of resources, the government has passed laws prohibiting monopolistic practices.

This analysis of monopoly provides the key to a practical definition of allocational efficiency. Assuming the capital markets are informationally inefficient, they might be termed "allocationally efficient" if owners and potential purchasers of securities have and use devices such as voting rights to compel all firms to undertake every investment project some investor is willing to finance and no others. In the language of modern finance, every investment project promising an expected return that is at least as great as warranted by its underlying risk should be undertaken by some firm. Moreover, no firm should invest in a project with a smaller expected return. The amount of stock owned by institutions relative to that owned by individuals may be an important variable in measuring the capability and willingness of investors to influence management.

To make allocationally efficient investment decisions, managers of firms must know what returns investors would expect or require from any project under consideration as a function of its risk. It is one of the roles of the secondary market to provide some of this information.

If all investors correctly perceive the expected cash flows and risks of all the investments undertaken by firms, the market might be expected to price each issue correctly. Specifically, any two securities or claims of the same risk would be priced so as to yield the same expected return. If not, no investor would purchase or hold the security with the smaller expected return, thus driving its price down and its expected return up. Similarly, the price of the asset with a larger expected return would be driven up, with a resultant decrease in its expected return. Likewise, the expected returns on any two portfolios of comparable risks must be the same, even if composed of securities of disparate risk.

Since managers of firms generally are not intimately familiar with the risk factors of the projects of competing firms, informational efficiency also demands the ability of managers to utilize the information from the secondary markets for the proper assessment of their cost of capital. This second property of informational efficiency would not appear to be any more or less plausible than that of investors to perceive correctly the risks and expected cash flows of the projects of a firm, since managers would have access to the same or more information than would investors.

The investors' ability to perceive correctly the true risks and true expected cash flows of a firm is based on the presupposition that each investor evaluates each company in the same way. However, this in itself does not guarantee that the evaluations are correct. It is possible for all investors, even though they judge everything equally, to be wrong altogether. If their judgments are sufficiently wrong, their investment behavior could lead to speculative excesses and ultimately to classical bubbles like the tulip mania that raged through Holland between 1634 and 1637, when a single tulip bulb allegedly could be exchanged for a carriage and its horses.

Without homogeneous expectations, it is highly unlikely that the market would be inefficient. One could construct scenarios in which the prices of securities would be the same regardless of whether all investors held the same expectations. Even so, the market in a broad sense would probably not be efficient since the consumption and saving decisions of individuals with false expectations would tend to be different from what their decisions would be if they had correct expectations. Thus homogeneous and correct expectations on the part of all investors would almost seem to be a prerequisite of a perfectly efficient market.

Compared with allocational and informational efficiency, operational efficiency is a very precise concept. A market is operationally efficient if there are no explicit or implicit transaction costs to the investor.[1] This definition of operational efficiency provides an absolute benchmark—namely, the absence of trading costs.

An alternative definition states that an operationally efficient market is one in which the transaction costs borne by investors are as small as possible given factor costs. This alternative definition is useful in identifying monopolistic practices, but perhaps less useful for our purposes than the absolute definition of overall market efficiency. Whether caused by monopolistic practices or factor costs, the absolute value of the transaction costs borne by investors determines how closely the net prices of buy-and-sell orders might be expected to approximate equilibrium prices.

Allocational, informational, and operational efficiency are not independent of each other. Without informational efficiency, it would be virtually impossible for firms to allocate their resources optimally. To the extent that the market is operationally inefficient, the quoted prices might deviate from those that would prevail if there were no transaction costs. Furthermore, the level of operational efficiency as it bears on liquidity would be expected to have a direct impact on the costs of funds extended to firms.

The Role of the Individual

It can be argued under some assumptions that the transfer of stock ownership from institutions to individuals would increase market efficiency, but under other assumptions that such a transfer would reduce market efficiency. What actually will happen ultimately is an empirical question.

Spokesmen for the NYSE have frequently espoused the advantages of an auction market over a dealers' market. In its idealized form, an auction market would assemble all the holders or potential buyers (called the "crowd") of a particular issue at one location. Each buyer or holder would be ready to buy or sell the issue the instant its price deviated from what he perceived as the fair market value. In this way, the price would reflect the consensus of all investors. Two points should be noted in this conception: (1) the location could be a common electronic network or a single physical location (which of these two approaches to location would lead to a more efficient market is currently a subject of debate) and (2) the requirement that everyone be at the same location implicitly assumes that individual investors evaluate the impact of new information differently. If all investors evaluated the impact of new information on the price of an individual issue similarly, the next trade between any two investors would take place very simply at the new perceived price.[2] Thus the presumed desirability of an auction market hinges on heterogeneous expectations that in themselves would generally be inconsistent with a perfectly efficient market.

Recognizing that not all investors would, in practice, be at the same location at the same time, proponents of the auction market have argued that the greater the number of participants at, or represented at, a single location, the more closely the actual price would approximate the true consensus price. If correct, it is easy to conclude, although not as a logical necessity, that for a given volume of trading it is better to have a large number of small trades than a small number of large trades. Since the trades of individuals are usually smaller than those of institutions, the greater the participation of individuals, the better the auction process functions. The emphasis in this view is on the amount of trading and not on the amount of stock owned, although these two quantities may be correlated.

The alternative to an auction market is a dealers' market. In this type of market one or more dealers quote prices at which they are willing to buy and sell. The buying price is called the "bid price" and the selling price, the "ask price." The market for government securities is one such example of a dealers' market, and the market for OTC stocks as well as the so-called third market are other such examples. It is not clear whether a dealers' market or an auction market would make for a more efficient market even though proponents of the auction

Market Efficiency and the Individual Investor

market act as though the choice is clear. Perhaps one reason that the superiority of the auction market is often accepted with little question is that, at least outwardly, such a market seems to epitomize perfect competition. In fact, however, the differences between the two are differences only of degree—perhaps so sufficiently minor that there are no important differences between the two. The specialist on the floor of the exchange performs some of the functions normally associated with a dealer. He quotes prices at which he will buy and sell an issue and often trades on his own account. Since the average investor is not allowed on the floor of the exchange, he must engage a member to act as his agent. In the case of an order to transact at the best available price, this agent can try to match the order with another member who may be acting as an agent for some other investor or for himself, complete the order by buying or selling to the specialist, or leave the order with the specialist to be executed at his discretion. In the case of an order to transact at a specific price, the agent generally gives the order to the specialist, who then has the responsibility of executing it.

These actions of participants on the floor of the exchange do not seem to be very much different from those in the so-called dealers' markets. Dealers would sometimes be buying and selling for their own accounts and sometimes acting as agents in matching orders. Indeed, in 1962, a year in which the required data were publicly available, only 18.6 percent of the share volume on the NYSE attributable to trades in which the public represented one or both sides was due to non-prearranged matches on the floor. Another 6 percent of share volume was due to matches arranged off the floor of the NYSE but executed on it to clear the "book."[3] These prearranged matches are not part of the normal action process as that process is usually understood.

The recent relaxation of rules prohibiting NYSE-member firms from dealing on this third market would seem to make such prearranged matches more attractive, since they no longer have to be executed on the floor to clear the book. Moreover, these figures are for 1962, and it is dangerous to extrapolate from these to the current date, but the rapid growth of institutional investors with their larger orders makes it seem unlikely that the proportion of nonprearranged matches would have increased.

It has been argued that the members of the NYSE are more closely regulated than are participants in other markets. Without judging the validity of this argument, it would seem that the issue of regulation is separable from the desirability of auction versus dealers' markets—a comparison that would make sense only if there were some substantive differences between these two markets as they have actually developed.

Three main differences stand out: (1) in a market dominated by individuals, the average size of an order or a transaction for a given level of volume is likely to be smaller, but the number of orders larger; (2) the information available to individuals and institutions, as well as the way in which they use it, might differ; and (3) individuals and institutions might differ in their ability and willingness to influence corporate decision making. It is one thing to state that the market correctly prices a company, no matter how it is managed, and quite another to state that the market forces a company to pursue optimal strategies.

Apart from the distinction between auction and dealers' markets, the difference between markets dominated by individuals and those dominated by institutions may affect efficiency. Some differences between these two types of markets are obvious, but the importance of these differences must be determined empirically.

Operational Efficiency

Of the three types of efficiency, operational efficiency is the most straightforward. An operationally efficient market is simply a market in which there are no explicit or implicit costs of or barriers to trading. Explicit costs would include commissions, taxes, and some allocation of the bid-ask spread between buyer and seller. Implicit costs would include the value of the investor's time in managing his portfolio as well as any temporary impact his trading might have on price.

Except for the costs associated with temporary price impacts, the meaning of each of these factors is clear. To illustrate the meaning of a temporary price impact, consider a stock quoted at a bid or buying price of $20 and an ask or selling price of 20^{1/4}$. A purchase order for 200 shares might drive the ask price temporarily to 20^{3/8}$, since the first 100 shares were purchased at 20^{1/4}$, but the second 100 at 20^{3/8}$. If the ask price immediately returned to 20^{1/4}$, the transaction cost associated with this temporary impact would be $^{1/16}$ of a dollar per share—a cost in addition to any others. This same type of cost can obviously occur on the selling side.

In practice, this particular kind of implicit cost cannot be measured as precisely as this example would suggest, since the change in price from any temporary imbalance should be measured relative to the equilibrium price, which may change over time. Likewise, the im-

Market Efficiency and the Individual Investor

plicit costs of managing a portfolio cannot be measured precisely. In contrast, direct costs like commissions or bid–ask spreads are fairly well defined.

Before moving on to a more detailed analysis of the impact of a potential shift of stockownership from institutions to individuals on the spread between the bid and ask prices and on the magnitude of temporary price fluctuations, let us look briefly at commission costs and the costs of managing a portfolio.

Until April 1975, NYSE members used a fixed noncompetitive schedule of commission rates. In recent years at the fixed rates, institutions, which have relatively large orders of relatively high-priced stocks, have generally paid a smaller proportion of the value of their orders as commissions than did individuals. The NYSE has attempted to justify these differences in commissions by differences in costs, but certainly some of the differences reflected the greater ability of institutions to utilize the third market, where commissions have been competitive. Individuals with fewer options had less bargaining power.

The competitive pressures that the institutions brought to bear on the NYSE were undoubtedly an important factor in the final demise of the fixed commission rate schedule. Competitive commissions have brought a reduction of commission rates for many types of orders, including those of the smallest individual investors if they wish to take advantage of them. Although some rates have increased, revenue figures published by the NYSE indicate that the overall effect has been a reduction in commission rates as a percentage of the total value of stock traded. Such a reduction in commission rates should bring an increase in operational efficiency, providing other trading costs borne by investors (e.g., bid–ask spreads) did not increase as a result. Even if this overall reduction in commissions were partially offset by increases in other tradings costs, operational efficiency would still be enhanced, but to a smaller degree. Since the bid–ask spreads and the magnitude of temporary price impacts have experienced only minor changes during the last several years, it is reasonable to conclude that the freeing of commission rates has led to some increase in operational efficiency.

Although the costs of managing money may differ for individuals and institutions, it is impossible to estimate such differences accurately. The cost of an individual investor's time can only be determined arbitrarily. Nonetheless, the management of money does involve economies of scale. The original Wharton Mutual Fund Study and the more recent Institutional Investor Study of the Securities and

152   The Changing Role of the Individual Investor

Exchange Commission found a definite negative correlation between the amount of money under management and management fees and other expenses as a percentage of that amount.[4]

This brief discussion of commission rates and management expenses gives no reason to believe that a shift of ownership from institutions to individuals would enhance the operational efficiency of the market. If anything, this analysis would suggest just the opposite. The subsequent examination of bid–ask spreads and temporary price impacts also provides no support for the belief that increased relative ownership or participation in the stock market by the individual investor would enhance operational efficiency.

Bid–Ask Spreads

Just like any other merchant, a dealer in securities or specialist on the floor of the NYSE who stands ready to trade from his own inventory will demand some compensation for this service. The compensation is the difference between the net amount a dealer pays for a security and what he receives by selling it. The reason a dealer demands and receives compensation for the readiness to trade on his own account is that in providing these services he incurs costs and possibly exposes himself to certain risks.

A stock dealer's direct expenses generally include office rental, supplies, telecommunication devices, and, perhaps most important of all, staff salaries. These expenses might be subject to economies of scale, both in terms of overall activity and activity in a specific issue. Unlike the inventories of dealers in many other commodities, securities are productive assets that would normally be expected to yield a return roughly equivalent to their carrying costs.[5] For this reason, a dealer in securities would bear little, if any, of the usual direct costs that most dealers would incur in financing their inventories.

It has been pointed out, however, that this argument may not be strictly applicable to a dealer who must on occasion trade with investors who have information that he does not yet have. To the extent that a dealer cannot recognize such informationally motivated trades, he would expect to incur some costs. If the information were unfavorable and the dealer purchased stock from such an investor, he might find himself with a loss or at least a lower return than normal, and if favorable and he sold stock from his inventory, he might find that he had foregone a potential profit.

Counterbalancing this potential cost is the potential trading profits a dealer, and especially a specialist, might obtain because of his knowledge of the "book," which lists all orders to purchase or sell at specific prices placed with the specialist or dealer. The book thus provides valuable inside information about the supply and demand for a particular security. Since specialists and insiders appear to be the only groups of investors who have consistently outperformed the market, it would seem that knowledge of the book outweighs any possible disadvantages a dealer might have in not knowing with whom he is trading.

It also has been argued that to make a market, a dealer must on occasion hold more or less of a specific issue than he would normally want to for reasons of diversification. If so, he would require some compensation. But as his wealth increases, this factor should become less important.

On the basis of arguments such as these, the bid–ask spread, expressed as a percentage of the price of the security to eliminate obvious scale effects, might be hypothesized to be a function of the achieved economies of scale, the level of competition, the amount of trading by knowledgeable investors, the value of access to the book, and finally the degree to which a dealer's holdings might differ from what he would want to hold were he not a dealer.

Expressing the bid–ask spread as a percentage of the price of the security would eliminate obvious scale effects; however, this percentage bid–ask spread may still be a function of price for two reasons. First, most stocks listed on the NYSE must trade in units of 1/8, so that the minimum bid–ask spread is 1/8, which represents a larger cost for a low-priced than a high-priced stock. Second, the NYSE, in justifying its fixed commission rate schedules, has argued that the costs of a dealer may increase with the number of shares traded even if the dollar volume of trading is held constant. Even if this second reason were not valid, the first reason itself would suggest a relationship of the percentage spreads to price. Thus a given percentage increase in price would be expected to lead to a greater reduction in the percentage spread for a low-price than for a high-price stock. In the terminology of economics, the elasticity of the percentage spread with respect to price should be negative and an increasing function of price if this "one-eighth" effect is important.

Within this framework, it is useful to examine the variables used in previous studies. Such variables have included the dollar volume of trading, the number of stockholders, the market value of the stock outstanding, the number of markets, some risk measures, and finally the price of the stock. The dollar volume of trading is supposed to measure economies of scale. The number of stockholders and the market value of the stock outstanding may be seen as alternative measures of economies of scale. The number of competing dealers and the number of markets are designed to measure the degree of competition and again would be highly correlated with the dollar value of stock outstanding.

To create a market for a security, various risk measures have been used in previous studies to measure the additional risk a dealer may have to bear. Without going into detail, this study uses two measures of risk. One is the so-called beta coefficient, which has been defined in Chapter 2. The other is the standard deviation of total return.[6] By allowing both these variables to enter into the analysis simultaneously, one can allow the data to determine the importance of the distinction between total risk and nondiversifiable risk, a distinction frequently made in the academic literature.

This discussion of the determinants of the percentage bid–ask spread implicitly assumes that all trades are consummated through changes in the inventory positions of dealers or specialists. However, not all trades are actually so consummated. As pointed out earlier, some of the volume on the NYSE attributable to trades in which the public represented one or both sides was affected by chance matchings of public orders on the floor of the NYSE. Another limited amount was due to orders matched off the floor. The first type would more likely involve individuals and the second, institutions. A switch of shareownership from institutions to individuals would likely affect the proportion of trading through matched orders.

The possibility of a change in the proportion of matches in an institutionally dominated market would probably affect the percentage bid–ask spreads in various ways. First, the value of the book to specialists, and to a lesser extent dealers, will change. This would alter their profits, which, depending on competitive forces, may result in a decrease or an increase in the percentage bid–ask spreads. Second, if a greater percentage of informationally motivated orders are matched, it would reduce a dealer's or specialist's risk of trading with an insider and thus would be expected to reduce his bid–ask spread; if the percentage is smaller, the reverse would be true. Third, if the number of matches were to increase, a dealer or specialist would less often have to act against his wishes, leading to a lower bid–ask spread; in case of decrease, the reverse would be true. Although there may be other effects, these three are sufficient to suggest that the trading volume of institutions might affect the percentage bid–ask spreads, but, if so, it is not clear in which way.

To analyze the impact of institutional trading on bid–ask spreads, 200 companies listed on the NYSE were selected at random for each of six dates: November 10, 1932, December 10, 1941, August 4, 1955, December 24, 1959, January 25, 1968, and March 11, 1974. The dates themselves were not chosen at random but were picked so as to cover the entire 1932–1974 period and to represent different kinds of markets and also, particularly for the pre-World War II period, with an eye toward the availability of data. The percentage bid–ask spreads were related through regression techniques to various variables such as the price of the security, the dollar volume during the month, the market value of the stock outstanding, and the two risk measures discussed earlier.[7] For the last two dates, direct measures of institutional ownership and the number of exchanges on which the stock was traded were obtained. These measures were not available for the earlier dates. No risk measures were collected for the first two dates.[8]

As already noted, dollar volume and market value of stock outstanding are highly correlated—for example, 0.75 in 1974. Frequently, in view of such close correlation, only one of the two variables is used to explain the percentage bid–ask spreads. Since dollar volume would seem more closely tied to the costs of a dealer, this variable is used in the analysis, although it should be noted that the results using market value are almost identical.

As expected, the bid–ask spreads as a percentage of the stock prices tend to decrease with increases in price and also to decrease with increases in dollar volume. Since the risk variables are insignificant in each year, these variables were dropped to obtain more efficient estimates of the relationship of percentage bid–ask spreads to price and dollar volumes.[9] These more efficient estimates disclose some clear long-range trends. In 1932 these estimates would suggest that a doubling of dollar volume, holding price constant, would have been expected to result in a 29-percent decrease in the bid–ask spread as a percentage of the stock price (Chart 4-1). The corresponding percentage in 1941 was 31 percent. By 1955 this percentage dropped to 15 percent, with a still further reduction to 7 percent by 1974. A doubling of price, holding dollar volume constant, would have been expected to result in a 20-percent decrease in the bid–ask spread as a percentage of the stock price in 1932 (Chart 4-2). This percentage fluctuated within narrow bounds through 1960 and then increased dramatically and significantly to 44 percent in 1968 and 58 percent in 1974.

The change in the expected reaction of the percentage bid–ask spreads to the doubling of dollar volume appears to have preceded the

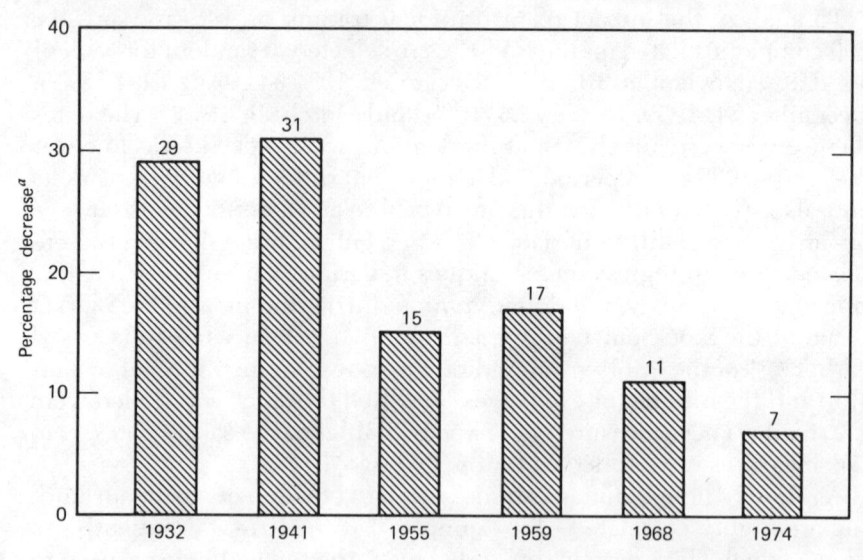

156 The Changing Role of the Individual Investor

[Bar chart showing percentage decrease values: 1932: 29; 1941: 31; 1955: 15; 1959: 17; 1968: 11; 1974: 7. Y-axis labeled "Percentage decrease[a]" ranging 0 to 40.]

[a] The t—values in chronological order are 7.8, 6.8, 4.6, 5.7, 4.0, and 4.3.

Chart 4–1. Expected percentage decrease in bid–ask spread as a percentage of stock price from a doubling of dollar volume holding stock price constant.

rapid growth of institutions that took place from the late 1950s to the present. This apparent change in the structure of the market of itself thus gives no reason to believe that the markets would be more or less efficient if individuals were to increase their share of stockownership. Nonetheless, it is interesting to speculate on some possible reasons for this change.

The percentage bid–ask spread for the average stock in the 1932 and 1941 samples was about six times that of 1955, 1959, 1968, and 1974. The average percentage bid–ask spreads in 1932 and 1941 were estimated to be 11.1 and 12.2 percent, respectively. In contrast, the average percentage bid–ask spreads in 1955, 1959, 1968, and 1974 were estimated at 1.7 percent, 1.6 percent, 1.2 percent, and 1.6 percent, respectively. Although there is a big gap between the average percentage bid–ask spread before World War II and after, the percentage bid–ask spreads of heavily traded stocks in 1932 and 1941, such as Standard Oil of New Jersey, were of the same magnitude as those of the postwar period.

This phenomenon suggests that the statistical finding that a dou-

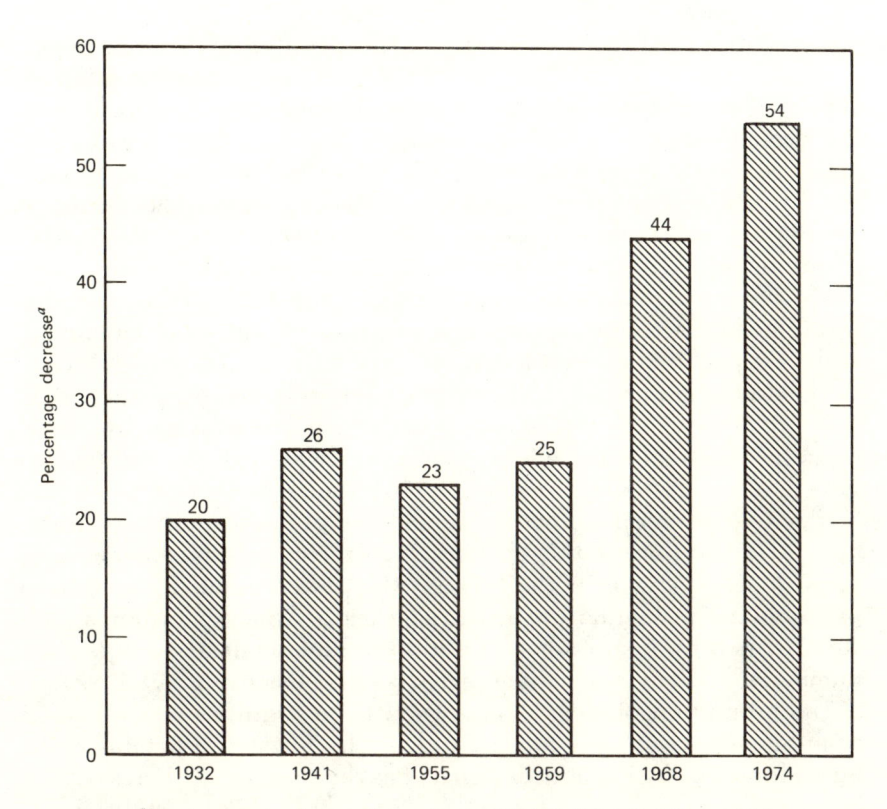

[Bar chart showing percentage decrease on y-axis (0 to 60) for years 1932, 1941, 1955, 1959, 1968, 1974 with values 20, 26, 23, 25, 44, 54 respectively.]

[a]The *t*-values in chronological order are 2.5, 3.9, 3.4, 3.3, 6.8, and 12.1.

Chart 4–2. Expected percentage decrease in bid–ask spread as a percentage of stock price from a doubling of stock price holding dollar volume constant.

bling of dollar volume would have been expected to have a greater impact on spreads prior to World War II than after should not be taken at face value. What may be happening is that the percentage bid–ask spreads for inactively traded stocks are relatively large. As volume increases, spreads may fall at a very fast rate and then at a slow rate. A much larger percentage of the stocks listed on the NYSE was inactively traded in the 1930s than after World War II, suggesting that perhaps a single number cannot adequately summarize the relationship of spreads to volume.

These declines in the average percentage bid–ask spread from 1932 and 1941 to the post-World War II period may be attributable to differences in trading activity; however, it might be argued that they were due to secular technological changes as well as increased regulation of the securities markets. To investigate this possibility, the average percentage bid–ask spread for July 2, 1928 was estimated for 103 randomly selected common stocks.[10] The average of these spreads was 2.5 percent—a little larger than today's averages, but considerably smaller than those for 1932 and 1941. Thus the relatively large bid–ask spreads for many stocks in 1932 and 1941 are more likely attributable to their low volume rather than to secular changes in the market environment. The fact that some high-volume stocks in these two years showed percentage bid–ask spreads comparable to those in periods of greater activity suggests that the more important economies of scale take place at the stock level and not at the overall exchange level.

The dramatic increase in the responsiveness of the percentage bid–ask spread to stock price, holding dollar volume constant, occurred over the 1959–1968 period—a span coincident with the most rapid growth of institutional ownership. This change could hence possibly be due to institutional growth. In an attempt to ascertain the importance of institutions to this change, the percentage bid–ask spreads of individuals' stocks in both 1968 and 1971 were related not only to price and dollar volume, but also to a measure of the proportion of each stock owned by institutions. In addition, the analysis included the number of exchanges on which each stock was listed as a variable.

The proportion of each stock owned by institutions was obtained from Standard & Poor's *Stock Guide*. The *Stock Guide* tabulates a figure for each stock that is designated as the number of shares owned by institutions, although in fact it covers only those institutionally owned shares that are reported in some way as part of the public record. As such, the figure in 1968 and 1971 would include only those shares owned by mutual funds; closed-end investment companies; and fire, life, and casualty insurance companies. Perhaps its most important omissions are holdings administered by banks. This measure is thus not a completely satisfactory one, but it is adequate to give some insight into the relationship between percentage bid–ask spreads and institutional ownership.[11]

In 1968 the correlation between the percentage bid–ask spread and the proportion of stock owned by institutions[12] was -0.16 and in 1974, -0.29. These negative correlations might be attributed to the propensity of institutions to hold higher-priced, more actively traded stocks; even before institutions became important, the percentage bid–ask spreads were negatively related to price and volume. Yet even if price, dollar volume, and number of exchanges on which the stock is traded are held constant, the percentage bid–ask spreads are still negatively related to the measure of institutional ownership.[13] However, in both years the relationship is not statistically significant.

Taken at face value, these results indicate that increases in institutional ownership would tend to reduce the percentage bid–ask spreads, everything else remaining the same. Even if this conclusion were true, the magnitude of the effect is virtually nil. For instance, in 1974 a doubling of the percentage of stock owned by the institutions covered by the *Stock Guide* would imply an expected decrease in the percentage bid–ask spread of only 0.5 percent.

Nonetheless, as institutional ownership increases, things do not remain constant, and volume may well increase. And a doubling of volume would imply a decrease of 11 percent in the bid-ask spreads. Thus, through this back door, institutional ownership may have increased the operational efficiency of the market in pricing of individual assets. However, since the bid–ask spreads fall at only a fraction of the increase in volume, the total resources devoted to trading to cover the bid–ask spreads probably increased. Such an increase would affect the allocational efficiency of the market. The absolute decrease in total commissions associated with institutional trading would be expected to offset these additional costs; whether in total or in part depends on the relative magnitudes of these two effects.

If the results are taken at face value, the greatest impact on the percentage bid–ask spreads would result from increasing the prices of individual shares, such as through reverse splits. The statistical analysis implies, for instance, that in 1974 a doubling of the price of a share would result in a 53-percent reduction in the percentage bid–ask spreads.

These results, however, should not be taken at face value. For instance, the level of the percentage bid–ask spread may be geared to a normal volume level, and the monthly volume figure used here may represent only an imperfect measure of this normal volume. The true amount of institutional ownership may well be correlated with the normal volume level, and thus its negative relationship to the percentage bid–ask spreads may in fact be due to volume. The competitiveness of the market-making function was measured by the number of exchanges on which a security was traded. This measure does not cover trading in the third market. Since institutions are the principal traders in the third market, it could be argued that the institutional ownership variable is in part a measure of competition.

The slight negative relationship between the percentage bid–ask spreads and institutional ownership may thus be due to factors other than institutional ownership itself. But what is important for this study is that this analysis gives no support to the belief that a shift of ownership of stock from institutions to individuals would enhance the operational efficiency of the market. Indeed, one could argue that the reverse is true, but that argument would not be persuasive. The safest conclusion to be drawn from this analysis is that at the current level of institutional participation in the market, the proportion of a particular stock owned by institutions is not an important variable in explaining differences in percentage bid–ask spreads among stock.

Before concluding this section, the strong relationship, particularly in recent years, between the price of a share and the percentage bid–ask spreads should be mentioned, since it would be easy to increase the price of a stock through reverse splits and perhaps benefit from a decreased percentage bid–ask spread. This policy prescription would work if it is the price of a security itself that affects the percentage bid–ask spread. It would not work, however, if the price of a security tended (e.g., for institutional reasons) to reflect more basic underlying variables.

The discontinuities in the bid–ask spreads caused by the requirement that most stocks be quoted in multiples of eighths of a dollar can only explain part of the relationship. For example, a stock quoted at a bid price of $10 and an ask price of 10^{1}/_{8}$ would have a percentage bid–ask spread of 1.2 percent—roughly of the same magnitude as the average percentage bid–ask spread in 1974. Thus only with the lowest-priced stocks, such as those under $10, would the "eighth" quotation requirement have a significant impact. Yet when the analysis of the percentage bid-ask spread was replicated in 1974 on only those stocks with bid prices in excess of $10, the strong negative relationship between the percentage bid–ask spread and price was still observed.[14]

The publication of indexes of low-priced stocks is in itself anecdotal evidence that the price of a stock itself conveys some information about fundamental variables to the market. For instance, in an analysis of all NYSE stocks going back to 1926, it was found that, more often than not, low-priced stocks became low-priced because of poor prior rates of return and not because of splits.[15] Moreover, poor previous rates of return tended to be associated with subseqent increases in the risk of the securities. In a similar way, perhaps for some institutional reason, price may tend to measure some fundamental factors other than those explicitly included in this analysis that are relevant to the determination of bid–ask spreads. In any case, more study is clearly needed to understand the reasons for the observed strong negative relationship between the percentage bid–ask spread and the price of an individual stock. One possibility would be that low-priced stocks are for institutional reasons more risky.

Price Impact

Since 1928 there have been marked changes in the volatility of the market as measured by the percentage fluctuations in the daily closing values of Standard & Poor's Composite Index. Not surprisingly, in the October 1929 through October 1933 period, the market showed its greatest volatility since 1928. The next greatest volatility was from September 1937 through roughly the middle of 1939. Until the mid-1970s, with the notable exception of September 1946, the market maintained a relatively low level of volatility, at least in comparison with the 1930s. Beginning some time in early 1973 the volatility of the market increased substantially but did not reach the heights of the 1930s. During 1976 the volatility of the market subsided again almost to the 1940-1972 levels.

This description of the secular changes in volatility is based on data prepared by the Securities and Exchange Commission, partly in conjunction with its program of monitoring the effect of competitive commission rates.[16] For sound statistical reasons, the SEC has decided to measure volatility within a month by the interquartile range of the percentage changes in the value of the market as defined by the daily close of Standard & Poor's Composite Index. The interquartile range is defined as the difference between the 75th and the 25th percentile, whereby, for example, the 75th percentile is determined as that daily return in which roughly 25 percent of the daily returns in the month would be greater and the remainder less.

This analysis has the merit of covering a long time span, but it is based on market averages that may hide significant differential effects among securities. To discover any such differential effects, a detailed analysis was made of daily prices for all common stocks listed on the NYSE in each of three six-month periods: one in 1962, another in 1969, and the last in 1976. In addition, more detailed analyses of daily price changes of most individual common stocks listed on the NYSE were undertaken for the months August 1972 and March 1975.

The volatility of daily returns of individual common stocks on the NYSE in the second and third quarters of 1969 appears to be about the same as in the last half of 1962. The daily volatility in the first half of 1976 appears to be slightly greater than in either of the two earlier periods. This apparent difference in volatility between 1976 and 1962 or 1969 is, however, small in comparison with the changes in the volatility of the Standard & Poor's Composite Index since 1928.

From July through December 1962, the maximum daily rate of return, adjusted for dividends, on the average common stock was 7.1 percent; the minimum was -5.8 percent. Of course, some stocks would have experienced higher returns and some lower (see Table 4.1). We derived our average maximum figure by averaging the maximum daily returns for each of 832 common stocks during the last six months of 1962. These 832 stocks represent all common stocks on the NYSE that, according to the files of the Rodney L. White Center, were traded every day during this six-month period and whose data were judged accurate by an extensive error-checking routine.[17] The additional statistics in Table 4.1 describe the distribution of daily returns of individual stocks in greater detail. For instance, 5 percent of the time, or five days out of 100, the average stock in this six-month period in 1962 would have had a gain in excess of 3.6 percent. The other statistics can be interpreted in a similar fashion.

During the six months from April through September 1969, the average common stock on the NYSE experienced a maximum daily return of 7 percent and a minimum of -6.3 percent. Based on estimates from 1133 stocks, this range is virtually the same as that observed in 1962. In contrast, the average stock from January through June 1976 experienced a somewhat greater range of returns than in 1962 or 1969, with a maximum of 8.9 percent and a minimum of -6.6 percent. The estimates for 1976 are based on an analysis of 1083 common stocks.[18]

The distribution of maximum and minimum daily returns for individual securities tells the same story as the distribution of the daily returns of the average stock, namely, that there was little difference in the volatility of individual issues between 1962 and 1969 and, in addition, that the volatility of individual issues in the first half of 1976 was somewhat greater than in either of these two earlier periods. The distribution of minimum daily returns for individual stocks (Table 4.2)

Table 4–1. Distribution of Daily Percentage Changes in Price of Average Common Stock on New York Stock Exchange, Various Dates

Statistic	July–December 1962	April–September 1969	January–June 1976
	(Percentages)		
Minimum	−5.8	−6.3	−6.6
First percentile	−4.2	−4.6	−4.8
Fifth percentile	−3.0	−3.3	−3.5
Mean	0.1	−0.1	0.2
Ninety-fifth Percentile	3.6	3.4	4.6
Ninety-ninth Percentile	5.1	5.1	6.5
Maximum	7.1	7.0	8.9

Market Efficiency and the Individual Investor 163

Table 4–2. Distribution of Maximum Daily Percentage Gains and Losses for Common Stocks on NYSE, Various Dates

Percentile	July–December 1962	April–September 1969	January–June 1976
	(Percentages)		
A. Maximum losses			
1	−14.4	−16.2	−19.9
2	−12.8	−13.6	−17.3
5	−10.6	−11.4	−13.3
10	−9.3	−10.0	−10.7
50	−5.2	−5.7	−5.8
90	−3.2	−3.4	−3.2
95	−2.8	−2.9	−2.8
98	−2.5	−2.5	−2.3
99	−2.1	−2.3	−2.1
B. Maximum gains			
1	2.6	2.2	2.2
2	2.9	2.4	2.5
5	3.3	2.9	3.0
10	3.7	3.4	3.8
50	6.2	6.3	7.8
90	11.9	11.6	15.8
95	13.7	14.3	19.2
98	18.7	17.2	22.7
99	20.0	19.4	25.1

shows that the maximum daily loss on 1 percent of all common stocks listed on the NYSE during the July–December 1962 period was 14.4 percent or more. In the second and third quarters of 1969, the corresponding figure was a loss of 16.2 percent. In the first half of 1976, the maximum loss on 2 percent of the stocks was 17.3 percent or more, a loss exceeding that for the first percentile in either 1962 or 1969. Not only were the maximum losses more extreme in 1976 but also the maximum gains.[19]

The conclusion that 1976 daily returns were somewhat more volatile than those of 1962 or 1969 does not appear to be due to differences in the overall volatility of the market. Even after removing the effect of the market on the daily returns of individual issues, the same pattern over time persists. These daily statistics adjusted for market movements are given in Tables 4–3 and 4–4.[20]

Another measure of volatility, which is sometimes used, is given by the ratios of the squared dollar price changes per share, adjusted for

Table 4–3. Distribution of Daily Percentage Changes Adjusted for Market Movements in Price of Average Common Stock on NYSE, Various Dates

Statistics	July–December 1962	April–September 1969	January–June 1976
	(Percentages)		
Minimum	−5.7	−5.8	−6.4
First percentile	−4.1	−4.2	−4.7
Fifth percentile	−3.0	−3.1	−3.5
Mean	0.0	0.0	0.1
Ninety-fifth percentile	3.2	3.2	4.3
Ninety-ninth percentile	4.7	4.7	6.2
Maximum	6.6	6.6	8.6

Table 4–4. Distribution of Maximum Daily Percentage Gains and Losses for Common Stocks Adjusted for Market Movements on NYSE, Various Dates

Percentile	July–December 1962	April–September 1969	January–June 1976
	(Percentages)		
A. Maximum losses			
1	−15.0	−14.8	−19.5
2	−13.2	−13.3	−16.8
5	−11.0	−10.7	−13.2
10	−8.9	−9.1	−10.6
50	−5.0	−5.1	−5.6
90	−3.1	−3.2	−3.2
95	−2.8	−2.8	−2.9
98	−2.4	−2.5	−2.6
99	−2.1	−2.4	−2.5
B. Maximum gains			
1	2.3	2.2	2.3
2	2.6	2.5	2.4
5	2.9	2.8	2.9
10	3.2	3.2	3.4
50	5.7	5.7	7.3
90	11.5	11.0	15.6
95	14.0	13.3	18.9
98	18.5	16.9	22.8
99	20.8	18.5	25.4

dividends, to the average of such squared dollar price changes over the nine preceding trading days, again adjusted for dividends. These ratios were calculated for every trading day for each stock, with the exception of the first ten days of each six-month period. These first ten days were used to start the process.

In terms of the average stock, there was not much difference in the distribution of these ratios among the three six-month periods (Table 4–5). However, the distribution of the maximum values of these ratios for any individual stock did show some changes over time. In 1962 1 percent of the stocks had a maximum value of this ratio in excess of 130, in 1969 the corresponding value was 194, and in 1976 the value was 245 (Table 4–6). The same trend is found in the higher percentiles.

One could argue that this trend is consistent with increased efficiency, and one could maintain the opposite view. The argument for increased efficiency holds that the price of a stock should adjust quickly to new information, and assuming that new information becomes available only occasionally, most price changes should be small, but sometimes they would be large. The argument for decreased efficiency is that these occasionally large price changes are due to the trading activities of institutions that temporarily may cause large destabilizing price changes. Although it is difficult to choose between these two arguments, there is some evidence favoring the first argument at the expense of the second.

If institutional trading results in temporary price aberrations, one would expect large price changes to be followed by large price changes

Table 4–5. Distribution of Ratio of Daily Volatility to Average Volatility of Prior Nine Days for Average Common Stock on NYSE, Various Dates

Statistics	July–December 1962	April–September 1969	January–June 1976
	(Percentages)		
Mean	1.52	1.62	1.55
Ninety-fifth percentile	6.63	6.99	6.75
Ninety-ninth percentile	14.11	15.62	14.51
Maximum	30.62	34.18	34.26

[a]If returns were distributed by a normal stationary process, the mean would be expected to be nine. If however daily returns are distributed by a process with greater kurtosis, such as a non-normal stable distribution or a subordinated normal, the mean would be expected to be less than nine.

166 The Changing Role of the Individual Investor

Table 4–6. Distribution of Maximum Ratios of Daily Volatility to Average Volatility of Prior Nine Days for Individual Common Stocks on NYSE, Various Dates

Percentile	July–December 1962	April–September 1969	January–June 1976
	(Percentages)		
1	8.8	8.3	7.7
2	9.0	9.0	8.8
5	10.2	10.5	10.4
10	12.0	12.0	11.6
50	21.1	23.2	22.5
90	55.4	56.6	61.7
95	73.7	90.2	91.1
98	111.3	144.7	163.5
99	129.8	193.6	244.7

but of the opposite sign.[21] It has been found that large price changes one day tend to be followed by large price changes the next day, but the sign is random.[22] This finding could be interpreted as implying that, on the receipt of new information by the market, the price of a security tends to adjust quickly to the market's best initial estimate of the new equilibrium price, but that on reflection the market finds that this initial estimate, as often as not, is too great as too small.

It is difficult to offer an unambiguous interpretation for the changes in the distributions of the ratios of daily volatility to average volatility. However, it is possible to ascertain whether there are differences in the value of this ratio among stocks in a particular cross-section as a function of the degree of institutional ownership. In investigating this possibility, the ratio of the high price to the low price for the same day was regressed on the following variables: the opening price for the day; the market value of the monthly volume; the standard deviation of monthly returns estimated from prior data; the proportion of stock owned by institutions, as determined from the Standard & Poor's *Stock Guide*; and the average amount owned by each institution, also determined from the *Stock Guide*. This regression in logarithmic form was estimated separately for common stocks listed on the NYSE for each of two months, namely, August 1972 and March 1975. For August 1972 the elasticity of the ratio of high to low prices with respect to the proportion of stock owned by institutions was -0.19 percent, and with respect to average-sized institutional holdings, it was -0.21 percent— both virtually zero from an economic point of view. The corresponding elasticities for March 1975 were 0.16 percent and -0.58 percent—again virtually zero. The only important variable was the standard deviation of monthly returns with elasticity estimates of 18.7 percent in August 1972 and 25.6 percent in March 1975.[23]

In contrast to these results using daily data, there is some weak evidence that sales of large blocks may have a small adverse effect on market price in the sense that prices recorded on the ticker may temporarily fall.[24] Purchases of large stocks apparently do not have a corresponding temporarily stimulatory effect. The adverse price effect of sales of large blocks in 1968 and 1969, according to this analysis, seems to have averaged somewhat over 0.7 of one percent, but since only blocks associated with down ticks were included and total sales of the stock were not held constant, even this relatively small figure probably overstates the block effect. Moreover, any such temporary price effect seems to have been largely dissipated by the end of the day since the analysis of daily data disclosed no important institutional impact.

Extensive analyses of all transaction prices on the NYSE for two months, August 1972 and March 1975, were undertaken in an attempt to obtain a more definitive insight into the impact of institutional growth on market efficiency. These analyses did not prove useful for a technical reason. Changes in transaction prices can occur for two reasons: (1) the true market price could change and (2) ignoring for the moment matched public orders, transaction prices will fluctuate between the prices at which the specialist or other NYSE members are willing to buy securities and those at which they are willing to sell them as public orders oscillate between buying and selling ones. Matched orders would reduce the frequency of such fluctuations.

Once daily volume, opening price, and number of transactions in the day were held constant, it was found that the price sequence for an individual stock became slightly more "continuous" as the proportion of a day's transactions due to 100-share trades increased.[25] This result is consistent with two propositions; one is that smaller transactions do indeed make the market more continuous, and the other is a technical explanation with no real economic substance. A specialist can change his inventory by executing some of the limit orders on his "book." If he wished to increase his inventory, he could execute some sell-limit orders on his book; if he wished to decrease his inventory, he could execute some purchase-limit orders. In addition, prearranged matched orders must first clear the book. Since smaller transactions would generally be involved in these adjustments to the book, there would tend to be a greater bunching of small purchase and sell transactions than would normally be the case. This bunching tendency would seem to give the appearance of greater continuity. For these reasons, the analyses of transaction prices did not produce very meaningful results. Although they were subject to some deficiencies, the analyses of bid–ask spreads and daily price movements thus provide more useful insights into the impact of institutional growth.

Another commonly used measure of the price impact of trading is the ratio of the change in price adjusted for dividends to the associated volume. Presumably the smaller this ratio in absolute value, the more liquid the market. Yet a little reflection suggests that this measure could alternatively be interpreted as a measure of heterogeneous expectations. If all investors agreed on the impact of new information, one would expect a large price change on little volume. Only if they disagreed would there be little price change on large volume. Another difficulty with this measure is that it is not invariant to stock splits, rendering comparison over a period of years treacherous. This ratio was calculated for this study, but for these reasons it did not provide any new insights.[26]

These various analyses, in summary, suggest that the growth of institutions has had little impact on the operational efficiency of the market.[27] The major changes, such as the marked reduction of the volatility of the market and of the average percentage bid–ask spreads from the 1930s to the post–World War II period, could not be due to institutional growth since these changes occurred prior to that growth. Moreover, a limited analysis of the average bid–ask spreads in 1928 and of particular stocks in 1933 and 1941 suggest that once volume is held constant, there may not have been important changes in the level of bid–ask spreads as a percentage of prices, but this conclusion is highly tentative, and verifying it would require a separate study.

Informational Efficiency

Most, and particularly the early, tests of the informational efficiency of the stock market were addressed to the question of whether all available information is reflected or incorporated into the prices of securities. Operationally, prices of securities are said to reflect all available information if an investor could not use this information to win abnormally large returns. It would, of course, be very damning to the hypothesis of informational efficiency if, for instance, investors could use such readily available information as charts of past prices to obtain abnormal returns. In an informationally efficient market, such information should already be reflected or discounted in the prices of securities.

Whereas the absence of opportunities to use available information to make abnormal returns is a necessary condition for informational efficiency, it is by no means sufficient. The absence of trading opportunities by itself does not imply that securities are correctly priced according to some normative evaluation model. John Maynard Keynes and, more recently, the second "Adam Smith" have suggested the possibility that speculative excesses may sometimes be a more important determinant of securities' prices than the underlying economic variables. If past information could not be used to predict the duration of a speculative excess or the time and place of its next occurrence, current security prices would be said, in a technical sense, to reflect or incorporate this information. Although the market would in this technical sense be termed "informationally efficient," such efficiency would have little economic substance for the ultimate allocation of real resources.

There have been only a limited number of tests designed to answer the more fundamental question of whether security prices conform to those that can be predicted by a normative evaluation model. Moreover, even if the market were to value a company correctly, there is no guarantee that the company would be well managed. It is one thing to evaluate a mismanaged company correctly, and another to force a change in management.

In examining informational efficiency, it has become customary to distinguish between different types of information. Prices of securities may be efficient with respect to one type of information but not to another. The narrowest definition of available information, on which many tests have been based, would refer to all past prices of a security and perhaps volume. This narrow concept corresponds to the information that would typically be used by a chartist. A broader definition would include, in addition to past prices and volum type of information that would be used in traditional security analysis. The broadest definition encompasses all information available to any actual or potential investor, including inside information.

This section is, to some extent, organized according to these various definitions of information. The principal deviation is a separate analysis of the alleged two-tier market. In a two-tier market, the expected rates of return of stocks held primarily by institutions differ from those of stocks held primarily by individuals even after adjusting for differences in risk. If true, the markets would be informationally inefficient. It might be noted that the finding that there are no differences in expected returns after adjusting for risk may or may not be consistent with informational efficiency, it only indicates that there is no difference in informational efficiency among stocks held by individuals and institutions.

Efficiency with Respect to Past Prices

The earliest tests of informational efficiency examined whether there were any dependencies in the historical record of prices that could be used to predict future returns more accurately or, holding operational efficiency constant, could be used to implement a successful trading strategy. Without delving into the explicit statistical details, these early tests found that there were some dependencies in the sequence of historical prices that could be used to predict future prices more accurately. However, the transaction costs in implementing any trading strategy based on such forecasts would far exceed any potential gain.[28]

Since these early tests were generally confined to short periods of time in the post-World War II era, they are of only limited value in determining whether the market experienced any marked changes in the informational efficiency after institutions became an important factor. To provide a longer-term perspective, the monthly returns for all individual stocks listed on the NYSE for at least two consecutive months were examined for the period 1926–1975. The number of stocks ranged from 497 at the beginning of 1926 to 1477 at the end of 1975.

The relationship between the rates of return for, say, November 1975 and the returns for the same securities, but for the next month, December 1975, was determined. The correlation coefficient for these two months was -0.19. Similar correlations were calculated for every consecutive pair of months going back to February and March 1926. This process yielded 598 correlation coefficients ranging in value from -0.53 for the September-October comparison of 1939 to 0.40 for the January–February comparison of 1943.

If the prices of all securities adjusted instantaneously to new information, so as to eliminate all consistent leads or lags, and if all securities were of the same risk, these correlation coefficients should have an expected value of zero and be symmetrically distributed about the mean. However, securities are not all of the same risk. Since the returns on high-risk stocks should, on average, be larger than the returns on low-risk stocks, one would expect that stocks with the larger returns one month also would tend to have larger returns the next month. One would thus expect these correlations coefficients to be positive on the average, although the magnitude may not be great. If the returns of securities did not all adjust to new information instantaneously, one would expect these correlation coefficients to be less positive, on the average, and perhaps even negative. To illustrate, if the market receives favorable news but stocks do not all adjust at the same time, those that adjust first would have greater returns initially but lower returns subsequently, making for a negative correlation.

Over the entire 1926–1975 period 422 of the 598 correlation coefficients were negative, suggesting some degree of inefficiency.[29] In view of the generally small values of the correlation coefficients—83.7 percent were between -0.20 and 0.20—and the difficulty in predicting the sign of the coefficient, transaction costs may make it unprofitable to take advantage of these inefficiencies in a trading strategy. Nonetheless, it is interesting to note that since 1950 there has been a decrease in the percentage of negative coefficients. Prior to 1950, 77.4 percent of the 287 month-by-month comparisons had negative correlation coefficients; during 1950–1975 64.3 percent of the remaining 311 month-by-month comparisons had negative correlation coefficients. This drop, significant by standard statistical tests, would imply that the market has become somewhat more efficient since 1950. In view of the small magnitude of this inefficiency in the first place, one would be hard pressed to argue that further growth of institutional investors should be encouraged even if the rapid growth of institutional investors in the 1950s and 1960s was the cause of this apparent increase in efficiency.

Efficiency with Respect to Other Types of Information

The inability to obtain more accurate assessments of future returns from previous information or, after allowing for transaction costs, to implement a successful trading strategy is a necessary condition for an informationally efficient market, but it is not a sufficient one. Various studies (e.g., on the relationship between increases or decreases in the normal earnings of a firm and the associated price movements of the stock) have examined the reaction of the prices of securities to obviously relevant data.[30] Without an explicit evaluation model, these approaches usually can specify only the sign of the relationship—not the exact magnitude.

172 The Changing Role of the Individual Investor

Since these studies have not addressed the explicit question of whether the price adjustment was in some sense more efficient as the ownership or trading activity of institutions increased, these studies are of limited value for the purposes of this book. Of great relevance, however, are the well-documented findings that neither individuals nor institutions have consistently outperformed the market on a risk-adjusted basis.

These findings of no consistent differences in the past performances of individuals and institutions mean that neither group contributes relatively more to informational efficiency than the other. If institutions, with their presumably greater resources for security analysis, were better equipped than individuals to find mispriced securities, one would expect that they would consistently outperform individuals. This suggests strongly that the average institution's contribution to informational efficiency is the same as the average individual's.

The Two-Tier Market

In the past there has been little consistent difference in the investment performances of institutions and individuals; however, it has been argued that recent changes in the marketplace have segmented the market at least partially into two or more tiers. Even if such a segmentation has occurred, it should not affect the relative levels of informational efficiency in the different segments unless it is further assumed that what happens in one segment has little effect on what happens in another. Investors in one segment would then be assumed to be blind to development in the other segments and fail to take advantage of profitable opportunities in them. Though possible, such an assumption of irrationality seems implausible. Nonetheless, the publicity given the two-tier market justifies a careful analysis of its possibility.

Both individuals and institutions do tend to concentrate their holding in different sectors of the market. In the aggregate, individuals weight their portfolios more heavily than do other investors toward OTC or unlisted issues. For instance, figures from Chapter 2 show that in mid-1971 individuals owned 75.1 percent of all common stock. If they were to spread their investments evenly over all stock in proportion to the market value of each issue, individuals would have held 75.1 of OTC or unlisted stocks. Such unlisted stock would have included stock issued by investment companies. It is estimated, however, that individuals held fully 93.8 percent of such unlisted stock.[31] It follows that other types of investors, principally institutions, weight their portfolios more heavily toward securities listed on an exchange.

Market Efficiency and the Individual Investor 173

Since unlisted issues in mid-1971 represented 35.1 percent of the market value of all stock, individuals must have owned 65.8 percent of the market value of all shares listed on an organized exchange, such as the NYSE, to own both 93.8 percent of OTC issues and 75.1 percent of all stock. Thus investors other than individuals, primarily institutions, owned only 34.2 percent of all listed holdings. If some of the holdings in personal trusts are treated as institutional, this figure would approach 50 percent.

Although the evidence is fragmentary, it seems safe to conclude that institutions invest their portfolios more heavily in listed issues but even more heavily in the larger issues relative to the market value of the shares outstanding.[32] Thus in 1969 the percentage of total stock outstanding of the largest 500 NYSE stocks held by banks on behalf of pension and trust funds was roughly three times as large as their holdings of the remaining NYSE issues. There was also some tendency in 1969 for banks to weight their investments in the top 500 stocks more heavily toward the top 100 stocks within this group, but this tendency was so light that for most purposes it can be ignored.[33]

The pattern of concentration displayed in accounts managed by investment advisers differed somewhat from the pattern for banks. Investment advisers, who manage not only mutual funds but also a large number of other accounts, tended to concentrate their NYSE holdings in the bottom 400 of the top 500 stocks relative to a proportionally weighted portfolio of NYSE stock. The percentage of the stock outstanding of these 400 stocks held by them was roughly 1.5 times as large as the corresponding percentage for the top 100 stocks or the remaining NYSE stocks.

The pattern of concentration in NYSE issues of other institutional types, such as insurance companies, self-administered pension funds, and self-administered eleemosynary (charity) funds, was closer to that of banks rather than to investment advisers. Overall, therefore, institutional managers invested much more heavily in listed stocks, particularly the largest 500 issues on the NYSE, relative to the portfolio of all stock. This conclusion is based on data for 1969. There is, however, no reason to believe that structural changes have altered the qualitative nature of this result.

Some observers of the marketplace have postulated that this tendency of different types of investors to concentrate their holdings in different sectors of the market helps to explain the variation in realized returns among securities. It is an undeniable fact that different types of stock have shown substantial variation in returns in recent years. Specifically, many stocks of large market value have outperformed (or lost less than) stocks of small market value over some periods in the last six or seven years. Thus the equal-weighted Value Line Index declined 64.8 percent from March 11, 1968 through September 30, 1974, whereas the value-weighted NYSE Composite Index declined only 33.2 percent over this same period. In view of their propensity to concentrate their holdings in smaller issues, individual investors, at least before expenses, must have realized lower returns than institutions, particularly banks, during some parts of this six-year period. Over other periods, as from 1962 through 1968, the reverse occurred, with the expectation that individuals would have experienced larger returns than institutions.[34]

The hypothesis sometimes involved to explain these differences holds that the market consists of two or even more tiers and that institutions in recent years have been channeling their huge amounts of new funds into a limited number of so-called favored stocks, thereby supporting their prices. Since these stocks, which are said to constitute the upper tier, are generally stocks with higher market values, this allegedly explains the differences in returns between equal-weighted and value-weighted indexes or among different kinds of investors.

The rationale underlying the hypothesis of a two-tier market relies on a unique historical event to explain a presumably uncommon occurrence in the marketplace. The unique event is the rapid growth of institutional holdings, and the uncommon occurrence is the large differences in returns between those realized by the so-called favored stocks, primarily larger stocks, and those realized by out-of-favor stocks, primarily smaller stocks.

On the assumption that the actions of institutional investors were responsible for these differences in returns, some have argued that the rapid growth of institutional holdings and the tendency for institutions to concentrate their holdings in a select group of stocks has had deleterious effects on the equity market. Relative prices, it is alleged, may have become so distorted as to render the capital markets highly inefficient. Pursued to its logical end, this argument suggests that institutional holdings should be restricted and possibly at the same time individuals encouraged to increase their participation in the equity markets.

The presupposition of this policy prescription is that the often marked differences in returns between large and small issues in recent years is a unique, unprecedented phenomenon. If it were not unique, it would be difficult to argue that restrictions on institutional investors would preclude the future possibility of large differences in returns. Before examining the theoretical plausibility of a two-tier market, let us determine whether from a historical perspective the recent behavior of the market is unique.

Market Efficiency and the Individual Investor 175

A recent article[35] examined the rates of return on all issues on the NYSE from 1926 through 1971 and concluded that, even holding risk constant, the market value of an issue is an important variable in explaining realized returns, but that it is not an important variable in explaining expected returns once risk is held constant. In some periods the risk-adjusted returns on smaller stocks were substantially greater than on larger stocks. In other periods the reverse occurred; in still other periods there were no substantial differences. Therefore, the recent marked differences in the returns of large and small issues are not a new phenomenon.

Indeed, the larger issues on the NYSE performed relatively better than the smaller issues prior to 1950 than after. And it was only after 1950 that institutions became important. Four differently weighted indexes of NYSE common stock over the forty-five years from July 1928 through June 1973 serve to illustrate this fact.[36] One of these is the familiar equal-weighted index, in which the weight on each stock is the same; another is the familiar value-weighted index, in which the weight on each stock is proportional to the market value of the shares outstanding less treasury; and the final two are a more-than-value-weighted index and a less-than-equal-weighted index. The weights assigned to stocks in the more-than-value-weighted index are proportional to the square of the market values, and the weights in the less-than-equal-weighted index are proportional to the reciprocal of the market values of the stocks. The indexes are all appropriately adjusted for dividends.

The percentage of each index attributable to the top ten stocks by market value as of June 30, 1972 provides a perspective on the actual weights assigned to specific stocks (see Table 4-7). For the less-than-equal-weighted index the weight given to these top ten stocks was 0.01

Table 4-7. Percentage of Indexes Attributable to Largest Stocks as of June 30, 1972

Description (Stocks)	Less than Equal Weight	Equal Weight	Value Weight	More than Value Weight
	(Percentages)			
IBM	0.00	0.11	7.67	73.98
Top 10 stocks by market value	0.01	1.05	31.53	83.92
Top 50 stocks by market value	0.09	5.25	57.17	96.65
Top 100 stocks by market value	0.36	10.52	68.61	98.39

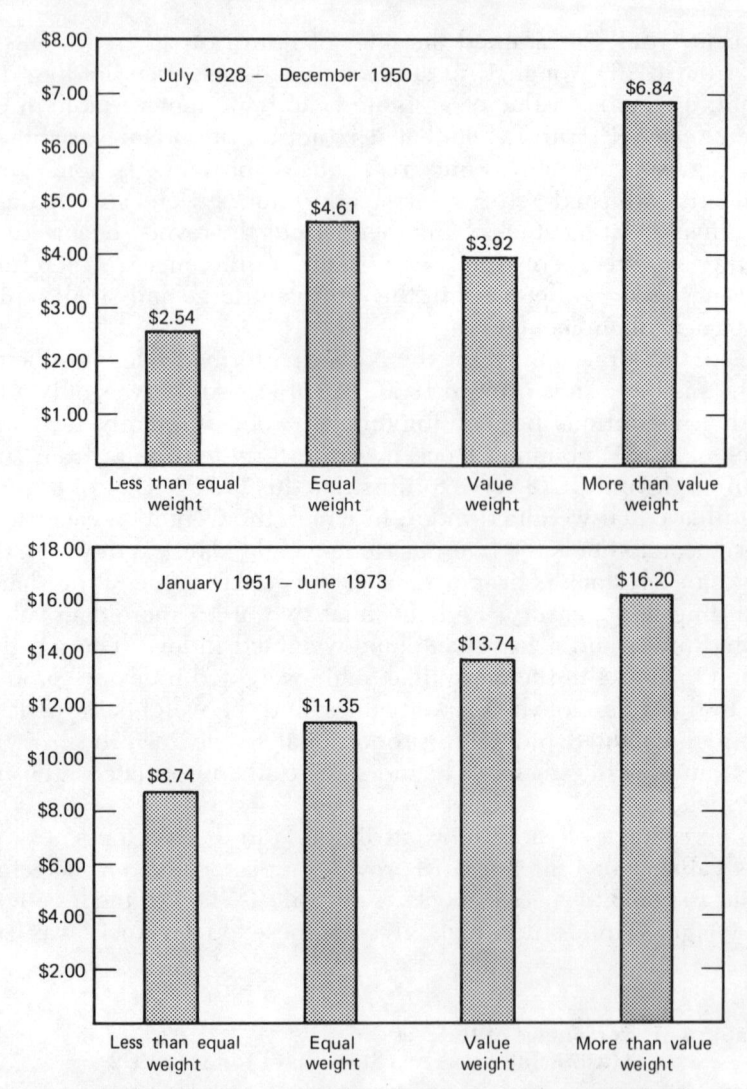

176 The Changing Role of the Individual Investor

Chart 4–3. Investment of $1.00 in various weighted indexes.

percent of the weight given to all stocks in the index, for the equal-weighted index the weight was 1.05 percent, for the value-weighted, it was 31.53 percent, and for the more-than-value-weighted it was 83.92 percent. Table 4–7 presents these percentages and similar percentages for IBM, the top fifty stocks, and the top one hundred stocks by market value. For dates other than June 30, 1972 the weights would, of course, be different, but they would still display the same basic pattern.

One dollar invested in the more-than-value-weighted index at the end of July 1928 would have increased to $6.84 by December 1950, whereas the same dollar invested in the value-weighted index would have increased to only $3.92 and in an equal-weighted index, to $4.61 (see Chart 4–3). The investment in the more-than-value-weighted index would have thus resulted in 74.5 percent greater wealth than in an equal-weighted index. Both the value-weighted and the equal-weighted index, in turn, performed much better than did the less-than-equal-weighted index.

In the post-1950 years, when institutions first became important and the two-tier market presumably began, there was less relative difference between the returns on large and small issues. One dollar invested in the more-than-value-weighted index at the end of December 1950 would have increased to $16.20 by June 1973, whereas the same dollar in a value-weighted index would have increased to $13.74. Thus the more-than-value-weighted index would have yielded 17.9 percent greater return than the value-weighted index—considerably smaller than the 74.9 percent recorded in the roughly twenty-two years prior to 1950. Also, the relative differences among the other indexes are less after 1950 than prior to 1950.

The even greater differences in returns between small and large issues before 1950 than after indicate the futility of restricting the behavior of institutions or encouraging the participation of individual investors as a way of preventing a so-called two-tier market. Even if the investment behavior of institutions were restricted or individuals were induced to return to the market, it cannot be presumed that the future would not see substantial differences among the returns of different sectors of the market.

Apart from the absence of any empirical basis in support of a two-tier market, the existence of such a market would require some type of market imperfection so as to permit two assets of comparable risk to have different expected returns. Without such an imperfection, investors holding overvalued securities would sell them, driving their prices down, and buy undervalued securities, driving their prices up. It would seem virtually impossible to devise some plausible type of imperfection that would permit the existence of such a two-tier market.

The two-tier market hypothesis is really an after-the-fact explanation of a pattern of market returns. An individual investor who foresaw the vast differences in returns on various assets would be foolish if he

178 The Changing Role of the Individual Investor

failed to buy those securities that promised a higher return than other securities. By so buying, he would immediately drive prices up and thereby reduce expected returns on those securities.

It is most implausible that any investor would knowingly sit by and watch institutions monopolize such highly favorably investment opportunities. Thus there is no economic basis for a two-tier market in which securities of comparable risks can offer different expected rates of return. Indeed, there are powerful economic forces, namely, the incentive for profits, to counteract such possibilities. This does not mean that institutional purchases were not responsible for the differences in returns, but only that these differences were not anticipated by the market.

Although this section sought to examine the rationale underlying the two-tier market, the empirical behavior of the indexes might on the surface suggest that an investment policy heavily weighted toward the larger issues would, in the future, be preferable to other policies. This conclusion, however, is not correct. Detailed statistical analyses of these variously weighted indexes show that the greater the weight on the larger issues, the lower the risk. Lower risk strategies theoretically should be associated with lower expected returns, and the available empirical studies confirm this proposition.[37]

In any particular period of time, there is some chance that a low-risk strategy will outreturn a high-risk strategy, and various statistical analyses suggest that it was just such a chance occurrence that the lowest-risk strategy produced the greatest returns in either half of the period from 1928 through 1973.[38] There is no guarantee that it will reoccur in the future. What can be said, however, is that if at all levels of probability a high-risk strategy will outreturn a low-risk approach, that high-risk strategy is not, in fact, a high-risk one. To call one strategy high risk and another low risk makes sense only if there are some probability levels at which the high-risk return is less than the low-risk one. Thus, at any particular time, there must exist some probability that a high-risk strategy would bring lower returns than a low-risk strategy; if not, it would not be more risky.

Allocational Efficiency

Although operational and informational efficiency are important properties of an efficient market, perhaps the most important property of an efficient market from the viewpoint of society as a whole is allocational efficiency. A market is said to be allocationally efficient if firms undertake those investments that optimize the welfare of the stockholders. More precisely, an informationally efficient market would be termed "allocationally efficient" if all firms undertake all investments that some investor would wish to finance and no others. Translated into the language of corporate finance, all projects whose expected rates of return equal or exceed their cost of capital should be undertaken; a project with an expected rate of return less than its cost of capital should not. Equivalently, a project with a positive net present value should be undertaken; one with a negative net present value should not.

Although the concept of allocational efficiency is fairly clear in principle, it does not readily lend itself to quantitative measurement. For instance, it would appear to be virtually impossible to measure the expected return on projects not undertaken to ascertain whether all projects whose expected rates of return equal or exceed their cost of capital are, in fact, undertaken. Perhaps the most that can be expected of a direct test of allocational efficiency is to find out whether the expected rates of return of projects undertaken exceed their cost of capital.

To construct such a test, one would need measures of the true expected rates of returns on specific projects and the cost of capital, or equivalently the returns that investors expect from such projects. If investors are on balance risk averse, they would expect a rate of return proportional to the perceived risks. In the case of common stocks, it would seem plausible to assume that the return expected by investors would be, on average, a positive function of historically estimated risk measures. Thus it would be assumed that a stock, such as PanAm, historically an above-average risk, would in future tend to be perceived of like risk.

In some previous works, including a study sponsored by the Twentieth Century Fund,[39] the true expected rates of return were measured by the ratio of subsequent earnings to the current price of the stock, adjusted for differences in dividend payout. The statistical relationships of these ratios to various risk measures were estimated over long period of time going back to 1954. No significant changes in these relationships were detected over time. This test is really a joint test of informational and allocational efficiency. In view of the large variability in the ratios of subsequent earnings to price and the corresponding difficulty in estimating the true expected returns, these analyses do

180 The Changing Role of the Individual Investor

not permit one to conclude that there was no change, but only that the tests used could not detect a change.[40]

This type of direct test measures the impact of institutional growth at its current stage. If institutions were to continue to grow and become a more important part of the market, some further insight into the likely effects on market efficiency can be gained from an extensive survey conducted recently by the SEC of major institutional investors, including the largest banks, insurance companies, and so on.[41] That study found that, whenever possible, institutional investors tended to express their displeasure with management not directly through a mechanism like the proxy, but rather indirectly through stock sales. Institutions tended to become involved directly with management only when their holdings were so large that they felt they could not dispose of the stock without substantially affecting the price. In addition, bank-trust departments at the current time consciously appear to avoid potential conflicts of interest between themselves and the commercial loan departments.[42]

Since institutions, in particular, tend to invest in larger companies, there is little danger in the foreseeable future that they will employ their potential power to any great extent to control managements—either for their own benefit or for that of their beneficiaries. Rather, they will generally try to sell their holdings if they are displeased with management. If a larger number of institutions were to sell a particular stock, the price of that stock would presumably fall. Even if management did not have stock options or other incentive programs, it would be concerned that such a drop in price would make the company a more likely target for takeover bids and thus place their jobs in jeopardy.

In sum, institutions tend to avoid an active role in the management of a company. They generally do the same as individuals who are displeased with a company and whose holdings are not large enough to make use of the proxy mechanism—they would, for example, sell their holdings, thereby putting pressure on the stock's price.

If institutions were better able than individuals to detect mispriced securities, a shift of stockownership to institutions would be expected to enhance the allocational efficiency of the market. The inconsequential differences in the historical performances of these two groups suggest, however, that institutions on balance are neither more nor less able than individuals to find mispriced securities. Based on this and the other analyses in this chapter, there appears to be no economic reason for encouraging greater relative market participation by the individual investor.

NOTES

1. It might be noted that, quite apart from any new information, a purchase or sale might affect the level of prices if such a purchase or sale were associated with a change in the overall propensity of the market to bear a specific type of risk. Although any transaction motivated by a desire to change one's exposure to risk would alter the market's propensity to bear that type of risk, the effect on the overall market would in most cases be so negligible that this effect could be ignored. However, a transaction accompanied by an immediate change in price followed by a return to the old price would normally be inconsistent with an operationally efficient market.

2. If investors foresaw not only the immediate impact of the new information on price, but also the secondary impact of the rebalancing of portfolios which may occur in response to a change in price, the new price would represent the final equilibrium price. If they did not foresee this secondary impact, the final equilibrium price might differ somewhat from the price that would clear the markets, assuming that no rebalancing had yet taken place.

3. Testimony of M. E. Blume before the Securities and Exchange Commission, December 5, 1974.

4. *A Study of Mutual Funds*, U.S. Congress, House, Committee on Interstate and Foreign Commerce, House of Representatives No. 2274, 87th Congress, Second Session, 1962, and the *Institutional Investor Study Report of the Securities and Exchange Commission* (Washington, D.C.: U.S. Government Printing Office, 1971).

5. This statement holds even if the dealer has taken a short or negative position by borrowing shares from somebody else to satisfy his customers. Unlike most investors, a dealer can reinvest the proceeds from such short sales. The expected returns on the reinvested proceeds would be expected to offset, at least on a risk-adjusted basis, the expected losses on the short position.

6. The standard deviations of total returns were estimated from the 60 monthly returns immediately preceding the date of specific analysis. If 60 months of data were unavailable, the standard deviation was still estimated if there were at least 48 months of data. The beta coefficients were estimated by regressing the same monthly returns on the market returns as measured by the Fisher Combination Link Relative.

7. All variables were expressed in terms of their natural logarithms so that the coefficients in the regressions can be interpreted as elasticities.

8. If any portion of the data could not be found or was of questionable accuracy, that security was dropped. Sixty-one securities were dropped for this reason in 1932, thirty-one in 1941, eleven in 1955, six in 1959, two in 1968, and five in 1974. The primary difficulty in 1932 and 1941 was that one could not always be certain that data collected from different sources referred to the same security. When there was any doubt, that security was dropped.

9. Theoretical arguments suggested that the elasticity of the percentage bid–ask spreads to price should be a decreasing function of price. Such a relationship was observed in each of the post-World War II years analyzed, but in only one was it significant at the 5-percent level. The elasticity of the percentage bid–ask spreads to dollar volume appeared to be constant in each of the four post-World War II periods. Thus the subsequent analysis assumes that these elasticities are constant. The actual regressions run were of the following form:

$$\frac{\ln(P_A - P_B)}{P} = a + b \ln P + c \ln V \cdot P,$$

where P_A and P_B are the bid and ask prices, respectively; P is the average of these two; and V is the volume in shares. The coefficients of determination adjusted for degrees of freedom were, in chronological order, 0.52, 0.53, 0.29, 0.36, 0.39, and 0.68 for the six days covered.

10. The stocks were selected by taking every ninth stock from the daily list of NYSE stocks as published in the *Journal of Finance and Commerce*. The first stock was picked from the first nine at random, the second by counting nine further stocks down the list, and so on. If that were not a common stock, the next common stock was used. These bid–ask spreads are closing bid–ask spreads and thus may differ conceptually from those used since 1932, which are midday spreads. To examine the potential bias, the average bid–ask spread for February 16, 1931 was estimated from the *Journal of Finance and Commerce*, but from 124 securities. The estimate of 5.7 percent indicates an increase by 1931, but not as great as would be implied by the 1932 figures. It would have been desirable to calculate the average of the closing bid–ask spreads for November 10, 1932, but the data were not available.

11. Specifically, this measure of institutional ownership will almost always be equal to or less than the true measure, and the discrepancy between the two will differ from stock to stock. These errors in measuring institutional ownership would generally introduce bias into a regression of the percentage bid–ask spreads on this variable and other independent variables. In the case of a regression on this incorrectly measured variable and another correctly measured one, the consistent understatement in the measured institutional-ownership variable would by itself bias its coefficient away from zero. Assuming that the differing amounts of understatement are not correlated with the underlying variables in the regression, the differing amounts of understatement would bias the coefficient of the institutional-ownership variable toward zero. These two sources of biases will alter the magnitude of the absolute value of the coefficient on the institutional-ownership variable, but they will not change its sign. To ascertain what would happen to the coefficient on the other variable would require additional assumptions about the structure of the variables in the problem.

12. As in the previous regressions, all variables have been measured by their natural log transformation. Any stock with no indicated institutional holdings was dropped.

13. In 1968 the regression was:

$$\frac{\ln(P_A - P_B)}{P} = -1.30 - 0.39 \ln P - 0.13 \ln V \cdot P + 0.02 \ln N - 0.003 \ln I, \bar{R}^2 = 0.33,$$
$$(-2.58)(-4.70) \quad (-3.46) \quad (0.33) \quad (0.14)$$

where P_A and P_B are the ask and bid prices, respectively; P is the average of these two; V is share volume; N is the number of exchanges on which the security is traded; and I is the ratio of the number of shares owned by institutions as reported in the Standard & Poor's *Stock Guide* to the total number of shares outstanding. The numbers in parentheses are t-values, and $\bar{R}^2$ is the coefficient of determination adjusted for degrees of freedom. The number of observations is 141.

The corresponding regression for 1974 is:

$$\frac{\ln(P_A - P_B)}{P} = -1.25 - 0.53 \ln P - 0.11 \ln V \cdot P - 0.09 \ln N - 0.005 \ln I, \bar{R}^2 = 0.65,$$
$$(-3.57)(-9.44) \quad (-3.47) \quad (-1.84) \quad (-0.26)$$

where the symbols are defined as in the 1968 regression. The number of observations is 177. Adding both the natural logarithms of the two risk variables, the β coefficient and standard deviation, leads to a decrease in the value of $\bar{R}^2$ in either 1968 or 1974.

14. The regression was:

$$\frac{\ln(P_A - P_B)}{P} = -1.43 - 0.58 \ln - 0.08 \ln V \cdot P - 0.12 \ln N - 0.001 \ln I, \bar{R}^2 = 0.51,$$
$$(-3.32)(-6.76) \quad (-2.22) \qquad (-2.06) \qquad (-0.05)$$

where the symbols are the same as used in note 13 of this chapter. The number of observations is 143.

15. M. E. Blume and F. Husic, "Price, Beta, and Exchange Listing," *Journal of Finance*, (May 1973), pp. 283–299.

16. R. H. Marcotte, Jr., "Analysis of the Impact of Competitive Commission Rates on Aggregate Price Volatility of NYSE Stocks," Securities and Exchange Commission, Economic Staff Paper 75—No. 2.

17. This routine was designed to detect any errors in the data, such as a missing split, misplaced decimals, and so on.

18. The error-checking routine discovered a large number of errors in the data filed for the first quarter of 1976. This explains the drop in the number of stocks analyzed in 1976.

19. The SEC frequently publishes dollar changes instead of percentage changes. Because of movements in the average price of a share of stock over time, an increase or decrease in the volatility of dollar changes may be consistent with an increase, decrease, or no change in percentage volatility. For instance, the minimum daily dollar change for the average stock was -1.67 during the last half of 1962, -1.99 for the two mid-quarters of 1969, and -1.15 for the first half of 1976. For the corresponding dates, the maximum daily dollar change for the average stock was 1.95, 2.09, and 1.36. One percent of the stocks had maximum decreases in dollars per share of 5.75, 6.50, and 4.25 for these dates; and 1 percent had maximum increases in dollars per share of 6.38, 6.88, and 5.00 for these three dates expressed in dollars. These changes would indicate misleadingly that 1969 was the most volatile period.

20. A daily return was adjusted for market movements by dividing 1 plus the daily rate of return for the stock by 1 plus the daily rate of return for the market as measured by Standard & Poor's Composite Index. The adjusted daily return was finally obtained by subtracting 1 from this ratio and expressing the resulting number in a percentage form. The market return was not adjusted for dividends.

21. If the destabilization persisted over several days, large price changes would tend to be followed by large price changes of the same sign—not a random sign.

22. E. F. Fama, "The Behavior of Stock-Market Prices," *The Journal of Business* (January 1965), pp. 34–105.

23. The explicit regression for August 1972 was:

$$\ln \frac{P_H}{P_L} = 0.073 - 0.011 \ln P - 0.005 \ln V \cdot P + 0.187 \ln s$$
$$\qquad (58.8)(-37.0) \qquad (-39.1) \qquad\qquad (49.1)$$

$$\qquad -0.0019 \ln I - 0.0021 \ln H + \text{dummy variables}, \bar{R}^2 = 0.34$$
$$\qquad (-5.0) \qquad\quad (-8.4)$$

where P is the opening price; P_H is the high price for the day; P_L is the low price; V is the number of shares traded in the month; s is the standard deviation of monthly returns as estimated from the sixty months prior to August 1972 providing there were at least thirty six months of data; I is the porportion of outstanding stock held by institutions; and H is the average amount held by each institution. This regression was based on 16, 765 observations—somewhat over 730 stocks for up to twenty three trading days. To control for day-to-day changes in the overall market environment, twenty two dummy variables were added. The *t*-values in parentheses should not be taken at face value in view of the

184 The Changing Role of the Individual Investor

potential impact of a specification error on their values in a regression of so many observations. The regression for March 1975 was:

$$\ln \frac{P_H}{P_L} = 0.106 - 0.019 \ln P + 0.008 \ln V \cdot P + 0.256 \ln s$$
$$(59.2)\,(-44.3) \qquad (40.1) \qquad (37.2)$$

$$+ 0.0016 \ln I - 0.0058 \ln H + \text{dummy variables},\ \bar{R}^2 = 0.39,$$
$$(6.6) \qquad (-16.0)$$

where s was estimated on the sixty months prior to March 1975. This regression was based on 16,759 observations.

24. A. Kraus and H. R. Stoll, *Price Impacts of Block Trading on the NYSE*, Rodney L. White Center for Financial Research Working Paper No. 3-71, University of Pennsylvania. See also *Institutional Investor Study Report of the Securities and Exchange Commission* (note 4, this chapter).

25. Continuity was measured by the number of runs of price changes in the same direction within a day. Various definitions of the same direction were used, but a typical one would be as follows. Determine the opening price. If the price of the last trade within the next fifteen-minute interval was greater than the opening price, assume an up run. If less, assume a down run. If equal, determine the direction of the run at the end of the next fifteen-minute interval, and so on. On the assumption of an up run, the up run was assumed to continue through the next fifteen-minute interval if the last price in that interval was greater than or equal to the price in the previous quarter of an hour less $0.25, otherwise; it was assumed that the up run had terminated and a down run had begun. The use of a number, such as $0.25, was an attempt to abstract from the fluctuations in price resulting from the bid–ask spread. The same procedure was used for a down run, except that $0.25 was added to the previous price.

26. The SEC publishes a variant of this measure for the market as a whole as represented by Standard & Poor's Composite Index. The variant is a function of the ratio of the square of logarithm of the price relative to turnover rate, where turnover rate is defined as the ratio of share volume to stock outstanding, but this measure is still subject to the same ambiguity in interpretation.

27. Since the start of this study, the Comptroller of the Currency has started to collect data on large trades of bank-trust departments. These data have not as yet been thoroughly analyzed. The published analyses to date of these data have examined activity within the quarter and thus are of little value in determining whether banks reacted to past price movements, caused concurrent price movements, or anticipated subsequent price movements. With a more careful analysis, these data may ultimately be able to shed light on this lead–lag issue.

28. E. F. Fama, "Efficient Capital Markets: A Review of Theory and Empirical Work," *Journal of Finance* (May 1971) contains an excellent review of this early literature. Few academic pieces of which we are aware conclude that there are potential trading profits. One was an article by R. A. Levy, "Relative Strength as a Criterion for Investment Selection," *Journal of Finance* (December 1967). However, a subsequent article, "Random Walks and Technical Theories: Some Additional Evidence," by M. C. Jensen and G. A. Benington, appearing in the *Journal of Finance* (May 1970), suggests that Levy's results were unique to his particular sample period and did not generalize on subsequent periods. Another was an article by S. S. Alexander, "Price Movements in Speculation Markets: Trends or Random Walks," in the *Industrial Management Review* (May 1961). In a subsequent article he reworked his earlier results to remove a bias in their calculation, and the profitability of his trading technique was drastically reduced.

E. F. Fama and M.E. Blume, "Filter Rules and Stock-Market Trading," show that when Alexander's filter is applied to individual stocks rather than market indexes, all potential profit disappears.

29. It might be argued that these predominatly negative correlations are the result of an artifice and not of a true lead–lag relationship. First made by Lawrence Fisher, the argument was as follows: quoted stock prices as opposed to true prices are changed only when there is a trade. For inactively traded stocks, the rates of return calculated from quoted prices would tend to lag behind the true rates of return. Thus a negative correlation would be induced. The Rodney L. White Center developed, as part of some other analyses, several data files that would allow a determination of the importance of this effect. The first data file contains all securities listed for four or more years prior to 1970 and the monthly returns for those securities in 1971, but only where the returns are based on closing prices set by trades on the last day of the month. From this file, eleven correlations were calculated. Similar files for 1972, 1973, and 1974 yielded thirty-three more correlations. Thirty of these forty-four correlations were negative. For the correlations discussed in the text for the same months, but for the more comprehensive list of securities, twenty-eight were negatives. Thus the Fisher effect is probably not the explanation for the predominately negative cross-sectional correlations.

30. R. Watts, "Comments on 'The Impact of Dividend and Earnings Announcements: A Reconciliation,'" *Journal of Business* (January 1976), contains numerous references to this literature.

31. I. Friend, M. E. Blume, and J. Crockett, *Mutual Funds and Other Institutional Investors: A New Perspective* (New York: McGraw-Hill, 1970).

32. Such listed holdings would have included a small number of closed-end investment companies.

33. M. E. Blume, "Changes in the Structure of Share-Holders and their Impact on Decision making within the Firm," *Gesellschaft für Wirtschafts und Sozialwissenschaften—Verein fur Socialpolitik* (Aachen, Germany: September 9, 1975) contains a full discussion of the procedure followed in obtaining these estimates for banks and the subsequent ones for other types of investors.

34. Compare Friend, Blume, and Crockett, *Mutual Funds*, p. 53, and the *Institutional Investor Study Report*. From 1962 through 1968, small NYSE issues not only outperformed large NYSE issues, but OTC issues also outperformed NYSE issues.

35. Blume and Friend, "Risk, Investment Strategy and Long Run Rates of Returns," *The Review of Economics and Statistics* (August 1974).

36. Much of the subsequent discussion is taken from M. Blume, "Two Tiers—But How Many Decisions," *The Journal of Portfolio Management* (Spring 1976). This paper describes in detail the construction of the indexes and the statistical tests.

37. The evidence in Blume and Friends, "Risk, Investment Strategy and Long Run Rates of Returns," confirms this theoretical proposition and makes reference to other studies on the same subject.

38. Blume, "Two-Tiers" contains a detailed description of the statistical tests.

39. Friend, Blume, and Crockett, *Mutual Funds*.

40. Friend, Blume, and Crockett, ibid., discuss this test and other types of tests based on the true expected rate of return. These tests have been updated and show similar results.

41. Securities and Exchange Commission, *Institutional Investor Study Report*.

42. The most comprehensive treatment of this subject available raises some question even about the existence of serious damage to trust beneficiaries. See E. Herman, *Conflicts of Interest: Commercial Bank Trust Departments* (New York: The Twentieth Century Fund, 1975).

CHAPTER 5

Implications and Recommendations

The preceding analysis has implications for regulation and legislation that would affect the stock trading and holdings of institutions and individuals in a number of ways. Various mechanisms for improving the efficiency and equity of the stock market have been proposed and must be examined.

Limitations on Institutional Stockownership and Trading

The preceding analysis has indicated that the institutionalization of stock trading and ownership in the United States is likely to continue, though probably at a more moderate pace. However, that analysis provides no basis for believing that market efficiency and, hence, the quality of prices paid or received by either institutional or individual investors have been or will be impaired by institutional trading. The same holds true for market liquidity and transaction costs. Thus the occasional examples of large institutional purchases and sales associated with substantial and lasting changes in the price of a stock probably reflect the inflow of significant new information. In an efficient market, such information should be instantaneously incorporated into the price.

Even if institutional trading does occasionally have a temporary impact on price, the effect of such trading seems to be minor and should properly be regarded as an increase in the transaction costs of the institutional trade necessary to overcome a short-term supply–demand imbalance. Although the institution in these instances may have to bear a small cost for speedy execution of its order, there is no significant harm to other investors on a net basis. Investors on the other side of the institutional trade would as a whole benefit from the temporary aberration in the purchase or sale price.

Although there is no evidence that past institutionalization of trading has resulted in a deterioration of stock-market efficiency, concern has been expressed about the potential dangers involved in the continuation of this trend. This concern has focused both on the possibility that activity and prices in the stock market will in the future be determined by a handful of institutions, with little market impact by the individual investor, and on the supposed deficiencies of the bond markets, now dominated by institutions, large transactions, and dealers. However, there is little basis for the fear frequently expressed in financial circles that individual investors will virtually disappear from the market. The number of individual stock investors in the United States continued to rise until the early 1970s, and the absolute volume of stock transactions by individuals recently has been as high as in the 1950s or 1960s despite the decrease in individuals' proportionate share. There is no reason to believe that the absolute volume of individuals' stock transactions is likely to decline appreciably in the foreseeable future. Nor is it clear that the bond markets are generally inferior to the stock market. The argument made is that the bond markets—especially those for U.S. government and corporate issues—are largely institutional and dealers' markets; that individuals have been relatively unimportant in these markets since the 1920s, possibly due to factors associated with the growing institutional participation; and that these markets are hence inferior to the auction markets associated with individual trades.

It is not clear in what sense the market for U.S. government issues can be considered inferior to the more heavily auction-oriented markets.[1] The government bond market handles the largest volume of any of the securities markets at probably the lowest transaction costs, reflecting the ability of dealers with substantial capital to manage successfully the problems posed by large blocks. The market for corporate bonds is characterized by significantly higher transaction costs with more sizable bid–ask spreads, but even here there is no evidence that comparable costs are on the average higher than those for corporate stock.[2]

Transaction costs are, of course, higher for inactive issues,[3] whether they be stocks or bonds. Thus the market for municipal bonds, in which individuals are relatively much more important than in the other bond markets,[4] is probably characterized by the largest bid–ask spreads, but this reflects mainly the general lack of trading activity in most issues, and not the investor composition. To the extent that relative importance of individuals' and institutional trading does affect stock-market activity, an increased proportion of institutions in the market would probably tend to increase the volume of activity since in recent years, as noted earlier, institutions have had a higher turnover ratio on the average than individual investors.

Moreover, there does not appear to be any reason to ascribe the diminished role of individuals in these markets to factors associated with the growing institutional participation. Individuals probably found U.S. government and corporate bonds less attractive, at least in part because bond yields remained extremely low for several decades in comparison with other yields. Increases in personal income-tax rates further lowered the effective yield on these bonds, since virtually all return from bonds is subject to the full income-tax rates, whereas much of the return on stocks enjoys the more favorable capital gains rates. Until about 1950, major groups of institutions were largely legislated out of the stock market in the United States and were not subject to the same income-tax deterrent. With the rapid rise of bond yields in recent years, individuals have become a more important part of the bond market, especially for corporate issues. Thus for corporate (and foreign) bonds, the share of households in total holdings rose from well under 10 percent in 1965 to 20 percent in the early 1970s.

Any inference that the comparative absence of individuals from the corporate bond market has impaired its usefulness for raising new capital for corporations is contradicted by the substantial rise in the share of new corporate financing accounted for by bonds at the expense of equity securities since the 1920s. Again, however, noninstitutional factors—such as the increase in corporate income taxes, which makes debt financing relatively less expensive—may have played a more important role in this development.

Fear has also been expressed that the growing institutionalization of stock trading and ownership might harm new equity investment, apparently in part because of its allegedly adverse effect on the market for outstanding stock issues. However, as noted earlier, there is no indication that the market for outstanding issues would be adversely affected, and indeed the growth in institutional stockownership in the 1950s and 1960s may have contributed to the marked rise in stock prices during this period and to the apparent decline in the relative cost of equity financing. Institutions may have had such an effect in two different ways: (1) by adding to the overall demand for stock and (2) by reducing transaction (and information) costs.

As for the new issues market, the decline in the relative importance of new equity financing in the United States immediately after the

Implications and Recommendations 189

1920s obviously had nothing to do with the institutionalization of equity markets, which really did not begin until after 1950. Only starting in 1969—1970, at a time when the institutionalization of markets was close to its present peak, was there a marked resurgence of new equity financing, with only a temporary dip during the depressed stock market in 1974. This resurgence has apparently not been effectively deterred by institutionalization.

Whereas the growing institutionalization of the market probably has not depressed the total supply of new equity financing, it may have had adverse effects on the supply of unseasoned or risky new issues. It is true that institutions tend to concentrate in the larger NYSE issues. As a result, other things being equal, a shift in stockownership to institutions might lead to an increase in the relative cost of capital to smaller firms, which would typically include the more risky seasoned and unseasoned new enterprises, types of businesses preponderantly financed by individuals. As noted earlier, the NYSE Census of Shareholders shows a significant decline between 1970 and 1975 in the number of investors in issues not listed on the NYSE, in contrast to virtually no change for NYSE issues.[5] However, for reasons discussed earlier, institutions may have served to lower the overall cost of equity financing, so that the actual cost of equity to the riskier enterprises that largely depend on such financing may not have been adversely affected. Moreover, there is no reason to believe that any possible adverse effect on the cost of capital to risky and unseasoned companies has been large; perhaps the main result may have been the reduction or elimination of a possible historical inefficiency in the U.S. new-issues market, where the rates of return realized on unseasoned new issues have generally been lower than for seasoned stocks.

Historically, from the early 1920s to the early 1960s, the rates of return on new and especially unseasoned common stock issues were lower than on outstanding issues over five- and ten-year periods following their offering, although in view of the greater subjective risk usually attributed to unseasoned new issues, the opposite result might have been anticipated.[6] Although the inferior performance of the unseasoned new issues persisted over this period as a whole, it had become less pronounced by the early 1960s. The comparative experience of outstanding and unseasoned new issues since that time appears to be more mixed. One study found little difference in the performance over the 1960-1969 period between outstanding and unseasoned new issues registered with the SEC.[7] Another devoted to unregistered (Regulation A) issues again found the long-run performance of unseasoned issues inferior to outstanding issues for stocks issued during the period 1957–1963.[8] The most recently available study also found that the subsequent performance of new unseasoned issues registered with the SEC in 1971 was inferior to that of outstanding registered issues.[9] Although comparative results for the years subsequent to 1971 are not available, the evidence through 1971 does not give any indication that the capital markets in this country are characterized by significant discrimination against risky or unseasoned stock issues. However, in view of the decline in the number of individual investors in such stock over recent years and the concentration of institutional investors in the large seasoned issues, future developments in the comparative cost of financing the riskier, smaller, and unseasoned companies bear close watching.

The preceding discussion has suggested that there is no cogent evidence that the rapid growth of institutional equity investment has had or is likely to have any appreciable undesirable effects on the efficiency of the stock market.[10] It is conceivable, of course, that this might change if individual equity investors were virtually to disappear from the market, but no such withdrawal appears likely in the foreseeable future. The situation might also change if a substantial deterioration were to occur in the relative terms of financing risky, small, and unseasoned firms, but again there is no evidence that this has taken place and no strong reason for believing that it will in the foreseeable future. It is true that, as noted in Chapter 3, individual investors indicated they would increase their stock holdings modestly if new securities legislation were passed limiting the role of institutional investors, but even if individuals did increase such investment, there is no reason to believe that this would result in a more efficient market. Consequently, there does not appear to be any compelling economic reason for placing new limitations on institutional stockownership and trading.

However, two other important sets of reasons have been advanced to support the need for controlling the level or rate of growth of institutional equity investment and associated institutional policies and practices.[11] The first of these arises from the social concern over the growing concentration of potential power over American industry in the hands of a relatively small number of financial institutions. The second relates to a whole range of issues of equity or fairness involving potential conflicts of interest between individual investors and institutions as owners of the same portfolio companies (corporations whose shares are owned by the individual or institution) or between individual investors and management in these institutions.

The concentration of power over portfolio companies, implicit in the growth of giant institutions heavily invested in common stock, has given rise to concern totally apart from any other economic implications of the growth of institutional stock investment. Excessive concentration of power not only may have adverse economic consequences, but is even more commonly regarded as detrimental for reasons of social policy. However, institutions in the United States have not been especially active in holding stock and have usually reacted to portfolio-company management by purchasing or selling the company's shares rather than by attempting to influence its policy. There is, however, at least the theoretical danger that as insitutional investors acquire increasing amounts of the available stock and it becomes more difficult to dispose of the increasingly large blocks of stock involved, they may begin to play a more dominant role in the affairs of portfolio companies. But this danger does not seem to be sufficiently great at the present time or the foreseeable future to warrant restrictions on the size of institutional investors.

If some limitation on institutional investment should become desirable at some future time to avoid excessive concentration of power over portfolio companies, it might perhaps be best to impose restrictions on the proportion of stock in a portfolio company that can be held by a single institution. A single mutual fund (or other diversified management-investment company) is already restricted in 75 percent of its investments to holdings not exceeding 5 percent of its own assets, or 10 percent of the voting stock of the portfolio company. Moreover, if a mutual fund owns more than 5 percent of the stock of a portfolio company, most transactions between the fund and the company require prior SEC approval. Comparable types of restrictions might be enacted for other institutional investors, but, in the absence of data on the investment policy of such investors, especially of pension funds, we have little basis for assessing the need for, or potential effect of, such legislation. Moreover, the justification for such restrictions on liquidity grounds, as in the case of mutual funds generally, does not apply to other institutional investors. Fortunately, periodic information on portfolio and related data from pension funds and other important groups of equity-oriented institutional investors should become available shortly as a result of the Securities Act Amendments of 1975. Under present plans, periodic reports made public under this legislation will provide data for individual fiduciaries.

If the role of institutional equity investors continues to increase and they begin to take a more active part in the affairs of portfolio companies, it may become desirable to place further restrictions on their activities in these companies. Even then, however, there may be no adequate reason for limiting the size of the institutional investors.

The operating costs of mutual funds and other institutional investors for which data are available exhibit significant economies of scale. There appears to be little difference in the investment performance of large and small funds, however, suggesting that the reduced operating costs of the larger organizations may be offset by greater investment inflexibility. Perhaps the best approach to averting the dangers of monopolistic control of portfolio companies by large institutional investors, if and when such action should become desirable, would be to broaden and perhaps make more restrictive the current limitations on the percentage of voting stock of individual portfolio companies that may be held by a single institutional investor or an affiliated group of institutions.

An alternative mechanism that has been proposed would limit institutional holdings of equity issues in portfolio companies to nonvoting stock (i.e., nonvoting while held by institutional investors). The latter approach has the advantage of avoiding arbitrary percentage restrictions on stockholdings, but it seems undesirable on several grounds. First, if the institutional investors were truly divested of power by the use of nonvoting stock, it would be much easier for other stockholders (regardless of the wishes of the institutions) to gain control, with a relatively small investment, of portfolio companies largely owned by institutions, and proxy fights would probably erupt. Second, it is doubtful that institutional investors with very large blocks of stock would be divested of power simply because their stock was nonvoting, since a threat to liquidate such holdings would be enough even though the institutions might incur some costs in the process. Third, mutual funds and perhaps certain other institutional investors must have portfolio liquidity. Fourth, institutional investors may well be more informed stockholders than most of those enjoying voting rights.

Institutional ownership of large blocks of portfolio-company stock also raises a number of equity-related questions about the need for protecting other stockholders from the consequences of institutional activities, quite apart from any possible impact of institutional trading on stock prices. Institutions, because of their resources, may have readier access to information about a company's affairs. This could work to the disadvantage of most of the other smaller stockholders. There have been a number of news stories suggesting that, despite the safeguards under present securities regulation, institutions as well as other large investors may have a significant advantage over the smaller investors in the dissemination of corporate information (though, as noted earlier, there is no evidence that the investment performance of institutions as a whole has been superior to that of individual shareowners). It seems reasonably clear that securities regulation should attempt to ensure that to the extent feasible[12] no stockholder be given access to important information that is not made available to any other stockholder. This appears to be a simple matter of equity that should not be violated simply because some stockholders have large holdings while those of others are negligible.

Only one real issue seems to be in question here. Should management make available on demand to one stockholder significant information not available to another simply because he does not request it? Despite the costs involved in interfering with the free flow of such information, simple fairness would seem to require that to the extent possible no important information be given to one group of stockholders that is not made available to all stockholders at the same time (or where given, for example, to insiders who are also stockholders, that restrictions be placed on their ability to profit by it). Obviously, one way to minimize the effects of this policy on market efficiency would be to ensure that all important information be disseminated to stockholders as soon as feasible.

As a practical matter, dissemination of information to stockholders in a large publicly owned corporation is equivalent to public disclosure. A problem arises, and exceptions to the general rule of immediate disclosure might be warranted, when management desires to withhold information for a limited period for the company's welfare as distinct from the welfare of a particular group of stockholders. However, since equity as well as current securities regulation require fair treatment of potential as well as actual stockholders, there may be a conflict between the responsibility of management to potential stockholders (to provide relevant disclosure of material facts) and its responsibility to actual stockholders (to maximize their risk-adjusted returns). Presumably, the legal basis for resolving this conflict should take into account the prospective damage and benefits to the two groups. The most satisfactory resolution of the conflict depends largely on the relative responsibility of management toward actual and potential stockholders.

One tenable resolution—which rests on the premise that the basic responsibility of management is to maximize risk-adjusted return or market value for the company as a whole—would permit the temporary withholding of material information, so long as there is a legitimate reason for doing so from the viewpoint of the company's welfare, with no group profiting from advance knowledge. This apparently is close to present U.S. law. The rationale for this position, from the viewpoint of the potential stockholders who might be adversely affected, would be that the temporary withholding of information for the company's welfare may be regarded as an ordinary market risk (which enters into the pricing of stock) and management should not be expected to protect potential stockholders from such risks at the expense of its actual stockholders. The prospective damage to potential stockholders might possibly be lessened by a stricter construction of the legitimate business reasons for withholding material information and of the justified withholding period.

One last set of issues revolves about the question of whether the existence of stock-oriented institutions raises significant conflicts of interest between investors and management in these organizations and whether, as a result, legal restrictions on the activities of institutional management beyond those applicable to other corporate management are desirable. The establishment of institutional investors as intermediaries between the ultimate individuals and business firms who supply and demand capital does raise the possibility of conflicts of interest that would not exist in the absence of these institutions.

In the United States the conflicts in the post-World War II period were especially troublesome in mutual funds for reasons discussed in detail in various studies.[13] Perhaps the most notable of these reasons was the customary control of fund management by external investment advisers whose interests often were at odds with those of the fund shareholders. In recent years, the amendments to investment-company legislation and the government's prescription of competitive commission rates for stock transactions have significantly diminished the potential damage to shareholders from conflicts of interest in the management of these funds. An earlier study discussed further measures, especially those in the field of performance disclosure, that might be taken to reduce conflicts of interest and enhance competition in the operation of mutual funds.[14]

With respect to pension funds—the most important single group of stock-oriented institutions—corporate sponsors of externally managed funds and external investment advisers (typically commercial banks) are independent of each other, and the corporate management and the fund's beneficiaries are both interested in maximizing fund return and minimizing costs of operation.[15] The conflicts of interest in insurance stock companies are probably not very different from those of other corporations of comparable size. The conflict problems of mutual insurance organizations are presumably similar generally, though not specifically, to those of internally rather than externally managed mutual funds.

Like externally managed mutual funds, bank-trust departments, which administer personal trusts as well as pension funds, and whose stockholdings (and assets generally) are much larger than those of mutual funds, have been accused of being subject to significant potential conflicts of interest. As a result, serious consideration has been given from time to time to legislation mandating that organizations carrying out the trust functions of banks be separate and independent from those engaged in commercial banking operations. However, whereas such a requirement would certainly diminish appreciably the potential for conflicts of interest in institutional stock investment, it is entirely possible that any associated losses in economic efficiency would offset, and perhaps more than offset, any gains in the equitable treatment of trust beneficiaries. Unfortunately, there is not sufficient information on either the extent of damage to trust beneficiaries or the possible economic efficiencies associated with the joint operation of the commercial banking and trust operations to resolve this issue.[16] This also holds true for a related problem, that is, the advisability of separating the investment management and brokerage activities of securities firms.

To summarize, there does not appear to be any economic or noneconomic basis for restricting institutional stock trading. To ensure equity in the treatment of institutional investors in a corporation and other actual and potential stockholders, all important corporate information should be disseminated to the marketplace as soon as feasible. Whereas material information could be temporarily withheld for legitimate business reasons, private profiting from advance knowledge should be prevented to the extent possible, and stricter guidelines on what constitutes legitimate withholding might be established. If it seems necessary in the future to introduce new safeguards to prevent the undue concentration of power in the hands of institutions, probably the best approach would be to expand the current limitations (now applicable only to mutual funds) on the percentage of stock of individual portfolio companies that a single investor (or an affiliated group of institutions) may hold.

Stimulation of Individual Investment in Stock

No evidence has been found to support the contention that a shift of stockownership and market activity from institutions to individuals through changes in the composition of their portfolios would enhance economic efficiency in the markets for outstanding or new stock issues. However, even if market efficiency were not affected, many people apparently believe that the long-run prospects for the U.S. economy would be substantially improved by a more buoyant and active stock market, especially one patronized by large numbers of relatively small individual investors. This view seems to be based on two different premises; the first stems from a conviction that there is a serious shortage of equity capital to finance the extremely large capital requirements over the next decade or two, and the second rests less on economic than on sociopolitical considerations.

Equity capital, it is felt, will be required in part to expand the supplies of energy and basic materials, to provide for antipollution controls, conservation, and so on. The need for equity capital as against debt is stressed for several reasons, including the belief that it is more difficult to raise large amounts of equity funds in the capital markets and that they are needed to enable the issuance of debt. Moreover, equity funds are a primary source for financing risky (including new and small) investments. Finally, it is felt that the corporate capital structure as a whole would be much sounder if the ratio of equity to debt were increased. Actually, this ratio has increased appreciably over the past two years, reflecting much higher corporate profits and hence retained earnings and a more buoyant market for new stock issues, but it is still considerably below its average historical level in the United States.[17] Obviously, if the demand for common stock is substantially increased, the cost of equity capital, and probably the overall cost of financing risky investments, would be lowered, thereby probably stimulating investments in risky real capital goods, which are believed to have a higher economic return than other investments.

Implicit in the argument about a relative shortage of equity capital is the belief that the terms on which equity funds can be obtained, particularly those needed to finance the riskier investments, have deteriorated secularly as compared to the terms for debt capital. Information presented in Chapter 3 and earlier in this chapter does not lend much support to this belief. There is no evidence that the spread between the required rate of return on common stocks as a whole and on bonds at the end of 1975 or 1976 was significantly different from its historical values. There is, however, evidence that the perverse risk differential between the realized rate of return on unseasoned new stock issues and on outstanding issues may have narrowed in the 1960s, but as noted earlier in this chapter, realized returns on unseasoned new issues still remained below those on outstanding stocks in the early 1970s, providing no indication of capital rationing at the expense of risky ventures. The somewhat depressed level of common-stock financing in 1974 may have been due to cyclical rather than secular conditions in the

Implications and Recommendations 197

economy and stock market. The increased equity financing in 1975 and 1976, when the economy and market improved, is consistent with this view.

Although there has been no obvious secular deterioration in the relative terms on which equity financing has been available, it is still true that a more buoyant stock market and greater demand for stock would probably increase the demand for plant and equipment through a cost of capital effect. However, the effects of increasing the demand for stock are likely to be mainly cyclical rather than secular, unless the overall propensity to save in the economy is affected. Economists have generally concluded that the overall saving–income ratio is not importantly affected by changes in the overall rate of return on assets,[18] and the saving ratio is likely to be affected even less by differential changes in these rates of return. There is no reason to believe that savings would be directly affected in a substantial way by changes in rates of return associated with policies to stimulate stock purchases. Similarly, there is no reason to anticipate that such policies will have a substantial impact on saving through their effect on the value of assets. The expected increase in the market value of stocks, which would tend to depress saving, would probably be offset in large part by a decrease in the market value of other assets.

Even cyclically, there appear to be a number of more effective direct ways of encouraging business investment than by stimulating stock investment, such as investment tax credits. Similarly, in a period of secular stagnation when a low propensity to invest rather than a low propensity to save seems to be the limiting factor on the level of national income, most existing firms would probably find direct incentives to invest in capital goods more effective in increasing the level of capital expenditures than indirect incentives through stimulation of stock purchases. However, if it is desired to stimulate investment by small new firms for reasons other than those analyzed in our study, encouraging stock purchases by individuals, who have traditionally been most active in this market, might prove effective.

The present system of "double taxation" of dividend income does result in higher taxes on the income of corporations, and particularly on that portion paid out as dividends. As a result, although it is difficult to quantify the effects of this differential taxation on corporate and other income, there may well be a significant cost to the economy in terms of efficiency and productivity because of the tax-induced stimulus of both noncorporate investment and corporate investment financed by bonds or retained earnings. Much of this cost to the economy might be justified by other public policy considerations, such as the desire to encourage widespread homeownership or mom-and-pop businesses; however, it can be argued that there are more efficient ways, such as direct subsidies, of achieving this objective.

With respect to the second, or sociopolitical, rationale for a shift in stockownership from institutions to individuals, it is frequently assumed that the larger the number of investors, other things being equal, the smaller the potential concentration of control over U.S. corporations. Most Americans are suspicious of excessive power. Assuming no significant loss in economic efficiency, therefore, people generally would feel more comfortable if ownership of industry were widely dispersed. However, such greater dispersion may actually contribute to a concentration of management control over U.S. corporations.

Widely dispersed stockownership is also frequently championed not only to distribute economic power, but also as a means of giving the largest possible number of workers a direct stake in the free-enterprise system. This is one of the main arguments used in support of Employee Stock Ownership Plans (ESOPs) in the Tax Reduction Act of 1975 and related plans proposed in 1976 in a staff study of the Joint Economic Committee of the U.S. Congress.[19] Both liberal and conservative leaders in Congress strongly supported legislation in 1976 to give workers a "piece of the action" to promote productivity and labor peace, and in the eyes of liberals, to achieve a more equitable distribution of wealth. However, there does not as yet appear to be any evidence of a significant effect of ESOPs in increasing productivity or reducing labor problems.[20] Of course, the small investment normally likely to be involved in such plans would not expectedly have a substantial impact either on the employee's wealth or attitudes, since both will be vastly more affected by wages and wage-related incomes, notably pension and fringe benefits. Moreover, any sizable stimulation of ESOPs requires some form of tax subsidy, so that the total impact on the distribution of wealth is far from clear. The justification of government incentives for ESOPs, therefore, would seem to rest on presumed beneficial effects on labor.

Still another sociopolitical reason that could be adduced in favor of proposed tax changes designed to stimulate stock purchases is that the implied redistribution of the burden of taxation from stockholder to non-stockholder would result in a shift in the burden from the aged to the younger population groups. This might be considered equitable in view of the serious impact of inflation on the aged. On the other hand, for any age group, most tax mechanisms that have been proposed to stimulate stock purchases would result in a redistribution of income from the poorer to the richer sectors of the population.

Implications and Recommendations 199

As a whole, the arguments for changes in government policy to stimulate individuals to shift their investments into stock do not appear to be compelling. Yet where no significant costs are involved or where existing policies discourage or discriminate against stock investments by individuals, or if new findings were to demonstrate highly desirable labor effects, new measures to stimulate such investment may be justified.

Therefore, on the basis of available information, economic, equity, and social-policy considerations do not provide sufficient justification for encouraging the shift of individuals' assets into stock and institutional assets out of stock. Moreover, even if it is desired to increase overall saving, it does not appear that most of the changes in tax laws discussed in Chapter 3 as ways of encouraging the shift of individuals' assets into stock would have any substantial effect on saving.

Even so, many in both industry and government feel that it would be highly desirable to make stock investment relatively more attractive. Thus the Carter administration in its first year in office has given serious consideration to a tax program in which part of corporate income distributed as dividends would essentially be taxed at the personal income-tax rates applicable to the recipient (with the recipient receiving credit for taxes paid by the corporation) and capital gains would be taxed at the same rates applicable to normal income. On the basis of existing knowledge, it is difficult to forecast the net effect of so comprehensive a change in our tax system, but the data analyzed in Chapter 3 suggest that the elimination of the present favorable tax treatment of capital gains might offset a substantial part of the stimulating effect on stock prices of the exclusion of all, rather than some fraction of, dividend income from personal income taxation.[21]

There is, however, a less risky, less comprehensive, but still promising possibility (mentioned in Chapter 3) that would entail granting corporations a partial tax reduction for dividend payout (through an appropriate tax credit or deduction from taxable income) approximately equal in the aggregate to the amount of the additional taxes that would be paid by individuals on their increased dividend income. On grounds of equity and feasibility, these tax incentives for dividend payout should probably apply to all dividends paid out by a corporation rather than merely to any increase over some base period. The increase in individuals' dividend income after taxes would be equal to the decrease in retained earnings if the tax credits given corportions are set equal to the increase in taxes paid by individuals. In view of the currently favorable tax treatment of capital gains, which tend to be concentrated in an even smaller sector of the population than stocks generally, these offsetting changes in corporate and individuals' tax payments would probably make the after-tax distribution of individuals' income (including capital gains) somewhat more progressive than under the present system of taxation.

The responses to the Wharton questionnaire strongly suggest that such a change in tax policy, sufficient to induce corporations to raise appreciably the proportion of their income paid out as dividends, might substantially increase the demand for stock by individuals at this time, lowering the cost of external equity financing.[22] It appears from the reactions of stockholders discussed in Chapter 3 that, at least under present circumstances, they would greatly prefer the higher dividend payout, even at the cost of lower retained earnings. With any prolonged buoyancy in the stock market, stockholders' preference for higher payout might be dissipated in the future, especially if capital gains continue to receive a more favorable tax treatment than ordinary income. But if this turns out to be true, the encouragement of dividend payout over the cycle could be regarded as an anticyclical policy measure with no significant efficiency cost. Moreover, even if increased payout did not increase the demand for stock, the cost of such a tax change would be insignificant. Finally, encouraging dividend payout might also facilitate a subsequent move toward the elimination of the double taxation of corporate income if this is considered desirable.

This proposed change in the taxation of corporate income gives rise to several questions. First, there is the practical problem of estimating the effect of any tax-reduction plan on dividend payout, although such an estimate should not be too difficult to obtain.[23] Another question is whether the decline in retained earnings associated with the higher dividend payout would not offset the effect of a lower cost of external equity financing on the overall cost of capital, and hence on the level of corporate investment. This is a real possibility, since some business executives seem to regard retained earnings as low-cost financing. However, if retained earnings are thought of as low-cost financing for reasons other than the minimization of transaction costs, it can be argued that retention reduces market efficiency. Perhaps most troublesome is the question of whether the capital markets, in providing external equity to corporations, allocate capital more or less efficiently than corporate management through the investment of retained earnings. The available evidence, though not conclusive, suggests that the capital markets are about as efficient as corporate management in directing the flow of capital.[24]

Consequently, a change in the tax laws that would give corporations an appropriate tax reduction for paying out dividends would seem to constitute a relatively attractive approach to the stimulation of stock

Implications and Recommendations 201

investment and to the promotion of stockholder welfare. To minimize transitional problems and unforeseen complications, the tax reductions could, and probably should, initially be set so as to induce only a moderate increase in dividend payments and a moderate decline in retained earnings.

Of the other nontax developments (discussed in Chapter 3) with potentially favorable effects on the level of stock investment, a large reduction in interest rates or in the rate of inflation and, to a lesser extent, a substantial increase in stock-market prices would also serve to bolster the demand for stock. The remaining institutional or regulatory changes covered in Chapter 3, though generally easier to implement, would be far less effective. The creation of an Investor Protection Office by the SEC and, to a somewhat lesser extent, new legislation limiting the role of institutional investors would moderately stimulate stock investment, whereas the establishment of price and wage controls would moderately discourage such investment. The liberalization of margin-trading and short-selling regulations and the establishment of a maximum limit on the percentage movement in any stock during a single day would have only slight effects, positive and negative, respectively, on the level of stock investment.

The most promising of these different regulatory approaches to the stimulation of stock investment, if that is the desired goal, is the SEC Investor Protection Office, since neither the costs nor risks involved need be large, even though the impact on stock investment is likely to be only moderate. Such an office would process investors' complaints about trade execution and related problems, including allegations of discrimination between individual and institutional investors either as stockholders of corporations or as customers of brokerage firms.

Finally, mention should be made of one other possible institutional development that could affect stock investment and, even more so, trading. This development—a change in commission rates or other transaction costs—was not covered in Chapter 3 and this was not included in the final Wharton School Survey of Investors, but it was part of the pretest survey of relatively active customers of NYSE member firms, who would presumably be more sensitive than other investors to transaction costs. The pretest results indicated that the respondents would react moderately favorably to a 25-percent decrease in commission rates, not nearly as strongly as to a substantial increase in the proportion of corporate earnings paid out as dividends, but somewhat more strongly than to the liberalization of restrictions on margin trading and short selling.

It may be possible to reduce commission rates and other transactions costs (primarily bid–ask spreads) for a given volume of transactions through further computerization of brokerage operations, more widespread unbundling of those services not desired by many stockholders, and increased competition that might come from an integration of the exchange and OTC markets[25] or from the limited entry of commercial banks into the brokerage business. The current movement toward an integrated central market system may help to reduce transaction costs from all these sources. On the basis of the preceding analysis of the comparative impact of individual and institutional trading on the market and economy, there does not appear to be much justification for the argument commonly heard before the introduction of competitive commission rates that it is desirable to provide small or all individual stock investors with lower than competitive rates.

Disclosure: Basic Mechanism for Efficient and Equitable Markets

The preceding analysis suggests that neither curtailing the growth in institutional stock investment and trading nor stimulating stock purchases by individuals is expected to increase stock market efficiency or to contribute significantly to a sound market and economy. The rest of this chapter deals with the potential contribution of other mechanisms to efficient and equitable markets, that is, with securities disclosure, the most basic mechanism of securities regulation (which has recently been under attack not only by antiregulatory sectors in the academic and business communities, but apparently also in 1976 by the SEC chairman);[26] with restrictions on stock-trading activity; with the implications of the movement toward a central market system; and with some new institutional arrangements for improving the market, especially for small investors.

The basic argument for disclosure is the belief that the prompt provision of information to actual and prospective stockholders is a necessary condition for efficient and equitable markets. If we lived in a world in which management could be relied on to make all relevant information available, promptly and at no cost, to all stockholders and to the market place, there would be little need for disclosure requirements, but we do not. Thus, the public enactment of disclosure rules may well help to create a more efficient and more equitable market by reducing heterogeneity of expectations based on the inaccessibility of available information to major groups of stockholders.[27] However, although most people would agree that the case for disclosure requirements is quite strong on equity grounds, the economic basis for disclosure requirements must ultimately rest on empirical tests of their market effects.[28]

Some of the most convincing evidence on the need for disclosure and related aspects of securities regulation in the markets for new and outstanding issues is provided in the Pecora hearings,[29] two other U.S. government pre-World War II studies,[30] and the postwar SEC *Special Study*,[31] all of which document the massive abuses of the earlier period and the much healthier post-SEC experience. This evidence provides substantial reason for believing that the effects of disclosure requirements and related securities regulation have been beneficial. Vast amounts of money were lost in the pre-SEC period as a result of activities that have been greatly reduced by securities legislation. These amounts would appear to exceed greatly any reasonable estimate of the costs of such legislation.

Stock-market pools, bucket shop operation, misuse of insider information, and other types of manipulation and fraud, which frequently relied on the deliberate use of misinformation and the absence of full disclosure, were widespread in the pre-SEC period, involved vast sums of money, and seem less prevalent today. In the earlier period, enormous losses were sustained by the public in new issues of public-utility holding companies, investment companies, and foreign bonds frequently sold under disclosure conditions bordering on fraud. It is true that the general economic situation bears substantial blame for such losses, but an important part is attributable to inadequate and deliberately misleading information and to widespread violations of fiduciary responsibilities by market and corporate insiders. Inadequate disclosure facilitated such violations.

The post-World War II *Special Study* gives additional evidence of the beneficial effect the full disclosure requirements under the SEC had on new issues. For example, during the early 1960s, Regulation A issues, which do not require full disclosure, appeared to fare better with respect to price in the short run but worse in the long run than did issues registered with the SEC, which require full disclosure. Similarly, a substantial portion of the public monies raised through a number of Regulation A offerings made under the auspices of a single interest group was siphoned off to persons affiliated with that group, whereas registration statements filed at about the same time by the same group never became effective. This evidence suggests that in the short run full disclosure prevents unwarranted price rises and in the longer run protects against dilution of the stockholders' interests and ensures a closer correspondence between initial price and intrinsic value.

The effectiveness of full disclosure is further borne out by a compar-

204 The Changing Role of the Individual Investor

ison of the market experience during 1958–1963 of unregistered new industrial common stock less than $300,000 in size issued in 1958 with otherwise comparable registered issues between $300,000 and $5,000,000 in size, where the returns on both groups of stocks were adjusted by movements in the market averages.[32] This test again covered only a limited time period, but it also pointed to a superior after-issue price performance of the registered issues. The returns for the registered small issues did not differ much from those typically found for the larger ones but were appreciably better than the returns for the very small issues not subject to registration.

A series of tests of the relative performance of new and outstanding common-stock issues from the early 1920s to the early 1970s, referred to earlier in this chapter, may be viewed as consistent with greater efficiency of the new issues market (compared to the market for outstanding issues) in the post-SEC than in the pre-SEC period. Mandatory disclosure was in force only in the post-SEC years, and effective disclosure was much greater in that period, especially for new issues. The disclosure requirements, which are more rigorous for new issues, would be expected to affect the new issues more than outstanding issues even for seasoned companies, and obviously much more for unseasoned companies. In both pre- and post-SEC periods, it will be recalled, the intermediate or long-run rates of return were on the average higher for outstanding than for new stock issues, even though on the basis of risk considerations the reverse might have been expected. However, in the post-SEC period this perverse risk differential appeared to have narrowed. These tests cover a much longer period than the direct comparisons for registered and unregistered issues in the post-SEC period but provide only indirect evidence on the effect of disclosure, in view of the other institutional changes from the pre- to post-SEC period.

An additional significant result of this comparison of pre- and post-SEC price performance of new common stocks, relative to those outstanding, concerns the variances of the price ratios, which for each of the five years after issue date were much larger in the pre-SEC period. In other words, there was much less dispersion in relative price performance of new issues in the post-SEC period; this, too, is consistent with theoretical expectations of the effects of improved information and a reduction of manipulative activity.

Another comparative test of market performance, this one by George Stigler, also suggests a statistically significant improvement in the structure of new issue prices from the pre- to post-SEC periods.[33] Thus, the correlation in the pre-SEC period between new issue prices and prices one year later (with all new issue prices deflated by the price index for outstanding issues) seems to have been significantly lower than the average correlation for adjacent pairs of years after issue, whereas these correlations are identical (and higher) in the post-SEC period. In other words, after adjustment for movements in the market, new-issue prices in the post-SEC period seem to have anticipated subsequent price movements more accurately than in the pre-SEC period.

The sum total of this evidence on disclosure requirements for new issues seems to support the thesis that disclosure had improved market efficiency.[34] Nor do the costs of such disclosure, to the extent they can be measured, appear to have been excessive.[35] This does not mean that the evidence in favor of new-issue disclosure is conclusive or that the SEC disclosure requirements have been the best possible ones, but simply that the evidence that disclosure as a whole has benefited the market for new issues is considerably stronger than evidence to the contrary. Further study is required to determine the usefulness of specific current disclosure requirements or how they could be improved.

For outstanding stocks also, the evidence seems to lend greater support to the conclusion that disclosure has improved market efficiency than to the conclusion that it has had no effect or an unfavorable effect. This evidence includes indirect tests drawn from market equilibrium theory that suggest an improvement in market structure from the 1920s to the post-World War II period and, more importantly, direct tests indicating that published accounting data can be useful in making investment decisions, thereby contributing to market efficiency.[36] Several tests conducted to determine whether accounting data provide useful new information to the market found it highly probable that they do.[37]

A recent study casts further light on the effect of a specific type of SEC-mandated disclosure on the efficiency of the market for outstanding stocks. This study analyzed the consequences of recently initiated new regulations requiring multiproduct firms to disclose revenues and profits by product-line in their annual reports.[38] The results for two out of three years tested indicate that product-line data are more useful in anticipating changes in total firm earnings than are accounting data combining all product lines; thus here again we have evidence of the value of disclosure requirements for stock market efficiency.

Another recent study provides additional insight into the need for SEC-mandated disclosure.[39] This study found that, where the SEC reporting requirements grant management flexibility within a fiscal year in reporting unusual events that might affect earnings, favorable items tended to be reported early in the fiscal year whereas unfavorable items tended to be reported late. This strongly suggests that mangement is eager to disclose favorable information as soon as possible and to delay the disclosure of unfavorable information, although prompt reporting in both cases would be more conducive to the maintenance of an efficient market.

It should be noted that, as in the case of new-issue disclosure, further study is needed of specific disclosure requirements applicable to outstanding stock to determine whether they are useful and how they can be made more useful. There is reason to believe that in some cases the SEC had mandated disclosure while paying insufficient attention to the comparative costs and benefits, such as in the recently mandated corporate disclosure of replacement-cost data. Whereas replacement-cost data may be extremely useful to investors in view of the great differences in an inflationary period between book and true earnings, the implementation of this requirement is likely to be very costly, and there is as yet no consensus on the techniques for making the necessary calculations or on the magnitude of the resulting benefits. In such instances, involving mandatory disclosure of information not normally compiled for internal purposes by the corporations, it would be highly desirable for the SEC to go beyond simply obtaining general reactions from the business, academic, and professional communities. It should also, whenever possible, conduct a small sample survey of cooperating business firms to determine the approximate costs of the proposal and its likely benefits (as measured, e.g., by the effect of replacement-cost accounting on a company's stock price relative to stock prices of otherwise comparable firms).[40]

A quite different example of the SEC inhibiting potentially useful voluntary disclosure concerns the area of management's earnings forecasts. Although such forecasts are inevitably subject to a wide margin of error and to occasional serious abuse, any indications of prospective earnings are of potential value to investors, and management is likely to be in a better position to provide such insights than are other sources.[41] Management is not likely to provide earnings forecasts on a voluntary basis so long as it is not protected against liability suits based on charges of erroneous and thus misleading projections. It should not be too difficult to provide investors with reasonable protection by highlighting the potential margin of error in such forecasts and at the same time to protect management against harassment. In general, securities (as well as other) legislation in recent years has tended to encourage nuisance suits against management, with appreciable costs to the corporate stockholders and to the court system. The law

Implications and Recommendations 207

firms that represent the plaintiffs and assume little risk seem all too often to be the principal beneficiaries.

As the preceding discussion indicates, quite apart from equity considerations, the trend toward increased disclosure mandated by the SEC has probably had in general, if not necessarily in every instance, a salutary effect on the securities market. It may be useful, therefore, to consider two theoretical arguments that have been adduced to question the economic rationale of compulsory disclosure.

First, it is sometimes asserted that since individuals learn from experience, they would not be expected to repeat their investment errors and that hence mandated protection is unnecessary. Unfortunately, the average investor in an unregulated market is likely to be at a substantial competitive disadvantage compared with market makers and corporate insiders (investment bankers, exchange specialists and company officers, directors, and principal stockholders). By the time he has learned from one expeience he is likely to be confronted by another situation that may be or at least seem quite different, and even if he himself has become a wiser man, new investors lacking his firsthand experience are waiting to take his place. Moreover, if the only lessons investors, old and new, learn from experience is that they cannot rely on the adequacy of disclosure, the cost of capital is likely to increase and the informational and allocational efficiency of the stock market to suffer since the relationship of market prices to the future returns on stock is likely to diminish.

Second, it is sometimes argued that to the extent that disclosure of information is valuable, management can be relied on to make it available to stockholders and the market, either because management is assumed to act in the best interest of stockholders or because competition will force it to make such disclosure to reduce the riskiness of its stock and thereby its cost of capital (and in the process to maximize stock price). Although management may and probably does generally act in the best interests of its stockholders, clearly there are times when these interests may conflict. Since managers have finite lives, they may take advantage of occasions when they can maximize their own long-range interests by actions not necessarily consistent with the long-range interests of their stockholders. Moreover, there are other times when maximal protection of the stockholders' interests can be attained at the expense of the market generally, as when management holds up the disclosure of unfavorable information.[42]

Nor does the record support the view that competition will force management to make disclosure, except perhaps over a period too long to be useful to most investors in their lifetime. Thus, whereas the proportion of NYSE corporations that reported so basic a financial datum as annual sales increased moderately in the second half of the 1920s from 55 percent in 1926 to 62 percent in 1930, it did not change thereafter through 1934, the last year before all registered companies were required to file such (and additional) information under the Securities and Exchange Act of 1934.[43] Under subsequent SEC regulations these companies were required to make public their quarterly as well as annual sales—data that virtually all well-run companies would regularly compile for internal purposes. Prior to another SEC regulation, relatively few firms regularly published product-line data in their annual reports, and as noted earlier, when management is given discretion in its reporting of unfavorable items, it tends to delay as long as possible. Disclosure mandated by the SEC is not only likely to take place earlier, but investors also tend to feel that it provides a more reliable picture of a company's financial position.

To summarize, economic as well as equity considerations seem to support the general value to investors of the greater financial disclosure that has taken place under the stimulus of Federal securities regulations. More research is required to evaluate the usefulness of a number of specific disclosure requirements, particularly those relating to information not generally compiled for internal use. However, even where the economic benefits do not appear to justify the costs, equity considerations would still have to be weighed in deciding on the desirability of specific types of disclosure.

Restrictions on Speculative Activity

In addition to disclosure, stock-market regulation has restricted several types of speculative activity to promote efficient and equitable markets. The economic as well as noneconomic reasons for regulations designed to prevent the more flagrant manipulation of securities prices require little explanation. Theoretically, such regulations might improve both efficiency and equity in the capital markets, even though empirical evidence may be required to assess whether the benefits justify the cost. Restrictions on certain types of speculation—margin trading, short selling, writing and buying of options, and trading by corporate and market insiders—are frequently rationalized on similar grounds, but theory alone cannot prove the existence of economic benefits from such policies; it requires evidence. For example, it is easy enough to use theoretical arguments to "demonstrate" that under plausible conditions speculators on the average must stabilize stock prices so long as it is assumed that their activities do not affect the demand for stock by other investors. This, however, is a heroic assumption and requires empirical verification.

Of the different types of restrictions on speculative activity, the regulation of margin trading has been subject to criticism by many economists because it interferes, at least theoretically, with the optimal adjustment of portfolios to desired levels of risk as well as with the ability of speculators to stabilize market prices, and because it has no obvious strong equity rationale. Margin regulation originally reflected congressional concern about the possible abuse of securities credit and its impact on the economy as a whole as well as on the stock market itself. Currently, advocates of margin regulation seem more concerned with the potentially adverse effect of margin trading on the market than on the economy.

The empirical evidence on the impact of margin regulation on market efficiency is conflicting, with some studies concluding that market efficiency has been improved as a consequence of such regulation, and others that it has not.[44]

The most recent, and perhaps most useful, of these studies since they are the only ones based on cross-section data,[45] indicate that the imposition of 100-percent margin requirements on individual stocks was associated with a halt of the marked upward price movement that had typically preceded the new margin requirement.[46] Moreover, these stocks, or at least those listed on the NYSE, did not rise again after the lifting of this special margin requirement, suggesting that this requirement not only reduced market volatility but may have contributed to market efficiency. However, the evidence is far from conclusive.

As in the case of margin trading, the available empirical evidence on the impact of short selling on market efficiency is rather mixed.[47] However, it is possible to improve on that evidence by a more careful analysis of time-series and, particularly, cross-section data.[48] The cross-section data for selected dates compiled for this study permitted the derivation of statistical relationships between the short position of *each* NYSE stock (available around the 15th of each month) and both preceding and subsequent movements in the stock price. Earlier studies using cross-section data were based on much smaller samples and did not explore the possible impact of short positions on stock prices of less than one month's duration. These earlier studies concluded that returns of one month and over on short positions were on the average less favorable than those achievable by a random timing of short sales of the same stock.[49]

Time leads and lags between short positions and price movements,

210 The Changing Role of the Individual Investor

ranging from one day to one month, were studied separately in our analysis for every NYSE stock with a short position and for each of three different months in 1970—February, April, and August. The first month represented a period of relative stability in the market as a whole, both preceded and followed by market declines; the second preceded a period of fairly strong decline in the market; and the third preceded a period of moderate gain.

In only one of the three months tested—April 1970—was there any indication that either the level of or changes in a stock's short position preceded or followed changes in its price. For that month the level of short positions showed a statistically significant tendency to lead the percentage change in price by about one week, with larger short positions followed by a decline in stock prices, even though the relationship was extremely weak.[50] This relationship is not appreciably altered when subsequent price changes over the following three weeks and three months are held constant to test whether short sales anticipate or cause price fluctuations over the following week. Yet when the percentage change in stock prices from the middle of a month (the time the short-position data are available) to one month, three or four months later is related to the initial short position, there is no evidence that short positions led stock prices over these longer time spans. Therefore, this new analysis suggests that short sellers may in certain periods possess the ability to anticipate short-term stock-price movements and thus may contribute modestly to market efficiency. However, any effect of short sales on market efficiency would appear to be very small and very brief.

Unfortunately, the available cross-section data do not permit the separation of the impact of changes in short positions of NYSE members, particularly specialists, from the impact of changes in short positions of public customers. It is known that for all NYSE stocks combined, specialists in recent years have accounted for about 50 percent, and public customers for about 20 percent, of short sales, with the trades of other Exchange members accounting for the balance.[51] There is also evidence that the NYSE specialists are one of the two groups in the market (the other being corporate insiders) that may exert some stabilizing influence on stock prices, presumably reflecting inside market information.[52] As a result, it seems probable that any favorable impact of short selling on market efficiency is more likely to reflect trading by marketing insiders than that of the general public.

A comprehensive time-series analysis of the relations between monthly short positions and monthly and weekly short sales in all NYSE stocks combined and the associated changes in NYSE stock

Implications and Recommendations 211

prices for the period 1974–1975 does not show any clear tendency for aggregate short positions or sales to either lead or follow stock-price movements. A similar result is obtained when short sales by public customers are analyzed separately. Thus it is doubtful whether the main regulatory constraint currently applicable to public short sales—that such sales cannot be made at a price lower than the last different price—has any appreciable effect on market efficiency.

Our new evidence in conjunction with earlier findings for the post-World War II period suggests that the current limitations on short selling are about as likely to detract from as contribute to market efficiency, but that the effect is not likely to be large in either direction. Yet an analysis specifically directed at the effect of pre- and post-SEC short selling concludes that in the pre-SEC days short sales "often had a temporarily disorganizing effect on the price movements of a particular stock and sometimes (in the early days of the NYSE) of the market as a whole—but that the regulation and policy of the Securities and Exchange and of the New York Stock Exchange itself seem, in recent years, to have eliminated such sporadic outbursts."[53]

Although option trading has become a substantial, increasing and apparently highly profitable part of the securities business, satisfactory tests of the impact of options on stock-market efficiency have yet to be carried out. The basic reason for this gap is that only in recent years, after the Chicago Board Options Exchange (CBOE) initiated its activities on April 26, 1973, have stock options become an important part of the securities business, and much of the data necessary for an adequate analysis of the impact of option trading on stock prices are not yet available. There have been a number of empirical studies of the profitability of writing and buying options and of the relationship between the actual pricing and theoretical value of options, but very little work has been done on the effect of option trading on stock prices. The most comprehensive study published so far covers only the CBOE's first nine months of operation, and only a handful of stocks, and must in every respect be regarded as preliminary.[54] However, its results suggest that for the brief period covered, option trading did not adversely effect the overall efficiency of the market for the underlying stocks.[55]

In view of the growing importance of option trading, clearly more information is necessary to assess its impact on market efficiency. In addition, the ease with which options can be purchased by investors who can ill afford to take risks and the comparative sophistication required to assess the risks and associated returns point to the need for collecting new information on the characteristics of option traders, on

212 The Changing Role of the Individual Investor

the use to which they put options, on their understanding of the risks involved, on the sales practices used, and on their investment experience. The SEC has apparently initiated a new study of option trading that should supply some of these data.

In contrast to the lack of impressive evidence on the effect of margin trading, short selling, and option trading, or existing restraints on such speculative activity on market efficiency, there is fairly strong evidence that corporate insiders (officers, directors, and principal stockholders) have fared better in their investment performance than has the market as a whole, tending to sell when the prices of their equity issues are relatively high and to buy when they are relatively low.[56] Since much of this above-average performance reflects relatively long holding periods,[57] it is likely that trading by corporate insiders has correctly anticipated (rather than caused) subsequent fluctuations in price and has thus contributed to market efficiency. It is hard to tell whether the superior performance by insiders reflects the more extensive and earlier corporate information available to them, a greater ability to make use of such information, or some combination of the two. However, even if this performance is regarded as the result of the monopolistic access of insiders to corporate information, their trading appears to contribute to a reduction in the disparities between current stock prices and their longer-run values.

From the viewpoint of the regulation of insider trading, mainly provisions for fairly prompt disclosure of such trading and corporate recovery of their short-term profits, the relevant question is whether it is desirable to maintain or change the present constraints on the exclusive advantages possessed by corporate insiders. On equity grounds and to minimize potential conflicts of interest, it would probably be regarded as desirable to minimize the monopolistic advantages enjoyed by corporte insiders. However, to the extent that this involves constraints on trading rather than disclosure alone, restrictions on insider trading might well reduce market efficiency. Thus appropriate adjustments in stock price associated with new information initially available to insiders alone may as a practical matter be possible only with longer time lags if insiders are either precluded or greatly discouraged from trading. Obviously, it is not feasible, and under certain circumstances may not be desirable, to release all information as soon as it becomes available. Even if the information is released, it is not clear that the general investor would be in as good a position as the insider to evaluate its significance. Thus a major potential conflict exists between equity and efficiency considerations.

If on equity grounds it is desired to minimize the ability of corporate insiders to profit from their monopolistic access to company information, one way of reducing the impact of such measures on market efficiency would be to encourage corporate repurchases and reissuance of its own shares. Such decisions made by corporate management with an above-average ability to tell when the price of their stock is undervalued or overvalued would, of course, contribute to market efficiency without raising serious equity and associated conflict-of-interest problems.[58] Corporate management possesses this ability, as is indicated by its own investment performance in its company's stock referred to earlier. A recent study indicates that, like corporate insiders acting on their own behalf, corporate officials similarly evidence an above-average ability to detect, and profitably exploit for their stockholders, price-value divergences in their companies' stock (as measured by the performance of the companies' net stock-purchase programs).[59] These divergences, it might be noted, do not appear to have been fully corrected for more than two years.

Another recent study has raised some questions about the usefulness of insider regulation even on equity grounds; that is, for the protection of stockholders, quite apart from market-efficiency considerations.[60] That study indicates that the resolution of two lawsuits involving the SEC (Cady, Roberts and Texas Gulf Sulphur), which might have been thought to lead corporate insiders to expect stricter enforcement of the insider trading rules, did not in fact have a statistically significant effect on the profitability and volume of insider trading. As a result, at least these specific changes in the prospects for regulatory constraints on insider trading seemed to have relatively little effect on the profitability and volume of such activity.

This new evidence is certainly relevant to the effectiveness of these legal actions; however, its relevance for the broader effectiveness of Section 16B of the 1973 Act (relating to corporate recovery of short-term profits by insiders) is not clear, nor does it seem to be relevant to the effectiveness of Section 16A (relating to full-disclosure provisions for insiders).[61] Thus, if these provisions of the 1934 Act had been effective well before the first of the relevant legal actions (the November 1961 Cady, Roberts decision), the interpretation of the results would be radically different. Given the extreme variability of stock-price changes and rates of return, it would not be surprising to find that new evidence of stricter enforcement of the SEC insider trading rules had little effect. Even before Cady, Roberts, there were the full-disclosure and short-term profit rules and the prospect of private litigation for recovery of insider profits.

Clearly what is required for a more convincing response to the effect of insider regulation on stockholder experience is a careful comparison of pre-SEC and post-SEC insider behavior from the scattered evidence available. A reading of the major U.S. government investigations of the stock market and related abuses of the 1920s cited earlier leads us to believe that insider abuses have declined substantially since then, probably in part due to the disclosure provisions and restrictions imposed on insiders by the 1934 Securities Exchange Act.

As noted earlier, there is significant evidence to suggest that the trading activities of stock specialists—notably those on the NYSE—as well as corporate insiders may stabilize stock prices and contribute to market efficiency.[62] Since specialists are held responsible for helping to maintain fair and orderly markets, their trading activity has not been subjected to the same restrictions imposed on other types of speculative activity. However, it should be noted that any stabilizing influence of specialist activity is likely to be of brief duration, reflecting their responsibility to maintain orderly markets in case of a temporary disequilibrium between bids and offers. A considerable portion of specialists' dealer profits is derived from the spread between the bid or buying price and the ask or selling price.[63] In view of their monopolistic access to the book listing all limit orders on both sides of the market on stocks in which they act as specialists, they have a significant advantage over most other investors in assessing the basic supply-and-demand conditions of a stock, although, as noted in Chapter 4, they may be in an unfavorable position in trading with investors possessing inside company information.

The monopolistic advantage of the specialists may be due—to a much greater extent than holds true for corporate insiders—not to the intrinsic nature of their position, but rather to the existing institutional arrangements, with the NYSE rules constraining competition by other members as well as nonmembers. A question increasingly asked in recent years is whether more competition among specialists should not be encouraged by extending specialist privileges. A more important change in specialist arrangements may be realized through the establishment of a central market system with all bids and offers available to all members of the system. This change may largely eliminate the privileged position specialists now occupy.

Movement Toward a Central Market System

Recent developments clearly indicate that a nationwide stock-market system that electronically funnels purchase and sale orders to a central

Implications and Recommendations 215

mechanism accessible to all participants in the markets is likely to supersede the present fragmented system. Most observers believe that this will improve market efficiency, especially through the reduction of bid-ask spreads and overall transactions costs. However, opinion in the financial community is divided on what form the central market system should take and on important details of its implementation.

Three plans have been proposed for the establishment of a central market system:

1. An order-routing or notification system, called an *order-indication system* (OIS) by the NYSE, that would electronically link the different existing exchanges and OTC markets, disclosing, for eligible securities, the best bid and offer in each market and also providing other markets an opportunity to participate in new public orders over some designated size;
2. A consolidated limit order book (CLOB) containing all unfilled orders by all specialists and other market makers in each eligible security;
3. A fully electronic market system in which a computer channels all unfilled bids and offers for eligible securities to a central point and makes them available to all interested parties and automatically executes transactions in accordance with a designated set of rules, including time and size priorities for execution of orders.

In our judgment, the most comprehensive of these plans, which would set up a fully electronic market system covering executions as well as bid and ask orders, is likely to have the most favorable effect on market efficiency.[64] Such a system could provide any investor, acting through a broker or dealer, with virtually instant information on outstanding limit orders and on the volume and market prices of transactions in eligible stocks. We agree with the proponents of a fully electronic central market that this sytem contains the promise of promoting effective competition and equity among different participants in the market, reducing transaction costs, facilitating detection of manipulation and fraud, improving monitoring of the trading activity of insiders, and eliminating the monopolistic advantages of the specialists.

Less ambitious systems, even if superior to present arrangements, have a much lesser potential for achieving these objectives. These less ambitious proposals are frequently supported on the grounds that since they entail less heroic departures from present arrangements, they are less likely to disrupt the market in ways that cannot be foreseen. However, the ultimate costs associated with their adoption may

216 The Changing Role of the Individual Investor

be greater than those for a fully electronic central-market system. Not only may the benefits associated with the more comprehensive system suffer substantial delay, but the money spent in the installation of a less ambitious system may prove wasted if a more comprehensive system should subsequently be thought desirable. Moreover, it is not even clear whether the success or failure of some of the limited proposals, such as the NYSE OIS, will cast much light on the feasibility or desirability of the fully electronic system.

Yet a number of serious questions have been raised by members of the financial community about the desirability and feasibility of many of the specific suggestions advanced for implementing a fully electronic central-market system. These range from questions relating to the most effective form of the system to those suggesting that any comprehensive system may substantially impair the efficient functioning of the stock market. The NYSE in particular feels that the absence of an affirmative obligation by market makers to maintain orderly markets, an obligation that is not part of the most comprehensive current plans,[65] will result in disorderly stock-price movements.

In view of the dilemma posed by the combination of potential advantages and risks, it seems to us that an optimum procedure at this time would be to test a fully electronic central-market system with a relatively small sample of different types of stocks. All the major issues—the need for affirmative obligations by market makers, limitations on the number of market makers, the appropriate role of and access to the book, problems raised by the imposition of customer and size priorities, and the types of stocks and transactions to be included in the system—could be explored without incurring excessive costs[66] or risks.

It is our belief, as well as that of many others in the financial and academic communities, that competition and efficiency in the stock market will be enhanced by some form of electronic central-market system and that all public customers are likely to benefit. A sample experiment appears to be the best way of testing the validity of this belief and of determining the appropriate form of such a system.

Other Changes in Market Arrangements

Two other recent developments have considerable potential for improving market efficiency. The first is the pressure, largely successful, on the NYSE by Congress and the SEC to remove the earlier NYSE ban on off-board trading by member firms (Rule 390) to make the stock

Implications and Recommendations 217

market more competitive. All such restrictions on agency transactions were eliminated as of January 2, 1977, and the SEC plans to review the restrictions on principal transactions in the near future. The second is the growth of index funds, which are essentially unmanaged diversified portfolios of stocks constructed to duplicate approximately, at minimum cost, the investment performance of the market as a whole or some substantial sector of the market, most commonly the 500 stocks in the Standard & Poor's Composite Index.

No new research on this subject has been carried out for this book; however, in our judgment, the removal of the restrictions on off-board trading by NYSE member firms will not only enhance competition among securities firms but will also improve market efficiency.[67] Here also, however, serious questions have been raised by the financial community about the possibly adverse implications of the elimination of these restrictions for fragmentation of markets. Again, it might be useful to carry out a test, based on a small sample of different types of stocks, of the extent to which such fragmentation does take place and whether it does adversely affect market efficiency. It should be noted that the abolition of Rule 390 will result in substantial revenue losses to NYSE specialists, thus involving equity as well as efficiency considerations, but any attempt, however, to delay the lifting of restrictions on off-board trading by member firms may involve equity costs to investors.

The recent surge of interest in index funds has reflected the widely publicized findings by the Wharton *Study of Mutual Funds* and other analyses on the investment performance of different groups of large institutional investors in stock, including pension funds and insurance companies. These studies have found that, except for management and trading costs, the performance of these large portfolios has generally conformed quite closely on a risk-adjusted basis to that of the market as a whole.[68] Once it became widely recognized that the main investment service provided by a participating interest in these stock funds or portfolios is efficient diversification of risk, the growth of "unmanaged" index funds permitting substantial reduction in management fees and trading costs was hardly surprising. Such funds have substantial potential utility, not only for direct investment by individuals, but also for pension funds and other large portfolios. In contrast to the steady but slow increase in the use of these indexed funds by pension plans, their availability to the general public has so far been relatively limited, reflecting both the poor market for mutual funds generally and the failure of the brokerage community to promote their sale.

It should be noted that, although most academic market experts feel that index funds provide a useful investment service, and hence enhance market efficiency, this viewpoint is not universally shared. Thus it has been argued by one well-known academician that, since the long-term trend in the stock market is upward, investors would be better off in the long-run by investing in riskier (i.e., higher beta coefficient) stocks with higher expected returns than in the market as a whole as represented by an index fund.[69] Moreover, according to this argument, in times of a weak market, investors should shift to low-risk stocks and increase their investment in fixed-income securities rather than index funds. The answer to this argument is self-evident. Those relatively few investors fortunate enough to be able to forecast movements in stock and bond prices should take advantage of their unusual insight to shift into and out of the more and less risky stocks and into and out of bonds in accordance with their forecasts. However, most investors in the securities markets are likely to find index funds useful. In addition, they can be formed not only for stock generally but for bonds generally, and for stocks and bonds in different risk classes, facilitating shifts into and out of these different classes by those investors who feel that they can forecast prospective trends in broad bond and stock prices even if not in the prices of individual securities.

Other critics of index funds have argued that, once index funds account for a substantial share of stockholdings, stock prices will represent the judgment of merely a subgroup of the universe of all stockholders and that this subgroup may not be representative of the universe and will possibly be less well informed and less risk averse. These critics have further alleged that less risk aversion would lead to a decline in output.[70] It is not clear to us why the universe of investors is preferable to a smaller but equally well-informed subgroup for setting the pattern of stock prices, or why the active investors in the market, once index funds become more important, would be expected to be less well informed than other participants in the market. The contrary would appear to be more plausible, since investors with access to new information are more likely than those who do not to anticipate movements in stock prices. Although it is possible that the active investors would tend to be less risk averse than the purchasers of index funds, it again is not clear why this would adversely affect the economy as a whole, and output in particular. Once more, the contrary effect might be expected since the lowering of the rate of return on risky economic investments referred to earlier would simply result from a reduction in the market cost of capital for financing these investments with the highest expected rates of return.

Implications and Recommendations 219

Another argument advanced against index funds is similarly puzzling, namely, that adjustment of the sample of stocks in these funds to match the composition of the universe of stocks would "require selling poor performers during weakness and buying market leaders on strength, thus aggravating existing trends."[71] It is not clear why sampling is needed at all when an index fund seeks to duplicate the performance of most specified groups of stock (e.g., those stocks contained in the Standard & Poor's indexes), since a proportionate share of all stocks in that group could be bought at the outset and then held. However, even if it desired to replicate the performance of a group of stocks by sampling, there is no reason to believe that the trading activities of the index funds would aggravate trends in the stock market. Thus, if the sample of fund stocks selected reflects the industry composition of the universe of all stocks—but the fund's stocks in one industry performed worse than all stocks in that industry, yet those in a second industry performed better than all stocks in that industry—the fund would presumably acquire more of the stock in the first industry and sell some of the stock in the second. If stock trends were affected at all, they would tend to be moderated rather than aggravated. Moreover, there is every incentive for the managers of index funds to trade in such a way as to minimize the effect of their trading activities on the market.

The final question that should be considered in connection with the adequacy of existing stock-market mechanisms is the possible existence of new institutional arrangements that might improve market efficiency significantly. Particular stress has been laid on two deficiencies in the set of investment opportunities now available to investors, namely, the absence of financial instruments that permit either a satisfactory hedge against the risk of inflation or a satisfactory international diversification of risk. However, it is not clear whether there are any changes in financial instruments, especially those issued by the private sector, that would adequately meet either of these two conditions.

Even in the heyday of the domestic mutual funds, U.S. investors showed only limited interest in mutual funds invested in securities of other nations. The reason, we believe, is not a failure of entrepreneurship in the private sector but the reaction of American investors to unpredictable political, and hence economic, risks associated with investment in other countries—risks that might be evaluated quite differently by investors in those countries.

The difficulty of devising hedges against inflation reflects the fact that the value of the bulk of marketable assets has turned out to be inversely related to the rate of inflation. Contrary to earlier economic theory and preconceptions of the financial community, the value not only of long-term bonds but also of stocks has been adversely affected by inflation, and the real value of these long-term securities has been substantially reduced. Inflation in the post-World War II period has tended to raise nominal interest rates and, more surprising, to depress somewhat nominal market rates of return on stock for the concurrent and following years,[72] and thus to depress substantially real stock returns over these time spans. The best investment hedges against inflation have been residential real estate, not a readily marketable asset, and short-term U.S. government issues, which require constant reinvestment. Attempts to market real-estate investment trusts of nonresidential real estate as a hedge against inflation were initially very successful, but over time their investment experience has been extremely poor, at least in part because of the extremely speculative, highly leveraged, and insufficiently diversified nature of most of these ventures.

It probably would be possible to make private financial instruments more readily available to serve as partial hedges against inflation, but the possibilities seem limited so long as inflation seems to have a damping effect on virtually all real corporate earnings. Corporations in the United States have been reluctant to issue indexed bonds (with the interest rate linked to the rate of inflation) in view of the absence of a strong positive correlation between company earnings and the rate of inflation.[73] One promising innovation that might profitably be tested in the capital markets is a new security based on variable-rate, rather than fixed-rate, residential mortgages. Variable-rate mortgages have multiplied at a rapid pace in recent years, particularly in California, and a variable-rate bond based on such mortgages would provide at least partial protection against inflation. However, more adequate protection against inflation would probably require governmental action, either through measures to curtail inflationary pressures or through indexed government securities.

Another new financial instrument that might somewhat improve the market's efficiency is a liquidation fund to buy up the marketable shares of companies more valuable in liquidation than in operation. Thus a number of closed-end investment and holding companies, whose assets consist of portfolios of marketable securities, have portfolio net-asset values substantially above the market prices of the company shares. The purchases of these shares would in many cases be the prelude to the liquidation of the company and the sale of its portfolio securities. The same objective might be achieved by converting closed-end companies with net-asset values well in excess of market prices into open-end.

By far the most ambitious proposal to improve the mix of securities

Implications and Recommendations 221

available to investors is that of creating a new type of financial intermediary, known as a *superfund*.[74] The basic idea behind the superfund is to expand the set of available investment opportunities by establishing a new type of index fund that would hold as assets some proportionate share of all marketable securities (the "market" portfolio) and periodically issue a series of fixed-term securities against these assets, each of which would pay off only if a previously specified rate of return on the "market" portfolio were realized. Each series of these fixed-term securities, which are called *primitive securities* in the technical finance literature, would be issued in the form of contingent claims to one dollar at some specified time, say, the end of the year, payable only if the realized rate of return on the "market" portfolio is at a specified level, which might be 5 to 6 percent, 10 to 11 percent, 15 to 16 percent, 50 percent or less, 100 percent or more, or any amount in between.

The number of different series of these primitive securities would depend on the estimated plausible range of returns on the market portfolio and how fine a break of this range is desired, but 100 might satisfy most purposes. The prices paid for each of these primitive securities would depend on the investors' evaluation of the probability distribution of returns on the market portfolio, on their attitudes toward risk, and on their wealth. By combining these primitive securities, investors might be better able to attain their desired goals than is possible under present market conditions.[75]

Although such a superfund has considerable theoretical attraction, we have substantial reservations about its practicability and usefulness in the restructuring of the capital markets. The average investor in such a fund might be at a more serious disadvantage than market professionals in assessing the probability distribution of returns. It could be argued that the superfund would attract much of the money now channeled into lotteries and gambling, but the average participant would probably be less able to assess the odds than in the usual games of chance. It also is possible that prior to their maturity, the securities issued by these funds would as a whole sell at less than the market value of the portfolio assets, as is true now for closed-end investment companies and dual-purpose funds. The main losers might be those investors with the smallest resources if forced to liquidate as a result of adverse circumstances.

Concluding Comments

Our analysis has concluded that the relative shares of individuals in stockownership and trading will probably continue to decline for some time, although at a more moderate pace than in the past twenty-five years. There is, however, no reason to believe that the absolute volume of the stockholdings and trading of individuals is likely to decrease appreciably or that individuals will not continue to constitute a major force in the stock market. Moreover, there is no evidence that their diminished share of the market has, or is likely to impair, the market's efficiency.

Until the end of the 1960s the declining shares of individuals in stockownership and trading were accompanied by a large increase in the number of individual stockholders. The decrease in individually held shares over the period reflected the lifting in the early 1950s of several legal constraints against equity investment by trustees, and both the subsequent accelerated inflow of investable funds into institutions (especially the pension funds) and the substantial upturn in their portfolio turnover. It did not reflect disenchantment with the market on the part of individual investors.

After the late 1960s, however, the decline in individuals' shares of market ownership and trading was accompanied by a moderate decrease in the number of individual stockholders and reflected a negative attitude on the part of individual investors. However, this negative attitude seems to be due largely to the sharp drop in stock prices, whose impact on individual investors was exacerbated by the rise in the price of goods and services purchased, by a depressed economy and higher unemployment for much of this period, and, for many investors, by undiversified portfolios that occasionally resulted in catastrophic losses. It does not appear that the deficiencies in institutional arrangements in the stock market were responsible to any major extent for the exodus of many individual investors from the market or for the reduced activity of others. Obviously, governmental fiscal policies could be changed so as to stimulate an increase in stock investment by individuals, but our analysis raises questions about the desirability of most of the measures proposed.

The future of individual participation in the stock market is likely to depend more on the course of stock prices and returns and the general state of the economy than on foreseeable or justifiable changes in institutional arrangements and governmental policy. However, a number of changes can be justified from the viewpoint of encouraging stock investment and improving the market's efficiency without placing a significant burden on other sectors of the economy.

Some of these changes, notably a fully electronic central-market system, are already under way but need to be accelerated. Limited progress also has been made in the area of index funds capable of offering investors a diversified portfolio of common stocks (or other securities) at minimal cost. So far, index funds have been used more extensively by corporate pension funds than by individual investors. However, they have great potential value for individuals, especially the smaller investors, who need an economical diversification of risk.

Perhaps the most promising idea for encouraging stock investment and promoting the welfare of individual investors without cost to other sectors of the economy is for the government to grant corporations some tax reduction as a function of their dividend payments, with the reduction set so as to avoid any loss in overall tax revenue.

Most other changes in official policies or market arrangements that would stimulate stock investment, according to our analysis of investor reactions, would either entail excessive cost or have relatively little impact. One possible exception is the establishment by the SEC of an Investor Protection Office, which would process complaints by investors, including cases of alleged discrimination against individual investors. Another step the private sector could take would involve the repurchase or liquidation of at least a portion of a company's shares where management considered the market price to be substantially below asset value.[76]

Finally, although our analysis has found no evidence that the stock market or the economy has been (or in the foreseeable future is likely to be) adversely affected by the relative growth of institutional stockownership and trading, it is, of course, possible for this situation to change. If it does, probably the best regulatory approach would be to limit the percentage of voting stock of individual portfolio companies that a single institutional investor (or affiliated group of institutions) is allowed to hold rather than to restrict institutional trading.

NOTES

1. It might be noted that even the NYSE is far from being a pure auction market.

2. Limited data on activity in these different markets are provided in I. Friend et al., *Investment Banking and the New Issues Market* (World Publishing Company, 1967).

3. Although increased activity in an issue tends to reduce transaction costs per trade, which is what is normally meant by transaction costs, it should be noted that the total of such costs is probably raised.

4. According to the Federal Reserve Board *Flow of Funds* data, individuals in 1975 owned 30 percent of all municipal bonds, 20 percent of corporates (including foreign), and 11 percent of U.S. government bonds.

5. The number of stockholders in NYSE issues declined 2 percent from 1970 to 1975, after a 47-percent increase from 1965 to 1970. In contrast, the number of stockholders in

224 The Changing Role of the Individual Investor

OTC issues other than mutual funds (who did not also own shares in issues listed on an exchange) declined 51 percent from 1970 to 1975, compared with 114-percent increase from 1965 to 1970. Thus the 1975 stockholder figure for NYSE issues was 44 percent higher than that a decade earlier, whereas the 1975 figure for OTC issues was only 5 percent higher.

6. I. Friend and E. S. Herman, "The S.E.C. Through a Glass Darkly," *Journal of Business* (October 1964); I. Friend and J. Longstreet, "Price Experience and Return on New Stock Issues," in *Investment Banking and the New Issues Market* (New York: McGraw-Hill, 1967). It might be noted that for the unseasoned—though probably not for the seasoned—new issues, this finding is perhaps explained by a low covariance and high co-skewness of return on such issues with the return on outstanding stocks, but this possibility has not been tested.

7. R. G. Ibbotson, *Price Performance of Common Stock New Issues* (Chicago: University of Chicago Press, 1973).

8. H. R. Stoll and A. J. Curley, "Small Business and the New Issues Market for Equities," *Journal of Financial and Quantitative Analysis* (September 1970).

9. C. A. Simmons, *Immediate, Short- and Longer-Run Performance of New Stock Issues*, Rodney L. White Center for Financial Research, University of Pennsylvania, 1974.

10. This is true even though for some stocks a few large institutions apparently now account for a substantial part of total trading. See R. A. Schotland, "Bank Trust Departments and Public Policy Today," *Securities Regulation Law Journal* (Winter 1977).

11. The discussion of these issues draws heavily on I. Friend, M. E. Blume, and J. Crockett, *Mutual Funds and Other Institutional Investors: A New Perspective* (New York: McGraw-Hill, 1970).

12. There may be circumstances where efficiency costs are major and potential inequities minor so that the former are the dominating consideration.

13. For example, see I. Friend, M. E. Blume, and J. Crockett, *Mutual Funds and Other Institutional Investors: A New Perspective* (New York: McGraw-Hill, 1970).

14. Ibid.

15. There is, of course, a similar coincidence of interests for internally managed pension funds.

16. The most comprehensive available treatment of this subject raises some questions about the existence of major damage to trust beneficiaries. See E. S. Herman, *Conflicts of Interest: Commercial Bank Trust Department* (New York: The Twentieth Century Fund, 1975).

17. There are some countries, such as Japan and Sweden, where the equity ratio is very much lower than in the United States, suggesting that a large equity ratio is not essential to economic growth.

18. I. Friend, "Determinants of the Volume and Composition of Saving," in *Impact of Monetary Policy*, Commission on Money and Credit (New York: 1963). Two recent papers imply on the one hand a negative effect of interest rates on saving [W. E. Weber, "Interest Rates, Inflation, and Consumer Expenditures," *American Economic Review* (December 1975)] and, in contrast, a positive effect on saving (Michael Boskin, *Taxes Saving, and the Rate of Interest*, NBER Occasional Paper #135, 1976).

19. *Broadening the Ownership of New Capital: ESOPs and Other Alternatives* (Washington, D.C., U.S. Government Printing Office, June 17, 1976). Other supporting arguments advanced in this document include the danger of a shortage of equity capital, especially of a risky nature, which has been considered earlier in this chapter.

20. Same as note 19.

Implications and Recommendations   225

21. Stockholders indicated that a 50-percent reduction in capital gains taxes might stimulate in the neighborhood of half the net stock purchases (or, more precisely, the percentage of assets expected to be in stock) that would be associated with the elimination of dividend income from personal income taxes. It should be observed that the proposed Treasury tax program may also include a 50-percent ceiling on marginal tax rates for all sources of income, which would probably also stimulate net stock investment. However, as noted in Chapter 3, stockholders indicated that a reduction of 10 percent in personal income taxes would have only a moderate effect on the percentage of assets held in stock.

22. There is some evidence that institutions have recently also increased their preference for dividend payout, perhaps reflecting at least in part the enactment of the Employee Retirement and Income Security Act of 1974.

23. The simplest, though not necessarily the optimal, procedure would be to require corporations to distribute a specified minimum percentage of their earnings and receive a level of tax credits set so as to leave unchanged the combined tax revenue from stockholders and corporations. Another posssibility that has been proposed for simplification of the tax system is to require that all corporate income be distributed and to abolish the corporate income tax, but this proposal is questionable because of the dangers implicit in cutting off abruptly the flow of internally generated funds from retained earnings, by far the most important source of equity financing, and because of the need to make up for the substantial decline in overall tax revenues implicit in this proposal.

24. W. J. Baumol, P. Heim, B. G. Malkiel, and R. E. Quandt, "Earnings Retention, New Capital and the Growth of the Firm," *Review of Economics and Statistics* (November 1970), and I. Friend and F. Husic, "Efficiency of Corporate Investment," *Review of Economics and Statistics* (February 1973). (See also reply by W. J. Baumol et al.)

25. The reduction in bid–ask spreads of NYSE issues growing out of increased competition in other markets is briefly discussed in I. Friend and M. E. Blume, "Competitive Commissions on the New York Stock Exchange," *Journal of Finance* (September 1973).

26. "Securities disclosure" refers in particular to the disclosure of corporate financial information and events affecting security value, but includes other types of disclosure as well (e.g., conflicts of interest, transaction costs, investment performance). The information is assumed to be made available generally to all stockholders and the marketplace.

27. For example, see J. F. Jaffe and M. Rubenstein, *The Value of Information in impersonal and Personal Markets*, Working Paper No. 16-75, Rodney L. White Center for Financial Research, University of Pennsylvania, 1975.

28. Part of the following discussion of these effects is based on a much more detailed analysis appearing in I. Friend, "Economic Foundations of Stock Market Regulation," *Journal of Contemporary Business* (Autumn 1976). As pointed out in that analysis, although the provision of new information entails additional costs, the required disclosure of information may reduce underwriting and other transaction costs and does reduce the private expense of investigations.

29. *Stock Exchange Practices*, Hearings before the Senate Committee on Banking and Currency, 72nd and 73rd Congresses, pts. 1–17 (1933–1934).

30. Federal Trade Commission, *Report on Utility Corporations*, Special Document No. 92, 70th Congress, 1st Session (1935), especially pts. 22, 71A, 72A, and 73A; and *Report of the Securities and Exchange Commission on Investment Trusts and Investment Companies* (1939–1942).

31. *Report of Special Study of Securities Markets of the Securities and Exchange Commission* (Washington, D.C.: U.S. Government Printing Office, 1963).

32. Friend and Herman, op. cit

33. G. J. Stigler, "Comment," *Journal of Business* (October 1964) and I. Friend and E. S. Herman, "Professor Stigler on Securities Regulation: A Further Comment," *Journal of Business* (January 1965).

34. A contrary opinion has been expressed by G. J. Benston in "Required Disclosure and the Stock Market: Rejoinder," *American Economic Review* (June 1975). The deficiencies in the Benston analysis are spelled out at length in Friend, "Economic Foundations of Stock Market Regulation."

35. Friend and Herman, op. cit.

36. A number of these direct and indirect tests are discussed in Friend, op. cit.

37. See, for example, N. Gonedes, "Capital Market Equilibrium and Annual Accounting Numbers: Empirical Evidence," *Journal of Accounting Research* (Spring 1974). The deficiencies in other tests in which it is concluded no such effect exists [notably in G. J. Benston, "The Value of the SEC's Accounting Disclosure Requirements," *Accounting Review* (July 1969)] are spelled out in detail in Friend, op. cit.

38. D. W. Collins, "SEC Product-Line Reporting and Market Efficiency," *Journal of Financial Economics* (July 1975).

39. A. Lurie and V. Pastena, "How Promptly Do Corporations Disclose Their Problems," *Financial Analysts Journal* (September–October 1975).

40. Obviously, it will be easier to estimate costs than benefits. Although normally it should not be too difficult to obtain a representative group of business firms to cooperate on a voluntary basis, such selective bias might greatly affect the accuracy of the estimated level of benefits, although even under these circumstances it may still be possible to determine whether benefits exist.

41. In spite of the legal constraints on their short-term trading, corporate insiders are one of the two groups of investors who are known to have above-average stock investment performance [see I. Friend, "The S.E.C. and the Economic Performance of Securities Markets" in H. G. Manne, ed., *Economic Policy and the Regulation of Corporate Securities* (Washington, D.C.: American Institute for Public Research, 1969)]. Exchange specialists comprise the other group.

42. Stockholders might benefit either through sales of at least part of their shareholdings or through long-term corporate gains achieved as a result of delayed disclosure of unfavorable information (e.g., through raising money from external sources at a lower cost than would otherwise be possible).

43. Benston, "SEC's Accounting Disclosure Requirements."

44. T. G. Moore, "Stock Market Margin Requirements," *The Journal of Political Economy* (April 1966); Friend, "The S.E.C. and the Economic Performance of Securities Markets"; G. W. Douglas, "Risk in the Equity Markets: An Empirical Appraisal of Market Efficiency," *Yale Economic Essays* (Spring 1969); R. R. Officer, "The Variability of the Market Factor of the New York Stock Exchange," *Journal of Business* (July 1973); and J. A. Largay, III, " 100% Margins: Combating Speculation in Individual Security Issues," *Journal of Finance* (September 1973).

45. An analysis based on cross-section data is able to hold constant the other economic and institutional changes that obscure time-series analyses of the effect of changes in margin requirements on the stock market.

46. See Largay, III "100% Margins." These findings were largely corroborated in an updated and somewhat more comprehensive analysis by W. L. Eckardt and D. L. Rogoff, "100% Margins Revisited," *Journal of Finance* (June 1976).

47. F. R. Macaulay and P. Durand, *Short Selling on the New York Stock Exchange* (New York: The Twentieth Century Fund, 1951); James S. Seneca, "Short Interest:

Implications and Recommendations   227

Bearish or Bullish," *Journal of Finance* (March 1967); I. Friend, "The S.E.C. and the Economic Performance of Securities Markets," T. H. Mayor, "Short Selling Activities and the Price and Equities: Some Simulations and Regression Results," *Journal of Financial and Quantitative Analysis* (September 1968); and J. G. McDonald and D. C. Baron, "Risk and Return on Short Positions in Common Stock," *Journal of Finance* (March 1973).

48. This is part of an analysis carried out by one of the authors in conjunction with Michael Granito and Bulent Gultekin.

49. McDonald and Baron, "Risk and Return on Short Positions in Common Stock." These authors point out that it is possible that these lower-than-average returns may have been associated with hedging of long positions in investors' portfolios, even though the only directly relevant evidence indicates that as of 1947 short positions established with a speculative motive comprised about two-thirds of the total short interest of NYSE members and customers combined, and an even higher ratio for customers alone (*Report of the Special Study of Securities Markets of the Securities and Exchange Commission*, pt. 2, pp. 246 ff.) It might be noted that the Special Study concluded that "it is probable that nonmembers' short selling consists mostly of speculation for the decline."

50. The best cross-section relationships derived from all NYSE stocks with short positions as of mid-April 1970 were:

$$P_{it} = -0.0041 - 0.00045 \frac{S_{it}}{A_{it}}, \quad \bar{R}^2 = 0.013; \text{ and}$$
$$(-2.14) \quad (-2.32)$$

$$P_{it} = -0.0030 - 0.00045 \frac{S_{i(t-1)}}{A_{i(t-1)}} - 0.062 P_{i(t-1)}, \quad \bar{R}^2 = 0.030$$
$$(-1.52) \quad (-2.30) \quad\quad\quad (-2.62)$$

where P_{it} is percent change in price of ith stock from the middle of April (t) to one week later; S is short position in shares as of middle of month; A is number of shares outstanding; $P_{i(t-1)}$ is percent change in prices of ith stock from mid-month March to mid-month April; R is the correlation coefficient adjusted for degrees of freedom, the number in parentheses represents t-values; and there are roughly 400 observations in the regressions. The $P_{i(t-1)}$ variable was introduced to adjust for serial correlation in price changes. Subsequent percentage price change over a three-month period, beta and sigma measures of risk, and log A were severally and jointly added to these equations with completely insignificant results. Other mathematical forms and other leads and lags yielded even weaker relationships between P and S.

51. In 1970 the proportion of NYSE short sales accounted for by public customers was somewhat higher.

52. Friend, "The S.E.C. and the Economic Performance of Securities Markets."

53. Macaulay and Durand, "Short Selling on the NYSE."

54. *Review of Investment Trading Experiences at the Chicago Board Options Exchange*, Prepared for the CBOE by Robert R. Nathan Associates, Inc., Washington, D.C. (December 1974).

55. The study provides limited evidence that bid–ask spreads in the underlying stocks might have narrowed relative to the market as a whole and thus operational efficiency might have been enhanced by the growth in option trading.

56. H. K. Wu, *Corporate Insider Trading, Profitability and Stock Price Movement*, Ph.D. Dissertation, University of Pennsylvania, 1963; J. H. Lorie and V. Niederhoffer,

228 The Changing Role of the Individual Investor

"Predictive and Statistical Properties of Insider Trading," *Journal of Law and Economics* (April 1968); S. P. Pratt and C. W. de Vere, "Relationships between Insider Trading and Rates of Return for NYSE Common Stocks, 1960–1966," in *Modern Development in Investment Management,* J. Lorie and R. Brealey, eds. (New York: Praeger, 1970); J. J. Jaffe, "Special Information and Insider Trading," *Journal of Business* (July 1974); and J. E. Finnerty, "Insiders and Market Efficiency," *Journal of Finance* (September 1976).

57. Sales by corporate insiders seem to have a much longer lead time than insider purchases in their relation to stock prices (Finnerty, "Insiders and Market Efficiency"). Most of the differential returns on purchases by insiders have been realized in the first six months.

58. There would still be a potential conflict between the interests of actual and potential stockholders, so there would remain a need for public disclosure.

59. S. S. Stewart, Jr., "Should a Corporation Repurchase Its Own Shares?" *Journal of Finance* (June 1976).

60. J. F. Jaffe, "The Effect of Regulation Changes on Insider Trading," *The Bell Journal of Economics and Management Science* (Spring 1974).

61. Actually Cady, Roberts involved activities which did not require corporate-insider disclosure.

62. *Special Study of Securities Markets of SEC,* pt. 2, pp. 83 ff., 162 ff., and 371 ff.; V. Niederhoffer and M. F. M. Osborne, "Market Making and Reversal on the Stock Exchange," *Journal of the American Statistical Association* (December 1966); and *Institutional Investor Study Report of Securities and Exchange Commission,* Vol. 4 pp. 1865 ff., 1923 ff., and 1956 ff.

63. *Special Study of Securities Markets of the SEC.*

64. One such plan has been developed by J. W. Peake, M. Mendelson, and R. T. Williams in a memorandum, "The National Book System: An Electronically Associated Auction Market," transmitted to the U.S. Securities and Exchange Commission on April 30, 1976. Two other, less ambitious, recommendations that have received substantial support in the Wall Street community are an OIS proposal by the NYSE and a proposal by the Securities Industry Association to explore further the feasibility of developing a CLOB system.

65. For example, those proposed by Peake, Mendelson, and Williams, and Merrill Lynch and Weeden.

66. Peake, Mendelson, and Williams roughly estimate the cost of carrying out such an experiment for up to 75 stocks as between $1 million and $1.5 million.

67. The argument is similar to that developed in I. Friend and M. E. Blume, "Competitive Commissions on the New York Stock Exchange," *The Journal of Finance* (September 1973).

68. For a particular year, the variation in performance among different groups of investors can be quite large.

69. R. F. Murray, "Index Funds—An Idea Whose Time Has Passed," *Pensions and Investments* (February 16, 1976).

70. J. A. Humback and S. P. Dresch, "Prudence, Information and Trust Information Law," *American Bar Association Journal* (October 1976), pp. 1310–1312.

71. T. Brown II, "A Great Idea, But It's Not Practical," *Pension and Investment Trusts* (February 1976).

72. J. F. Jaffe and G. Mandelker, "The 'Fisher Effect' for Risky Assets: An Empirical Investigation," *Journal of Finance* (May 1976).

73. However, it has been argued that in an inflationary economy, corporations might

Implications and Recommendations 229

be better off selling indexed bonds than nonindexed bonds (E. Kleiman, *Indexation, Risk, and Relative Prices in Israel, 1964–1975*, The Maurice Falk Institute for Economic Research in Israel, 1976).

74. N. Hakansson, "Efficient Paths Toward Efficient Capital Markets in Large and Small Countries," in H. Levy and M. Sarnat, eds. *Financial Decision Making Under Uncertainty* (New York: Academic Press, 1977).

75. This statement assumes that probability beliefs are not homogeneous and that the borrowing rate is not equal to the lending rate.

76. For a number of closed-end investment companies, such action would appear to offer obvious opportunities for enhancing stockholder welfare.

APPENDIX

Estate-tax Data

When evaluating the estate-tax data, various well-documented problems and biases must be taken into account.[1] First, it must be assumed that the balance sheets of the decedents are representative of those of living persons of similar wealth. This assumption may be invalid if individuals tend to make outright gifts in the expectation of death. Such gifts made within three years of death are supposed to be reported as part of the individual estate, but it is probable that some are not reported because for some technical reason they are not called "gifts" under the law or are simply misrepresented. Because the estate-tax data are collected before audit, such misrepresentation, even if caught, would not have been corrected. Also, the value of life insurance differs according to whether the insured is living or dead. Hence, to estimate the balance sheets of living persons, it is necessary to convert the face value of life-insurance policies as reported on estate-tax forms to cash value. The figures published by the Internal Revenue Service make such a conversion.

Second, the mortality rates, which are interpreted as sampling probabilities, may be in error. Recognizing that the mortality rates for the rich in given age groups may be lower than for the general population, the Internal Revenue Service has sought to determine these rates using the mortality records of the Metropolitan Life Insurance Company for policies of different values.[2] Although there has as yet been no outside validation of these rates, they have been carefully developed and, therefore, are used here.

Third, two types of assets, namely, lifetime transfers and annuities, were not allocated to the basic assets that they represent but were reported as single numbers. To make these assets comparable to other type of assets in the estate-tax data, it is necessary to allocate them to their component parts. This was accomplished by using the percentage composition of the assets of bank-administered trusts for year-end 1969, on the assumption that this composition is representative of mid-1962 and 1972.[3]

Fourth, the valuations of the estates are not all made on the same date. Each estate has a choice of two dates for the evaluation of assets, and these two dates in turn hinge on the date of death. Moreover, some of the estate-tax filings that will be used in estimating the wealth of the rich in 1972, for instance, may pertain to persons who died before or after 1972. Because of the price movements of assets, this bias can be reduced by the following procedure: increase the value of all assets in 1972 and mid-1969 by 2 percent, make no adjustment to the values in mid-1962, and finally take the 1972 data to represent year-end values, and those for 1962 and 1969 mid-year values.

Fifth, the value of the assets reported on the tax form may not reflect the true value. Such misrepresentation would most likely involve certain types of assets of the rich, such as closely held stock or large blocks of traded stocks. The value of assets may be understated in order to minimize estate taxes.[4] In an attempt to eliminate this bias, the value of the assets in the estate-tax data has been adjusted upward as follows: stock, 5 percent; unincorporated business, 25 percent; consumer durable goods and personal effects (jewelry, etc.), 15 percent; and all remaining types of assets except cash, bonds, and life insurance, 5 percent.

Finally, some types of trusts such as intergenerational transfers would escape the estate data every other generation. For example, a man might give assets to his grandchildren in the form of a trust with the provision that the income go to his children during their lifetime. Were it not for the obvious tax advantages, such a trust would probably have been set up directly for his children. Very little is known about the magnitude of such transfers.[5]

In an attempt to adjust the data for this omission, we made estimates of the total number of trusts that might reasonably be attributed to that part of the population with total assets in excess of $60,000, the threshold for filing an estate-tax form. From this figure, we subtracted an estimate of the value of trusts in the estate-tax data, and the residual furnished an estimate of those trusts not in that tax data. Although such an estimate may be inaccurate, it turns out empirically that increasing the amount of trusts by anywhere up to $20 billion has little effect on the long-range trends in concentration or in the percentage distribution of assets at any given time. That is so because trusts are distributed according to the percentage distribution of the assets of bank-administered trusts, and this percentage distribution does not differ that much from the balance sheets of the rich themselves—a little more in marketable financial instruments, a little less in other types of assets. An adjustment for these omitted assets would increase the overall level of concentration; however, any of the adjustments tried (up to $20 billion) would change the levels by at most 0.5 percent. Thus, regardless of whether an adjustment is made, the observed trends would be roughly the same.

Estate-tax forms are filed by individuals, not households, the more basic economic units. In estimating the wealth of the richest 0.5 percent and 1 percent of all families, two procedures were used. The first assumed that the richest spouse was married to a poor spouse; the second, which is probably closer to reality, assumed that the richest man was married to the richest woman. The first procedure would be expected to give an estimate of the lower bound of the amount of wealth held by rich households and the second, an upper bound.

In 1962 there were 54,652,000 households in the United States. The top 1 percent, therefore, numbered 546,520 and the top 0.5 percent, 273,260. To obtain the lower bound estimate of the top 1 percent, one would simply total the wealth of the 546,520 richest individuals as estimated from the estate-tax data. To obtain the upper bound, one would begin with the richest individual and then, if he or she were unmarried, would proceed to the next richest. If the subject were married, one would pair this individual with the richest married person of the opposite sex. Similar procedures were followed for the richest 0.5 percent of all households. The same procedures were followed for 1969 and 1972, except that the total number of households was taken to be 61,805,000 and 66,676,000, respectively.[6]

The margin of error in these estimates may be quite large for several reasons. First, the wealth of households cannot be precisely determined from the estate-tax data on individuals, as evidenced by the differences, often several percentage points, in asset categories between the lower-and upper-bound estimates. Second, the adjustments necessary to make the estate-tax data comparable with the balance sheets of the living, the allocation of trust assets, and the valuation adjustments can only be viewed as rough approximations. Third, the estate-tax samples themselves in any particular year may be unrepresentative. Despite all these potential sources of error, it is gratifying to note that the percentage composition of assets from the 1962 Federal Reserve Board Survey for households with net worth in excess of $1 million is roughly the same as the percentages for mid-1962 derived from the estate-tax data. For instance, the 1962 Federal Reserve Survey found that these households held 11 percent of their assets in bonds and mortgages and 59 percent in corporate stock[7]—almost the same as for the estate-tax data of that year. The similarity between these two sources of data thus reinforces one's confidence in the overall quality of both, at least for 1962.

NOTES

1. M. E. Blume, J. Crockett, and I. Friend, "Stockownership in the United States: Characteristics and Trends," *Survey of Current Business* (November 1974).

2. V. Natrella, "Wealth of Top Wealthholders—1972," paper presented at the Annual Meeting of the American Statistical Association, August 25, 1975.

3. In the published estate-tax data for 1969, which are comparable to that of 1962, lifetime transfers and annuities are combined with noncorporate business assets and various miscellaneous assets. This group of assets was reported under the heading "other assets." The Internal Revenue Service was kind enough to provide us with worksheets that for 1969 allowed the break-out of lifetime transfers, annuities, and noncorporate business assets from the "other assets." The remaining assets include physical assets such as jewelry and art and some trusts that could not be allocated from the information on the estate tax form itself. Assuming that 50 percent of the remaining assets are trusts, 46.4 percent of "other assets" were allocated both for 1962 and 1969 to component assets according to the 1969 composition of bank-administered trusts, 16.5 percent to physical assets, and 37.1 percent to noncorporate business assets. Since noncorporate business assets were separated in 1972, it was only necessary to assume that the relative proportions of physical assets and assets to be allocated in 1972 were the same as in 1969. Thus 26.2 percent of "other assets" in 1972 were assigned to physical assets, with the remainder allocated.

4. Since the estate-tax value provides the tax basis for calculating subsequent gains or losses, in some circumstances it may appear advisable to overstate the value of the assets, but such overstatement is probably not common.

5. G. R. Jantscher, in "The Importance of Gifts in the Transmission of Wealth," The Brookings Institution (undated mimeo.), examines the available evidence on this subject.

6. Since the basic estimates of wealth from the estate-tax data are aggregated by wealth class, it was sometimes necessary to interpolate for classes with incomes of less than $500,000. A linear interpolation was used in these cases. Since the classes below $500,000 are narrowly defined, such an interpolation is likely to introduce little error.

7. This estimate of 59 percent assumes that the value recorded for equity in unincorporated business in the 1962 Federal Reserve Survey is really corporate stock in privately held companies—a reasonable assumption in view of the way in which the 1962 survey solicited this information.

Index

Age
  net purchases of stock by (1973-1974), illustrated, 82
  percentage of stockholders by, illustrated, 75
  performance and age level, illustrated, 79
  population
    age profile, 10
    historical and estimated distribution, table, 34
    use of speculative mechanisms and, 16
    see also Regions
  and required rates of return, illustrated, 132
  of respondent, in evaluating stockholding families, table, 135
  risk, diversification and, illustrated, 122
  speculative mechanisms and, illustrated, 77
  stockholders increasing stock ratios by, illustrated, 106, 107
  stock purchase or investment plans and, 84
Allocational efficiency, 17, 20-21, 144-147, 178-180
American Stock Exchange (AMEX), 5-6
Assets
  in bonds, *see* Bonds
  categories expected to increase most, table, 88
  in common stock (1962-1972; and to 1980), 7
  composition of, table, 87
  effect of indicated economic and regulatory developments on percentage of, expected in stock, table, 102-103
  effect of other tax developments on percentage of, expected in stock, table, 98-99
  income and ratio of financial, in stock, illustrated, 92
  individual, 7-9, 23-60

and design of stockholder studies, 30-31
  percentage distribution (1962-1972), table, 24
  proportion of financial, expected in stock with 50 percent reduction in capital gains tax, table, 96
  of the rich, *see* Rich, the
  trends in proportions of, expected to be in stock (1975-1980), table, 89
Attitudes
  toward diversification, table, 121
  toward risk, table, 114
Auction market, 148-150

Bank-trust departments, 194-195
Behavior, 62-142
  1975, 66-78
    compared with earlier years, 80-82
    compared with earlier years, illustrated, 82
    comparison of value of purchases and sales, table, 70
    comparison of value of stock purchases and sales in 1973 and 1974, table, 81
    nature of stock transactions, table, 69
    reasons for net purchases, table, 83
    reasons for net sales, table, 84
    recency of stock transactions, table, 68
    sources and users of funds for stock purchases and sales, 78-79
    use of margin, option, or short sales, table, 73
    value of transactions, table, 71
  reasons for recent stock trading, 82-86
    net stock purchases, table, 83
    net stock sales, table, 84
β (beta) coefficient, 42-43, 154
  as measure of risk, 115
  published, illustrated, 128

236 Index

Bid-ask spreads, 17-19, 152-160, 201-202
  illustrated, 156, 157
Bonds
  assets in, 86, 94
    illustrated, 91
    1962-1972, 23
    tables, 26, 27, 87, 88
  investments in, by the rich, 9
  market in, generally, 187-188
  mean required rate of return on, 129-131
  the rich having investment in, 25-28
    tables of assets, 26, 27
  tax-exempt, stock sales for acquiring, 8, 79-80
Brokerage firms
  commission rates, 150-152, 194, 201-202
  use of, 8-9, 72-73

Capital gains
  change in taxes on, table, 98
  net stock sales and, 85
  proportion of financial assets expected to be in stock with 50 percent reduction in tax on, table, 96
  reduction in, 104
  return on stock and tax rate on, 188
  selling stock and realization of, 8
  support for reduction of tax on, 94-95
  taxes and increase in proportion of assets in stocks, 2, 3
Carter, Jimmy, 95
Cash
  assets in (1962-1972), 23, 25
  buying stock and availability of, 8
  holdings in, of the rich, 9
    tables, 26, 27
  resources in, as reason for stock purchase, 82
Central market system, movement toward, 214-216
Checking accounts
  financing stock purchases through, 7
  withdrawls from, as source of funds for trading, 78-80
Chicago Board Options Exchange (CBOE), 211
Commission rates, 150-152, 194, 201-202
Communications industry, income level and stock in, 37, 38
Composite indexes
  NYSE, 174

Standard and Poor's, 161, 217
Concentration, of ownership in common stock, 9-10
  patterns of, of individual holders, 172
  patterns of, of institutional investors, 172-173
  of power over portfolio companies, 190-192
  of stockownership, arrested, 81
  of wealth, 26-29
    trends in, 22
Conflict of interest, 194-195
Consolidated limit order book (CLOB), 215
Costs of trading, market efficiency and, 17

Dealer's market, 148-150
Debt financing of assets (1962-1972), 23
Debt repayment, stock sales for, 8, 79
Demand deposits, see Deposits
Deposits
  assets in, 23, 86, 94
    table, 87, 88
  selling stock to increase, 8
Disclosure, 193-194
  as basic mechanism for efficient and equitable markets, 202-208
Distribution, of common stock, tables, 162-165
  percent, of families transacting stock on NYSE, table, 69
  see also Regions
Diversifiable risk, 50
Diversification, attitudes toward, table, 121
  extent of, 46-58
    illustrated, 47, 48, 53, 54, 57
  measures of, 46-47, 49
  poor, 14, 22
  of previous holdings, trading and, 79
  and returns, 51, 52, 55-58
    illustrated, 53, 54, 57
  risk and, level of income, illustrated, 122
    market efficient and, 219, 220
    risk characteristics and, 38
  risk and portfolio diversification, 120-122
    table, 120
  risks inherent in undiversified portfolios, 50-58
    illustrated, 53, 54, 57
  selling stock for, 8
Dividends, diversification and, 51, 52

Index

percent of households listing stocks and dividend-paying stock, 46-47, 49
 illustrated, 47, 48
preference for income from, 106
as preferred over retained earnings, 3, 4
taxes on, "double taxation," 197
 elimination of taxes, 97, 100
 exclusion of dividend tax from income, 108, 112
 individual stockownership and reduction in, 3
 reduction in, 95, 96, 99, 199-200
 table on reductions, 96
Dow Jones Industrial Average, 12, 73, 74
Durable goods, stock sales for, 80

Earnings volatility, illustrated, 128
 as measure of risk, 116
Economic climate, as reason for stock purchase, 82
Economic developments, effect of indicated, on percentage of assets expected in stock, table, 102-103
Education, 8
 risk and, 124
 and level of education, 13
 risk, diversification and level of, illustrated, 122
 speculative mechanisms and level of, illustrated, 77
 stock sales for, 79
Electronic market system, 214-216
Eleemosynary funds, 173
Emergencies, stock sales for, 8, 79
Employed, the, 30-33
Employee Retirement and Income Security Act (1974; ERISA), 6
Employee Stock Ownership Plans (ESOPs), 198
Equity capital issue, 196
Equity financing cost decline, 188-189
Estates, income level and stocks held in, 37
Estate-tax data, 230-232

Families, buying or selling stock on NYSE, 66-67
 tables, 68-69
 characteristics of, holding stock, 133-137
 tables, 134-136
 median 1975 before tax income of shareholding, 64

percent listing stock-paying dividends, 46-47, 49
 illustrated, 47, 48
 region of respondent in evaluating stockholding, table, 135
 size of portfolio and income of, 71
 illustrated, 72
Federal Income Tax Form 1040, as source of financial information, 29-30
Federal Reserve Board, 25
 1962 survey of, 49
Females, risk-taking by, 13
Financial information, stockholder studies and source of, 29-30
Financing stock purchases, sources for, 7
 see also Stock purchases
Fixed-income securities, assets in, 86-94
 illustrated, 91
 table, 87, 88
Ford, Gerald R., 1

Home purchases, (or improvements), stock sales for, 80

Illness, stock sales for, 8, 79
Income, average realized returns by, table, 43
 change in tax on, 97, 100
 table, 98, 99
 characteristics of stock held by, 35, 38-39
 illustrated, 36, 37
 current, for financing stock purchases, 7
 family (1975), table, 134
 median 1975 before tax, of shareowning households, 64
 net purchases of stock by (1973-1974), illustrated, 82
 percentage of stockholders and level of, illustrated, 75
 performance and level of, illustrated, 79
 and ratio of financial assets in stock, illustrated, 92
 reduction of taxes on, 95
 and required rates of return, illustrated, 132
 risk, diversification and level of, illustrated, 122
 risk characteristics by occupation and, 39-40
 size of portfolio and family, 71
 illustrated, 72
 as source of funds for stock trading, 78-80
 speculative mechanisms and level of,

238 Index

illustrated, 77
stockholders increasing stock ratios by, illustrated, 106-108
Income taxes, *see* Taxes
Index funds, 216-219
Indexes
  Composite, NYSE, 174
    Standard and Poor's, 161, 217
    investment of $1.00 in various weighted, illustrated, 176
    percentage of, attributable to largest stocks as of June 1972, table, 175
Individual investment, stimulation of, 195-202
Individual investors, decrease in (1970-1975), 1
  decline in holdings (1970-1975), 5, 29
  holdings of, compared with those of institutional investors, 5
  increase in (1952-1970), 1
  numbers of, 187
Inflation, and change in trading activity, 85
  financial instruments permitting hedge against, 219-220
  net stock sales and, 82
  rate of return and expected rate of, 131, 133
  reduction of, and increased demand for stock, 101
    table, 102
  reduction in rate of, 201
  stock purchase and hedge against, 8, 82, 84-85
  risk and, 114-115
Informational efficiency, 17, 146, 147, 168-169, 193-194
  and past prices, 170-171
Inside trading, 212-214
Institutional changes, impact of, on market behavior, 94-113
Institutional Investor Study (SEC), 151
Institutional investors, effects of, on market efficiency, 17, 187
  impact of changes affecting, and market behavior, 94-113
  see also Market efficiency
  focus of, on NYSE issues, 5, 6, 189
  share of market, 4
  growth of, 4-6
    table, 102-103
Insurance companies, concentration patterns of investment of, 173

Interest rates, change in trading activity and changes in, 85
  reduction in, 201
  reduction of, and increased demand for stock, 101
    table, 102-103
  reduction of, stock holding and, 100-101
Internal Revenue Service (IRS), 2
Investment-company legislation, 194
Investment climate, as reason for stock purchase, 82
Investment performance of individuals and institutions, compared, 11-13
  net stock sales and, 85
  selling stock and, 8
Investment plans, 8, 82, 84, 86
Investor Protection Office (SEC; proposed), 4, 101, 104, 112, 201
  table, 102-103

Joint Economic Committee (Congress), 198

Keogh plans, 104
  table, 105
Keynes, John Maynard, 169

Life-insurance companies, as institutional investors, 5
Life-insurance policies, 9
  assets in (1962-1972), 23
  holdings of the rich in, 25
  assets, table, 26, 27
Liquidation fund, 220-221
Loans, as source of funds for trading, 7-8, 78-79
Long-term financial assets, investing in, by the rich, 24, 25

Males, risk-taking by, 113
Management expenses, 150-152
Margin accounts, investors using (1975), 16, 71
  risk and, 124, 126, 129
    illustrated, 125
  use of, 77-78
    illustrated, 77
    table, 73
Margin calls, 1973 and 1974, 86
Margin requirements, liberalization of, 101, 104, 112, 209
  table, 102-103
Market conditions, selling stock and

Index

technical, 8
Market efficiency, 16-21, 143-185
  allocational efficiency, 17, 20-21, 144-147, 178-180
  bid-ask spreads, 17-19, 152-160, 201-202
    illustrated, 154, 155
  common stock and, 16-21
  diversification of risk and, 219-220
    see also Diversification; Risk
  hedge against inflation and, 219-220
  index fund growth and, 217-219
  informational efficiency, 17, 146, 147, 168-169, 193-194
    and past prices, 170-171
  institutionalization of trading and, 17, 187
  liquidation fund, 220-222
  meaning of, 143-147
  operational efficiency, 17-19, 147, 150-151
  price impact on, 161-168
    tables, 162-165
  removal of ban on off-board trading and, 217
  with respect to other types of information, 171
  with respect to past prices, 169-172
  role of individual in, 147-150
  two-tier market and, 5-6, 172-178
    illustrated, 176
    table, 175
Market value, risk, diversification and, illustrated, 122
  stockholders increasing stock ratios and, illustrated, 106-108
  of stock holdings, table, 134
Market volatility, common stock and, 19-20
  1928-1976, 19
Monopoly, 145-146
Mortality rate, as measure of sampling probability, 24
Mortgages, assets of the rich in, 9, 25-28
  tables, 26, 27
Mutual funds, enhancing competition and reducing conflicts in operation of, 194-195
  income level and stock held in, 38
  percent distribution of families transacting in, table, 69
  and percent of families buying or selling stock, 66-67
    table, 68
  restrictions on, 191

risk and limited interest in, 219-220

New York Stock Exchange (NYSE), 1, 148, 149, 173, 214
  bid-ask spread and issues on, 18, 154, 160
  and commission rates, 151
  increase in aggregate volume of transactions on (1974-1976), 80
  increase or decrease in purchase of stock on (1974 and 1975), 80
  institutional focus on larger issues on, 5, 6, 189
  institutional investor share of market, 4
  investment in 500 largest issues of, 173
  level of income and investment in issues of, 35
  order-indication system of (OIS), 215, 216
  and past prices, 170
  percent of families buying or selling stock on (1975), 66-67
    tables, 68, 69
  portfolio turnover statistics of, evidence supporting, 82, 84
  removing ban on off-board trading and, 217
  returns on issues of, 11-12, 43, 44, 174
    table, 44
  risk measures and, 40
  short positions and, 209-211
  stockholder studies by, 2, 29, 62
    see also Wharton Survey
  transaction prices on, 161, 162, 167
    tables, 162-166
  turnover rate of stock on, 130
New York Stock Exchange Census of Shareholders, 62-65, 80, 133, 189
New York Stock Exchange Composite Index, 174
New York Stock Exchange telephone survey, 63-65
Nondiversifiable risk, defined, 50
Nondurable goods, stock sales for purchase of, 80
Nonvoting stock, limiting institutional holdings to, 192
NYSE, *see* New York Stock Exchange

Occupations, net purchases of stock by (1973-1974), illustrated, 82
  percentage of stockholders and type of, illustrated, 75

240 Index

risk characteristics by income and, 39-40
speculative mechanisms and type of, illustrated, 77
stockholders increasing stock ratios by, illustrated, 107, 108
Off-board trading, 217
Operational efficiency, 17-19, 147, 150-151
Optimal investment strategy, 145
Option plans, employee stock, increase in (1970-1975), 29
Options, *see* Stock options
Order-indication system (OIS; NYSE), 215, 216
Over-the-counter market (OTC), 148
individual investor portfolios weighted in favor of, 5, 172
institutional participation in, 18
level of income and investment in stocks, 35
returns on issues in, 11

Pareto, Vilfredo, 145
Pension plans, 104
concentration patterns of investment by, 173
conflict of interest and, 194, 195
and direct employee investment in stock, 6
private noninsured, as institutional investors, 5
restrictions on, 191
Population, age profile of, 10
historical and estimated distribution, table, 34
use of speculative mechanisms and, 16
Portfolios, concentration of, 127
diversification of, *see* Diversification
NYSE turnover statistics on, 82, 84
of the rich, diversification, 46-47
sizes, 45
sizes, illustrated, 45
risk and diversification of, 120-122
table, 120
risks inherent in undiversified, 50-58
illustrated, 53, 54, 57
size of, 45
illustrated, 45
size of, family income and, 71
illustrated, 72
Prices, and change in trading activity, 85
effect of increase in, 104

general decline in, as reason for sales, 85
impact on market efficiency, 161-168
· tables, 162-166
market efficiency with respect to past, 170-171
NYSE transaction, 161, 162, 167
tables, 162-166
Price volatility, illustrated, 128
as measure of price, 116
1960s, 20
risk and, 126, 128-129
Profits, as source of funds for trading, 7, 8
78-79, 82
see also Dividends; Returns
Profit-sharing plans, 104
effect of participation in, table, 105

Real-estate investments, stock sales for, 80
Recession, and change in trading activity, 85
net stock sales and, 85
Regions
characteristics of stock held by, 40-43
tables, 41, 42
net purchases of stock by (1973-1974), illustrated, 82
percentage of stockholders by, illustrated, 75
required rates of return by, illustrated, 132
of respondent, in evaluating stockholding families, table, 135
risk and, 124
stockholders increasing stock ratios by, illustrated, 107, 108
Regulatory approach to stimulate stock investment, 201
Regulatory development, effect of indicated, on percentage of assets expected in stock, table, 102-103
Residences, pattern of investments in, 25
as percent of assets, 9
Retained earnings, 3, 4
Retired, the, 31-34
risk portfolios and, 40
stock holdings by, 10-11
Retirement funds (state and local), 104
effect of participation in, table, 105
as institutional investors, 5
Returns, diversification and, 50, 51, 52-58
illustrated, 53, 54, 57
higher, as reason for stock purchases, 82
income and required rates of, illustrated,

132
  on NYSE issues, 11-12, 43, 44, 174
    table, 44
  rate of (July-December 1962), 161
  realized, on stock held by individuals, 43
    table, 44
  realized and expected, 11-13
  required and expected rates of, 129-133
    illustrated, 132
  risk and rate of, 113-115
  see also Market efficiency
Rich, the
  assets of, 9-10, 23-24
    percentage distribution, tables, 24-27
    ratio of stock to financial assets among, 91-94
    ratio of stock, illustrated, 91, 92
  bond investments by, 25-28
    tables, 26, 27
  cash assets of, *see* Cash
  corporate stock held by, tables, 26, 27
    waning importance of (1962-1969), 26
  increased importance of, 93
  net stock sales by, 85
  portfolios among, diversification, 45-46
    sizes, 45
    sizes, illustrated, 45
  preference of, for dividend income, 106-107
  purchases and sales by, compared (1973-1975; 1975), 69, 81
  reasons for stock purchases by, 85
  reducing holdings in common stock, 9
  regional distribution of, 40-41
  risk and, 122-123, 127, 128
  speculative mechanisms used by, 76
  use of brokerage firms by, 72
Risk, characteristics of, by occupation and income, 39-40
  characteristics of stock portfolios by region, table, 42
  disclosure and, 193-194
  diversification and, *see* Diversification and limited interest in mutual funds, 219-220
  reactions to, 114-129
    attitudes, table, 114
    attitudes toward diversification, table, 121
    degree of risk tolerance, illustrated, 123, 125

  diversification of portfolios, table, 120
  effect of price fluctuations and institutional buying on stock holdings, table, 118
  evaluation of risk, table, 115
  illustrated, 122, 123, 125, 128
  number of stocks held, table, 119
  reactions to different market developments, table, 117
  and stocks as hedge against inflation, 114-115
  see also Inflation
  in undiversified portfolios, 50-51, 52-58
Risk aversion among retired, 11
Risk-free assets, diversification and, 52-56
Risk management, poor knowledge of, 15
Risk measures, 39-40
  illustrated, 128
  and stock held by region, 41-43
Risk-taking behavior, 13-15

Savings accounts, as source of funds for stock trading, 7, 78-79
Savings ratio, and changes in rates of return of stock, 197
Securities Act (1933), 213
Securities Acts Amendments (1975), 191
Securities Exchange Act (1934), 213, 214
Securities and Exchange Commission (SEC), 63, 161, 189, 190, 202, 206, 208, 212
  inside trading, 213-214
Services, stock sales for, 80
Sex, of respondent, in evaluating stockholding families, table, 135
  risk and, 13, 124
Short sales, 16
  liberalization of regulations on, 101, 104, 112, 209-211
    table, 102-103
  risk and, 124, 129
    illustrated, 125
  use of, 71, 76-78
    illustrated, 77
    table, 73
Simon, William, 1
"Smith, Adam," 169
Special Study (SEC), 203
Speculation, mechanisms, illustrated, 77
  restrictions on, 208-214
  use of, 15-16

242 Index

Standard & Poor's Composite Index, 161, 217
Stigler, George, 204
Stock, current and prospective importance of, 86-94
    illustrated, 91, 92
    tables, 87-89
    percentage of indexes attributable to largest (as of June 1972), table, 175
    see also Assets
Stock Guide (Standard & Poor), 158, 166
Stockholder studies, design of, 30-31
Stockholdings, characteristics of families with, 133-137
    tables, 134-136
    effect of price fluctuations and institutional buying on, table, 118
    by employed and self-employed (1960-1971), 31-34
    illustrated, 32
    by individuals, 34-45
    institutional, limitations on, 186-194
    market value of, table, 134
    median portfolio size, in Wharton Survey and NYSE survey, 63-64
    1971, 10
    of retired (1960 and 1971), 31-34
    illustrated, 32
    risk and number of, table, 119
Stock options, 15-16, 211-212
    risk and, 124, 126, 129
    illustrated, 125
    use of, 71, 76-78
    illustrated, 77
    table, 73
Stock-purchase plans, 8, 82, 84-85
Stock purchases, cash resources as reason for, 82
    current income for financing, 7
    financing, 7
    as hedge against inflation, 8, 82, 84-86
    risk and, 113-114
    see also Inflation
    for higher returns, 82
    increase or decrease in, on NYSE (1974 and 1975), 80
    investment climate as reason for, 82
    net, of stock by income and region (1973-1974), illustrated, 82
    on NYSE, percent of families (1975), 66-67
    table, 68-69
    1973-1974, illustrated, 82
    by occupation (1973-1974), illustrated, 82
    reasons for, among the rich, 85
    and sales by the rich (1973-1975; 1975), 70, 81
    sources and users of funds for (1975), 78-80
    tax changes to stimulate, 198-201
    see also Taxes
    see also Stock trading
Stock ratios, percentage of stockholders increasing, illustrated, 105-110, 112, 106-111, 113
Stock sales, inflation and net, 85
    net sellers of (1975), 8
    and purchases, by the rich (1973-1975; 1975), 70, 81
    purposes in, 78-80
    recession and net, 85
    sources and users of funds for (1975), 78-80
    and technical market conditions, 8
    see also Stock trading
Stock trading, 1975, 66-78
    compared with earlier years, 80-82
    compared with earlier years, illustrated, 82
    comparison of value of purchases and sales, table, 70
    comparison of value of stock purchases and sales in 1973 and 1974, table, 81
    nature of stock transactions, table, 69
    reasons for net purchases, table, 83
    reasons for net sales, table, 84
    reasons for recent, 82-86
    recency of stock transactions, table, 68
    sources and users of funds for stock purchases and sales, 78-80
    use of margin, option or stock sales, table, 73
    value of transactions, table, 71
Stock value, in unlisted issues, 173
Superfund, 221
"Survey of the Financial Characteristics of Consumers, The" (Federal Reserve Board), 49-50
Survey method, 62-65
Surveys, as sources, 2

Taxes, bonds and rate of, on income, 188
    capital gains, *see* Capital gains
    change in, on income, 97, 100
    table, 98-99

Index

changes to stimulate stock purchases, 198-201
on dividends, "double taxation" on, 197
elimination of taxes, 97, 100
exclusion of dividends from income, 107, 112
individual stockownership and reduction in, 3
reduction of, 95, 96, 99, 199-200
table, 98
effect of other tax developments on percentage of assets expected in stock, table, 98-99
estate-tax data, 230-232
impact on market behavior of changes in, 94, 113
tables, 96, 98-99
incentives to corporations to raise dividends and, 4
income, exclusion of dividends from income, 107, 112
reduction of, 95
loss, net stock sales and, 85
lowering, on investments, as legislative and regulatory changes acting as stimuli, 112-113
median 1975 income before, of shareowning households, 64
tax-exempt bonds, stock sales for acquiring, 78-80
see also Bonds
Tax Reduction Act (1975), 198
Telephone industry, income level and stock in, 38-39
Time and savings accounts, *see* Deposits; Savings accounts

Time spent on investment analysis and financial decisionmaking, 71
Trusts, income level and stocks held in, 37
Two-tier market, 5-6, 172-178
illustrated, 176
table, 175

Unemployed, the, 30-33
Unemployment, net stock sales and, 85
Utilities, income level and stock in, 37-38

Value Line Index, 174

Wage and price controls, 104
effect of establishing, table, 102-103
effects on stock investments, 112
Wharton School, 2, 62
Wharton Mutual Fund Study, 151, 217
Wharton Survey, 2, 62-66
and actual investment performance, 73
and holdings of the rich in stock, 9, 10
institutional and tax changes and, 94-95
and investment performance, 12
liquidation of stockholdings (1975-1980) and, 90
pensions and, 6
and percent of assets in common stock (to 1980), 7
and risk-taking behavior, 13-15
and speculative mechanisms, 16
taxes on dividends and, 3
and risk aversion among retired persons, 11
and use of brokerage firms, 8
Work force, 6
employed and unemployed, 30-33

LIBRARY OF DAVIDSON COLLEGE

Books on regular loan may be checked out for **two weeks**. Books **must be presented** at the Circulation Desk in order to be renewed.

A fine is charged after date due

ions at the discretion of